Scribblin' on

THE GAME

By Jimmy Smothers

The Scribbler
Jimmy S.

Copyrighted articles used with permission of
The Gadsden Times and The New York Times.

Photographs are from the private
collection of the author, from the files of
The Gadsden Times and from other sources,
used by permission as noted.

Cover design by Jim Smothers
Talladega, Alabama

Edited by Randy Johnson
Albertville, Alabama

Copyright 2011
By Jimmy Smothers
Glencoe, Alabama
All Rights Reserved
ISBN 978-1466365735
CreateSpace Title 3691281

2009 and 2010

This book is about Alabama-Auburn football, particularly as it was played from 1963 through 2006, while author Jimmy Smothers was Sports Editor of The Gadsden (Ala.) Times. But one of the book's most salient points has to do with just how special that series is. Nothing could possibly make that point better than for the two schools to become the first from the same state to win back-to-back National Championships and have Heisman Trophy-winning players in successive seasons. The Tide and Tigers did just that in 2009 and 2010, and on the following pages Mr. Smothers recognizes and salutes those remarkable accomplishments.

The Publishers

2009

Alabama went into Jordan-Hare Stadium undefeated and ranked No. 2 nationally, harboring hopes of defeating unranked Auburn, then beating No. 1 Florida in the SEC Championship Game, and advancing to the BCS National Championship Game.

Those were lofty goals, even for the Crimson Tide, which had once been the dominant team in the Southeastern Conference. But before this year Alabama had not won the SEC since 1999 nor won a national championship since 1992. The Tide had beaten Auburn handily (36-0) the previous year, which was only its second win over the Tigers since the turn of the century.

Alabama, in its second year (2008) under Nick Saban, had won 12 straight games; then lost in both the SEC Championship Game and the Sugar Bowl. The third time around was the charm, and neither the coach nor his team was to be denied. They made no qualms about their goal – win it all.

That meant winning the last three games, beginning with Auburn. It was no easy task. Auburn was the underdog, with the mind of pulling an upset. And for much of the game the Tigers played that way, taking an early lead and outplaying the Tide most of the game.

Saban had told his players before the game that the strong can survive, but they can also get their butts kicked; or something similar. And it looked like that was going to happen until the fading minutes. With time running out Alabama was on the go, driving for the win. With 1:24 remaining Greg McElroy passed four yards to Roy Upchurch for the winning touchdown.

Upchurch said after the game that he had the feeling that he could get wide open in the end zone if he were in the game; so he started shouting, "Put me in! Put me in!"

No one seemed to pay any attention to him until they changed the play. It was his number and he was Johnny on the spot. After the game, a lot of people were paying a lot of attention to what Upchurch had to say.

Alabama had survived, relying a lot on its strong defensive stand earlier in the fourth quarter when Auburn was threatening to widen its 21-20 lead, but the story line was primarily that pass, and Upchurch sure had a story to tell.

It was said that Saban raised his right index finger as he walked off the field. But I didn't see it. Maybe it was for his first win in Auburn, or maybe it was an omen of what was to come — No. 1 in both the SEC and BCS championship games.

* * * * *

2009 in a nutshell:
Biggest Margin – Auburn 14, Alabama 0
Final Score – Alabama 26, Auburn 21
SEC Champion – Alabama
Heisman Trophy winner – Mark Ingram of Alabama
BCS National Champion – Alabama

2010

For some reason Auburn and Alabama football fans like to label various games between these two cross-state rivals. Just saying it was THE GAME of 1972, the Iron Bowl of 1985 or whatever year they are talking about doesn't get it; those games have come to be known as "Punt, Bama, Punt" or "The Kick" and a lot of other things, depending on the situation.

Thus it was with the game of 2010, which fans will remember as "Cam's Comeback". It could easily have been branded as "Believe It or Not" because Auburn quarterback Cam Newton led the Tigers to a come-from-behind 28-27 victory after trailing 0-24 in the second quarter.

It was the largest comeback in Auburn's history, and the largest ever allowed by the Crimson Tide. It was also unbelievable because it happened in Tuscaloosa; before the largest crowd (101,821) to ever see a game in this huge rivalry. Things like that just don't happen in Bryant-Denny Stadium, or to a defending national champion team.

But it did, and with a lot of similarities from the previous year when Alabama had been unbeaten going into the game at Auburn; and was focused on winning the SEC and national titles. The Tide had to score in the final two minutes to win the 2009 game, 26-21. Auburn took its first and only lead in the 2010 game on a seven yard pass from Newton to Philip Lutzenkirchen with 11:55 remaining.

Alabama had a 21-0 lead in the first quarter before Auburn made a first down, kicked a field goal to go up 24-0 in the second quarter, and was leading 24-7 at the half. But Newton didn't rattle, and the Tigers didn't choke. The quarterback led his teammates to comeback victories eight times that fall. In the comeback over the Tide, he ran for one touchdown and passed for three others.

For the second year in a row the home team came out strong, but the visiting team won in the end; the visiting team passed for the winning touchdown in the fourth quarter, and the visiting team kept its unbeaten record alive and went on to win the SEC Championship and the BCS National Championship.

For the second year in a row, the Iron Bowl proved to be the biggest challenge of the year for the winning team – it was a more severe test than either the SEC or BCS championship games.

The winning team's star player each year also wound up winning the Heisman Trophy – running back Mark Ingram of Alabama one year; quarterback Cam Newton of Auburn the next. But there was a difference in their play in THE GAME of 2010. Ingram did not perform up to his normal outstanding performance against Auburn; there is little hope that Auburn could have won without Newton.

* * * * *

2010 in a nutshell:
Biggest Margin – Alabama 24, Auburn 0
Final Score – Auburn 28, Alabama 27
SEC Champion – Auburn
Heisman Trophy winner – Cam Newton of Auburn
BCS National Champion – Auburn

Dedication

This book is dedicated to Dr. Ben B. Barnes,
whose inspiration and research made it possible.

ACKNOWLEDGEMENTS

A lot of people helped me with the publication of this book and I doubt that I can remember every one of them, but I'll try. Without them this book would have been a mission impossible for me. Since my retirement a lot of people have said, "Now that you are retired and have nothing to do, you should write a book."

Easier said than done. In fact, it has been so easy that I could not have done it alone. Here are some of the people who helped me along.

Dr. Ben Barnes, who holds degrees from both Alabama and Auburn, was the driving force behind this project. He was my principal sounding board -- when I could get him away from his television where he likes to while away the hours watching European soccer, playbacks of old football games, any level of baseball, sumo wrestling, and beach volleyball.

Glen Porter, publisher, and Ron Reaves, executive editor, of The Gadsden Times, obtained permission from The New York Times Company for me to use stories that I had once written for that newspaper, and a few old pictures found in some files.

Every effort was made to be factual so I sometimes went to former public relations people at both Alabama and Auburn for help and advice – people such as Kirk McNair, Larry White, Buddy Davidson and David Housel.

The primary proofreader was Betty McCoy, who also kept drinks and snacks on my desk as I wrote. Huntsville Times retired sports editor John Pruett worked with me closely and his input was invaluable. Randy Johnson, retired city editor from The Gadsden Times, was better than Google Search when it came to supplying details. Also, Clyde Bolton, formerly of The Birmingham News, offered some very helpful advice.

The cover was designed by my son, Jim Smothers, Jr., an award-winning employee of the Talladega (Ala.) Daily Home newspaper. The book was edited by Randy Johnson, who was once a member of my staff at The Gadsden Times.

Among the former players and coaches I spoke with are Terry Henley, Ray Maxwell, Freddie Kitchens, Toderick Malone, Jackie Burkett, M.L. Brackett, James Owens, Ray Perkins and Jack Crowe.

Time ran out before efforts succeeded in reaching others such as Patrick Nix.

INTRODUCTION

1961 was a significant year. As MAD magazine pointed out, it was the year that was still the same, still 1961, if you turned it upside down. And in many regards, it was a year when the old order was turned upside down and new beginnings took place. Some of those new beginnings had major input from and major impact upon the state of Alabama.

The United States space program made a major stride toward catching up with the Russians when astronaut Alan Shepard rode one of Huntsville's Redstone rockets on a sub-orbital space flight in 1961. And this was only the beginning of America's success in space. Also in 1961, President John Kennedy announced that an American astronaut would go to the moon and back before the Sixties were over. Thanks to Huntsville's Saturn V rocket, his confident prediction was accurate.

The civil rights movement brought forth violent reactions across Alabama in 1961 as the Freedom Riders attempted to integrate busses and bus stations in Anniston, Birmingham, and Montgomery. And this was only the beginning of the success of the civil rights movement, as Dr. Martin Luther King, Jr., of Montgomery, became a national and internationally recognized leader of those who sang with confidence "We Shall Overcome". Without the civil rights movement, Alabama and Auburn quite likely would not have won football national championships in 2009 and 2010.

1961 was the year that Alabama Crimson Tide football completed a remarkable resurgence. Only four years after losing 40-0 to Coach Ralph "Shug" Jordan's 1957 Associated Press national champion Auburn Tigers, Alabama won the AP's national title, completing an unbeaten season by defeating Auburn 34-0, a turnaround of some 74 points. This was only the beginning of a remarkable 25-year tenure at Tuscaloosa for Coach Paul "Bear" Bryant, during which he would lead the Crimson Tide to five more national championships, an accomplishment unparalleled in American college football.

In 1961 Jimmy Smothers, not long out of college, had become a professional writer, a young reporter in the sports department of The Gadsden Times, covering high school sports and doing it very well. Within only two years he would be covering "THE GAME" between Auburn and Alabama as the Times Sports Editor. This was only the beginning of a successful writing career spanning some 50 years in Gadsden, during which a special relationship would develop between Jimmy and the Bryant family. Jimmy would eventually join Coach Bryant, Coach Jordan, and other Alabama sports icons as an elected member of the Alabama Sports Hall of Fame, a signal honor indeed.

The following pages contain many of Jimmy Smothers' colorful words about THE GAME, as published in The Gadsden Times between 1963 and 2006: his pre-Game reports, Game day descriptions, and post-Game analyses. Happy reading! I hope you enjoy reliving these days with Jimmy as much as I did.

Ben B. Barnes, Auburn Class of 1956, Alabama Class of 1962

CONTENTS

2009 and 2010	v
Acknowledgements	xi
Introduction	xii
Prologue	xiv
THE GAME -- 1963 -- Auburn 10-8	2
THE GAME -- 1964 -- Alabama 21-14	9
THE GAME -- 1966 -- Alabama 31-0	17
THE GAME -- 1967 -- Alabama 7-3	26
THE GAME -- 1971 -- Alabama 31-7	36
THE GAME -- 1972 -- Auburn 17-16	48
THE GAME -- 1973 -- Alabama 35-0	62
THE GAME -- 1979 -- Alabama 25-18	67
Final Whistle for COACH JORDAN	79
THE GAME -- 1981 -- Alabama 28-17	85
THE GAME -- 1982 -- Auburn 23-22	94
Final Whistle for COACH BRYANT	105
Halftime	111
THE GAME -- 1985 -- Alabama 25-23	124
THE GAME -- 1989 -- Auburn 30-20	133
THE GAME -- 1992 -- Alabama 17-0	143
THE GAME -- 1993 -- Auburn 22-14	157
THE GAME -- 1995 -- Auburn 31-27	165
THE GAME -- 1999 -- Alabama 28-17	178
THE GAME -- 2000 -- Auburn 9-0	186
THE GAME -- 2002 -- Auburn 17-7	196
THE GAME -- 2004 -- Auburn 21-13	204
THE GAME -- 2006 -- Auburn 22-15	215
THE GAMES -- My Final Two	225
Epilogue	229
Finis by Rick Bragg	230
Overtime - Facts and Data	231
Listing of Names	242

Prologue

This book is an account of my professional and personal involvement with the Alabama-Auburn football series. It includes details about some of the games which were of particular interest to me, but I have not attempted to construct another complete history of the series. The book includes articles written at the time games were played, as well as commentary written this year.

The biggest football game in the state of Alabama each year is the one pitting the state's two largest colleges – Alabama vs. Auburn or Auburn vs. Alabama; depending on which is the home team on that particular year – Alabama on even years, Auburn on odd years. In sporting events the visiting team is always listed first. When game results are run on television the visiting team is first, and the winner is highlighted.

This is the top sports rivalry in Alabama, which has no major professional teams; and one of the top in collegiate athletics nationally, rating right up there with Oklahoma vs. Texas, Ohio State vs. Michigan; Army vs. Navy, Southern California vs. Notre Dame and Florida vs. Georgia.

There are a few other top rivalry games in major college football where both teams are from the same state, such as Florida State vs. Miami and Texas vs. Texas A&M. But neither of those rate with the Alabama vs. Auburn rivalry, which is a topic of conversation among fans in this state throughout the year.

Of all the well-known rivalries mentioned above, only two have had Associated Press national titles won by the two opponents in successive years -- USC and Notre Dame in 1966-67 and 1972-73, and Alabama in 2009, Auburn in 2010.

One year when I was sports editor of The Gadsden Times a readership survey was conducted by an out-of-state firm. One of the results listed was that if the paper ran an article on Alabama or Auburn football every day of the year, it would probably be the top-read story in the paper that day.

Because of the importance of that game to fans I always refer to it as THE GAME, which is easier than writing the Alabama vs. Auburn game or Auburn vs. Alabama game. Oh, I know that Harvard vs. Yale has been called "The Game" for many years, beginning back when those teams were dominating college sports. But today they are not major teams and don't draw the interest as do the Crimson Tide or Tigers. Neither does Stanford vs. California, which is known out West as "The Big Game".

Media and fans alike refer to the Auburn-Alabama game today as the Iron Bowl, although it isn't actually a bowl game, but one of 12 regular season games. Some fans erroneously refer to every game between the two schools as the "Iron Bowl" although the phrase doesn't date back past the 1964 season; and was not licensed and trademarked until 2000, when a shared logo was created.

The two schools wanted to protect the game's nickname, said David Housel, former athletic director at Auburn University. He says it is the money the schools get from the commercial use that may be the primary reason the name has stuck, although the game is no longer played in Birmingham, a city once noted for its iron ore and steel mills.

Housel also said the nickname may have stuck because the media has started using "Iron Bowl" when promoting the game; and so have the athletic publicity staffs. When Housel was sports information director he didn't use the term, nor does he call it the "Iron Bowl" today.

"Auburn-Alabama says it all for me," he said, adding that Iron Bowl might have been appropriate when it was played in Birmingham, the Iron City. But the term diminished in importance when the game was moved to Auburn and Tuscaloosa.

I've never liked the term "Iron Bowl" and rarely use it, although it has been said I may have had a minor role when Auburn coach Ralph Jordan coined the phrase. When I was doing research for this article I asked long-time Auburn employee Buddy Davidson, who was the sports information director back then, what he remembered about when and how the term was first used.

Here is his reply: "I'm reasonably sure it was in 1964. We had gone to the Orange Bowl the previous season and had been picked No. 1 by Sports Illustrated in preseason. But Jimmy Sidle got hurt and the season fell apart.

"The way I remember it, we were in Coach Jordan's office the week before the Alabama game. Somebody (I've always thought it was you) asked him about us not going to a bowl that year. He said something to the effect that 'We've got a bowl game to play and it is the Iron Bowl'."

I remember that press conference but didn't realize, until Buddy reminded me, that my question had prompted Jordan's first utterance of the phrase.

Mel Bailey, Jefferson County sheriff at the time, started giving an Iron Bowl Trophy in the mid-'60s. But Davidson says as the sheriffs changed over the years, that tradition faded away.

Coach Jordan also mentioned "Iron Bowl" during his Sunday television show and it caught on with the fans. Charles Land of the Tuscaloosa News had one sentence near the end of a lengthy pre-game article the following year saying Coach Jordan had referred to the game as the Iron Bowl.

Kirk McNair, former sports information director at the University of Alabama, said neither he nor Charley Thornton, long-time assistant athletic director, liked the term and never used it in press releases, game programs or media guides.

In recent years, the term has started showing up in game programs and media guides at the two schools. The newer generation of fans, publicity people and media have adopted it and it has become so ingrained that they may think the game has officially been the Iron Bowl since the teams first played in 1893, rather than when the name and logo were officially trademarked more than 100 years later.

Call it what you will, but to me, it remains THE GAME because that's what it is. It's the biggest, the best, the hottest rivalry, the most traditional football game played each year in Alabama. What more need be said? This is THE GAME. Ask anyone.

Seriously involved in one of many pre-game talks at Birmingham's Legion Field, Auburn's head coach (1951-1975) Ralph "Shug" Jordan (facing camera) and Alabama's head coach (1958-1982) Paul "Bear" Bryant (in hound's-tooth hat).

PAT TRAMMELL

In the long and storied history of THE GAME, there have been many impressive personalities with characteristics of determination and resourcefulness, coupled with respect for their opponents. They include Bo Jackson, who came to Auburn with the primary objective of ending Alabama's nine-year winning streak, and succeeded in his freshman year. They include Mike Shula, who overcame a seemingly hopeless situation in the final 40 seconds to lead Alabama to an astounding win in 1985.

This never-say-die spirit is perhaps best exemplified by Pat Trammell of Scottsboro, who was not deterred from playing at Alabama by their 0-40 loss to 1957 national champion Auburn in their most recent game before his arrival as a freshman at Tuscaloosa. As a senior quarterback in 1961, he led the Tide to its first ever 11-0 season, a 34-0 defeat of Auburn, the SEC title, and Coach Bryant's first national championship.

When he was only 28 years old, Dr. Pat Trammell, MD, died of cancer. His funeral in Scottsboro was attended by his Crimson Tide teammates and coaches, including Bryant. Also present were his former Auburn opponents and coaches, including Coach Jordan. Years later, when naming some of his all-time favorite players, Bryant singled out Pat Trammell as his "all-time favorite person."

THE GAME - 1963

By Jimmy Smothers, written in 2011

You won't find THE GAME of 1963 on a list of "notable games" in most places, but to me it was big. In a way it was the beginning of an era for me. Previously, I had seen five Alabama and Auburn games. I had covered two games as a photographer for other newspapers in the 1950s; I had been to two games as a sports writer after joining The Gadsden Times.

In fact, I wrote the "running" for the game story the previous year (1962) under another by-line. Bobby Hayes, a high school correspondent for The Times at that time, wrote the "lede". That might not happen today, but in a past era it was not unusual for sports writers to write stories for each other on certain occasions. I have written articles for others a few times; and other writers have covered for me. One year I got food poisoning at the Sugar Bowl and became extremely sick in the locker room after the game. David Housel wrote my game story that night as I lay in the bathroom thinking I would die.

In 1962 my sports editor and life-long friend, Jimmy Bryan, failed to make THE GAME at the last minute. I felt like the sports editor of a newspaper should have his by-line on the game story so I put it there. We never discussed it before or since. And as I look back now and read that story, I can see why.

Anyway, back to 1963. It was big with me because that was the first THE GAME that I covered as sports editor of the Times. Bryan had taken a job that summer with The Birmingham News and I was promoted to sports editor just before the beginning of football season. During that fall I switched back and forth, covering an Alabama or Auburn game each week.

On the last day of November I felt on top of the world as I made my way to the press box at Legion Field and sat there with some big-name sports writers that I'd read over the years. This was really big time – it was THE GAME of the year. And I had the top assignment for The Times.

Alabama was a slight favorite, but Auburn won, 10-8. In fact, some older fans still have T-shirts with 10-8 printed on them. Senior quarterback Mailon Kent replaced the injured Jimmy Sidle and led the Auburn offense. Howard Simpson stood out on defense.

This was the second time Auburn had scored against Bryant, since he first took the Alabama job before the 1958 season. Auburn won that year's game, 14-8, but Bryant's Tide shut out the Tigers the next four years – 10-0, 3-0, 34-0 and 38-0. That totals Alabama 93, Auburn 14 during those five years. (That almost made up for Auburn's 128-7 domination during the previous four years.)

The win in '63 gave the Tigers a 9-1 record (6-1 in the SEC) and earned them a trip to the Orange Bowl. I went along, covering my first major bowl game. Nebraska won, 13-7, robbing Auburn of a late win when a Cornhusker defender broke up a pass to Doc Griffith in the end zone that looked like a sure touchdown. The ball was almost in Doc's hands and I was thinking about leading my story focused on a hometown athlete from Hokes Bluff catching the winning touchdown pass.

Covering THE GAME at Legion Field and covering the Orange Bowl in Miami were big time assignments for a young sports editor at a small-town newspaper. They proved to be only the beginning of a career that carried over into the next century, and enabled me to crisscross the country to cover Alabama, Auburn and other teams. Before it ended my luggage was covered with a lot of decals from many teams and major sporting events.

-30-

Pre-game column

Spotlight on quarterbacks: Sidle, Namath

(Original version published in The Gadsden Times, Saturday, November 30, 1963)

BIRMINGHAM -- An unexpected cold front that swept into Alabama yesterday failed to chill a supersonic football fever which has spread across this Cotton State. But there's nothing to get alarmed about - no one expected it to.

Today Alabama's Crimson Tide and Auburn's War Eagles tangle at Legion Field in what may be the biggest head-knocker of the decade.

This is annually a sellout show, regardless of previous records and pre-game predictions. And this year, with the Southeastern Conference powerhouses squaring off with national ratings, major bowl bids and an outside chance for the loop's crown lying in the balance, scalpers are getting up to $100 a pair for good seats. And a little cold weather, rain, sleet or snow won't keep football followers away from this one.

Seventh-ranked Alabama is a one-touchdown favorite over the rival Plainsmen, who rate a ninth-place slot in the UPI poll. Each team is once beaten. Alabama fell to Florida, Auburn to Mississippi State. Both downed Tennessee, Georgia, and Georgia Tech.

Today's spectacular will be the rubber game of the cross-state rivals. Each team has won 13, there has been one tie. But in the modern series that began in 1948 Bama has a three-game edge. Both teams have been voted National Champions in The Associated Press poll -- Auburn in 1957, and Alabama in 1961.

Auburn has not scored on Alabama since the second quarter of the 1958 game, which it won, 14-8. But with substantial improvement on both offense and defense, any War Eagle fan will tell you this is the year to break the famine.

Auburn's attack is led by all-SEC Jimmy Sidle, the nation's rushing leader with 967 yards. The 200-pound junior needs only 38 yards to move ahead of Monk Gafford (1942) as the No. 1 Auburn rusher for a single season.

In total offense Sidle needs 43 yards to move ahead of Travis Tidwell, who gained 1,715 yards in a single season.

Chipping in at moving the pigskin for Auburn will be halfbacks Tucker Frederickson and George Rose and fullback Larry Rawson. There have also been unconfirmed rumors from the Plain that Mailon Kent may do the quarterbacking, while Sidle switches to halfback to pose even a bigger threat with his running.

Alabama will counter with Joe Namath, the "Hungarian Howitzer". He is one of the nation's better passers. And the last time out, against Georgia Tech, Joe also proved his worth as a field general in an infantry attack.

The other member of the Tide's one-two punch is all-SEC halfback Benny Nelson. The 185-pound Huntsville senior has averaged 6.4 yards per carry and has scored seven touchdowns.

Rounding out the Bama backfield will be Raymond Ogden or Hudson Harris at right half and Eddie Versprille at fullback. Mike Fracchia is listed as a doubtful starter.

While Alabama pits a passing attack against the Tigers' running game the defensive clubs will be knocking heads on almost an equal basis for the first time in years. The linebacking of Versprille and Paul Crane is rated on a par with that of Rawson and Bill Cody.

The ends should be about equal but Alabama should have a little edge at tackles and guards.

While the Tide and Tigers are battling it out in Birmingham an ear will be turned to the Mississippi State-Ole Miss battle. Ole Miss is a touchdown favorite, but if State can manage an upset, the SEC crown will go to the best of Alabama and Auburn.

Official announcements of bowl appearances are also expected after the game. The Crimson Tide is reported to have a Sugar Bowl battle with Mississippi cinched and Auburn has accepted an Orange Bowl date with Nebraska.

-30-

Game

Auburn turns Bama errors into victory

(Original version published in The Gadsden Times, Sunday, December 1, 1963)

LEGION FIELD, Birmingham -- It had to happen sometime. Yesterday it did. Auburn whipped Alabama 10-8 in what was listed as a major upset. But it wasn't. What else need we say?

Five years of football famine for the Plainsmen in the bitter cross-state rivalry ended as the mighty Crimson Tide came crashing to the ground before a record crowd of 55,000.

The weather, 55 degrees at game time, had dropped to near freezing as 30 mph gusts of wind and deep shadows knifed across the turf. But it didn't bother Auburn followers. Mailon Kent, Howard Simpson, Tucker Frederickson, George Rose, Doc Griffith, Chuck Hurston, Jack Thornton and the others saw to that.

Auburn came after the victory. Auburn got it. But it was no easy matter. Although the War Eagle gridders took the lead the first time they touched the ball and never trailed, Alabama kept the pressure on throughout the entire display of hard-nosed defensive football.

Fumbles and penalties proved to be the downfall of the Crimson Tide as the state's No. 1 football power. An alert secondary, hard charging linemen, and a dedicated Tiger crew earned the victory.

Mailon Kent, a 190-pound senior, who has played in the shadow of All-America Jimmy Sidle all season, came off the bench to engineer the Orange Bowl-bound Tigers to all 10 points.

The Lanett native, who had seen only six minutes of playing time prior to the game, came on when Sidle was injured on Auburn's second offensive play. He pushed his teammates 31 yards to the 14 in six plays. Woody Woodall entered the contest, swinging his trusty right foot, and Bama's magic spell was broken.

In the third quarter Kent flipped an eight-yard pass to Frederickson for a touchdown and that was it.

Bama's Benny Nelson put the Tide back within striking distance with an exciting 80-yard gallop up the middle. But Coach Paul Bryant's forces were unable to move it in for the fatal blow as Auburn's secondary refused to give Joe Namath a respectable target.

While defensive stars were numerous for the jubilant Tigers, Simpson stood out above the rest.

The 232-pound flanker killed an Alabama touchdown march at the five in the second stanza, and then put the Plainsmen in business at the seven in the third.

Although Alabama whipped Auburn in statistics, the Tiders were unable to overcome their mistakes.

Alabama lost the ball four times on fumbles. One doused a sure touchdown, one nipped a drive at the 26, another killed touchdown hopes at the 37, and the other set up Auburn's touchdown.

Penalties also played key roles in the game, as did the punting of Auburn's Jon Kilgore. Not once did he allow Alabama to field one of his boots in the air as he kept them coming out of the hole all day. In contrast, Buddy French, Alabama's kicker, averaged only 30 yards. One carried only 14 yards and set up Auburn's early field goal.

The game ended the season at 9-1 for Auburn, which officially accepted a bid to the Orange Bowl on New Year's Day. Alabama, now 7-2, has a Dec. 14 date at Miami remaining before meeting Ole Miss in the Sugar Bowl Jan. 1.

-30-

Post-game column

Kent proves to be top clutch player

(Original version published in The Gadsden Times, Monday, December 2, 1963)

In today's modern space age two-day-old news is often considered ancient history. But not so when speaking of Auburn's 10-8 triumph over Alabama last Saturday. That was a game which will never be forgotten, nor will War Eagle fans ever grow tired of telling of it.

Whenever talk arises of the big '63 game, the name Mailon Kent will forge high above all the others.

Auburn's All-America junior quarterback Jimmy Sidle and Alabama's All-SEC halfback Benny Nelson and highly praised Joe Namath were the ones booked to supply thrills for the epic-type football show.

That wasn't the case at all Saturday.

A five-year senior, who reportedly had considered giving up football this fall, was the bombshell who provided the punch for the shocking victory.

Sidle's excellent play, plus an injury, kept Kent sidelined three games after serving as the top signal caller in 1962. The Lanett native played one minute against Chattanooga and about five minutes in a later game. But he was ready, when and if the call came.

"Kent was the 'insurance policy' for us," Auburn publicist Bill Beckwith said after the game Saturday. "Today he paid off."

Kent had been billed as a clutch player throughout his entire stay at Auburn. Coach Jordan says he is the best drop-back passer for Auburn in years, and has the ability to hit a target when rushed hard. "He's at his best when the pressure is greatest," the coach said.

Saturday he proved both statements to be true.

In the third quarter after Howard Simpson had recovered Benny Nelson's bobble on the seven, Jim Simmons nailed Larry Rawson for a yard loss. Sidle threw incomplete. It was third down and eight.

Kent and assistant coach Buck Bradberry were standing on the sideline talking. Just as Sidle's pass fell incomplete they turned to one another and said, "Nineteen sprint pass." Coach Bradberry patted Kent on the back and he trotted onto the field.

If Bama's left defensive end rushed, Kent was to throw. If he stayed back, Kent was to run. The snap, the end shot in, Tucker Frederickson circled behind him into the clear at the goal line. Kent fired a strike and Auburn had the game.

Another example of Kent's value is his leadership. He has been team captain in two games in which he did not play, and his help to Sidle has been invaluable.

Sidle went into the game 37 yards short of Monk Gafford's All-Time Total Offense record for one season of 1,004 yards. He was 43 yards short of Travis Tidwell's total offense record.

He was expected to break both easily. He has been averaging more than 100 yards rushing per game this year. But Alabama had other plans, holding him to but 39 in 13 carries. However, it was enough to break Gafford's record by two yards. He failed to catch Tidwell who rolled up 1,715 total yards in 1946.

-30-

Auburn two-way back Tucker Frederickson (1962-64), shown with Auburn Coach Ralph "Shug" Jordan; Frederickson was No. 1 in the NFL 1965 draft.

THE GAME - 1964

By Jimmy Smothers, written in 2011

This year THE GAME was moved to Thanksgiving Day, Nov. 26, so it could become the first to be broadcast on television nationally. That seemed to be a big deal for a lot of people, but whether a game was on television or not didn't matter much to me. At least not at that time. Later, reporters had to change their style of reporting games because of what fans saw on television.

For example, the game stories didn't have as much play-by-play detail. Writers started getting more interviews in the locker rooms, where the TV camera did not go at that time. We started writing a lot of notes, trying to provide fans with as much detail and opinion as possible.

Going into that season Auburn was No. 1 in the pre-season ranking by Sports Illustrated; Alabama No. 6. But things began to turn around when the Tigers were beaten by Kentucky in Lexington the third game of the year. And by the time Auburn faced Alabama, it had also lost to Georgia Tech and Florida. Meanwhile, Alabama was winning every game and gradually moving up in the polls. Going into THE GAME, the Tide was No. 2.

The 21-14 win gave Alabama a 10-0 overall record, 8-0 against SEC teams. The Tide moved to No. 1 the next week and won the consensus National Championship, the second for Paul Bryant. But a 17-21 loss to Texas in the Orange Bowl resulted in the AP waiting until after the bowl games were played to name a National Champion. Other polls soon followed.

Oddsmakers increased the line during game week, moving the odds from 11 to 13 ½ during a two-day stretch before kickoff. But it didn't seem to matter to the players on either team if they were top dog or underdog. They had a game to play, and they all expected to win.

Alabama was going for an unbeaten season and another national championship; if Auburn won, the Tigers could claim a successful season regardless of failing to live up to pre-season expectation of being No. 1.

Coach Ralph Jordan had his team ready, and it played like champions most of the game. Auburn kept the ball much longer, and piled up more yardage on offense; and on defense it set school records.

Coach Paul Bryant, likewise, had his team doing what it always did best – making the big plays in key situations. While Auburn played ball control, Alabama scored quickly on big plays, both on the ground and in the air. Auburn's Tom Bryan passed for more yardage than either Alabama's Steve Sloan or Joe Namath, but they had better completion percentages.

While Auburn's defense set a new school standard; Alabama's defense made key plays that were factors in the win

For example, five times Alabama players broke through the line to make key stops which could have spelled the difference in the game.
1) Auburn was moving with the opening kickoff when Wayne Freeman stopped Jimmy Partin for a two yard loss on a third and five at the 39.
2) Later in that quarter Creed Gilmer tackled Auburn's Tom Bryan for a yard loss on a fourth and three at the 28.
3) On a goal line stand Paul Crane led a host of Tiders that threw Bryan for a yard loss on third and goal at the one.
4) In the fourth quarter Alabama's John Mosley intercepted an Auburn pass at the one.
5) A few plays later Gilmer threw Sidle for a two-yard loss at the Alabama 22.

By the way, this was the first in an Alabama five-win streak over Auburn, lasting until 1969 when Auburn won, 49-26.

-30-

Pre-game column

Tigers, Tiders poised for showdown

(Original version published in The Gadsden Times. Wednesday, November 25, 1964)

All-winning Alabama and rejuvenated Auburn will clash in Birmingham's Legion Field tomorrow before a capacity crowd of 68,000 fans. Millions more will be watching on national color television.

Alabama, the Southeastern Conference champion, is an 11-point favorite. But that doesn't faze Auburn. When these two teams meet anything can, and usually does, happen.

The Crimson Tide is undefeated, second-ranked in both wire service polls, and will officially announce its acceptance to the Orange Bowl after the game. Alabama is also still hoping for the national title, which it can grab with a big win over Auburn coupled with a Notre Dame loss to Southern California Saturday.

In addition, Coach Paul Bryant's crew is seeking its second unbeaten season in four years.

Auburn, 6-3, is unranked, although it opened the season listed at No. 8 among the nation's Top 20 teams. Although the Tigers haven't achieved pre-season expectations, a win over rival Alabama will now satisfy Tiger alumni.

A triumph over Alabama will also likely mean a bowl bid for Auburn. The Gator Bowl is still interested and yesterday the Sun Bowl in El Paso, Texas, talked with officials at the school.

Despite the odds, both coaches are confident of a win, but only if their respective teams "plays its best game of the year".

"We've got a lot done in sweat clothes this past week," Coach Ralph Jordan said yesterday of his Tigers. "We have an excellent chance to win. We know Alabama has a well-balanced football team, but in some respects their game films with Mississippi State and LSU have also been encouraging to our boys and coaches."

Meanwhile, down at the Capstone, Coach Bryant speaks highly of his team's Turkey Day opponent.

"We'll have to play our best game of the season to beat them," he said. "They have a tough defense, three or four great players and a lot of good ones."

Alabama worked out in the gym at Tuscaloosa yesterday. Today the team moves into the Magic City and its headquarters at the Bankhead Hotel. The team is scheduled to hold its final pre-game workout today in Birmingham.

While the Tiders stayed indoors, Auburn worked for about an hour and a half in the rain. Auburn will journey to Birmingham today and set up headquarters in the Town House Motel.

Tomorrow will be the final regular season game for 17 Alabama seniors, although defensive back Grady Elmore won't play due to a knee operation. These boys have seen the Tide win 29 games and lose only two in the past three seasons, starting with the 1961 national championship team.

Fourteen Tigers will be winding up their college careers. And they, too, want another shot at a bowl game, having lost to Nebraska in the Orange Bowl last Jan. 1. That will give the Auburn seniors an extra incentive, if it's possible to pick up any more incentive in this game.

The fans will also see two All-Americas lock up. Alabama guard Wayne Freeman and Auburn fullback Tucker Frederickson were named to the NEA's All-America selection last week.

Steve Sloan (1963-65), left, and Joe Namath (1962-64) led Alabama to three wins over Auburn in four games and SEC and National titles in 1964 and 1965.

* * * * *

Auburn will also be facing eight All-SEC performers. In yesterday's UPI All-conference selection Joe Namath was named on the first unit and seven other Tide players were mentioned among the 33 men named. Frederickson was the only War Eagle listed, being named to the first unit.

Alabama kicker David Ray, who has already broken a national record for scoring by kicking with 58 points, could mean the difference in this game. Last year Auburn won, 10-8. And despite the big point spread set up by odds makers this year; most fans expect a close game.

Ray, who was named to the 33-man All-America squad picked by the Football News, will also be shooting at a national field goal record set by former Auburn great Ed Dyas. He is only one field goal short.

Although Namath isn't expected to start for the Tide he'll be ready for heavy duty if needed. And his passing could spell the difference as it did against Georgia Tech in the last game.

Steve Sloan, who has kept Alabama on the winning trail since Namath's injury, will start. Tom Bryan, who has manned the quarterback duties for Auburn's injured All-America Jimmy Sidle, will again get the nod for the Tigers. Sidle will play tailback.

Frederickson will be the big man in Auburn's attack. He's the team's leading rusher with 459 yards on 107 attempts. He's also the leading pass receiver with 14 catches for 101 yards. And he's tied with Bryan as the team's leading point maker with 24.

Steve Bowman paces the Tide in rushing; having gained 450 yards on 97 carries. Tommy Tolleson is the top receiver, having caught 22 passes for 248 yards and two touchdowns. The top scorer is Ray, with 70 points.

The game will feature the conference's best offensive team against the conference's top defenders. Auburn has averaged giving up only 77.3 yards a game rushing while Alabama has averaged gaining 186.1.

-30-

Game

Tide thankful to escape Tiger stew

(Original version published in The Gadsden Times, Friday, November 27, 1964)

BIRMINGHAM – Alabama switched from the traditional Thanksgiving Day Turkey to a helping of War Eagle yesterday, roasting Auburn, 21-14, before some 68,000 chilly fans and a national television audience. But it was the victim, not the victor, which added the trimmings.

Auburn, a 13½ point underdog at game time, was expected to be an easy helping for the nation's No. 2 ranked football power. But the opponent from the Plain proved to be a tough ol' bird. And the Crimson Tide was a little extra thankful to escape with a victory of any sort.

Auburn almost doubled the Tide in first downs, 19-10; powered its way for a net 187 yards overland compared to 128 for Alabama; and trailed the Tide's great passing show by only seven yards, 114-121.

The score, however, is what determines the winner. And in that department Alabama was tops by a touchdown and extra point, thus winning the game.

Steve Bowman recovered an Auburn fumble in the end zone for a first quarter touchdown. Ray Ogden ran the second-half kickoff back 107 yards for the Tide's second touchdown. Joe Namath passed 23-yards to Ray Perkins for the final touchdown; capping a 71-yard drive in only three plays.

Other than that, Auburn allowed its biggest rival across the 50-yard line only three times. The deepest penetration came on the fourth play of the second quarter and was stopped when David Ray missed a 37-yard field goal. Alabama advanced to the 48 just before the half ended and had the ball on the 46 when the game ended.

Auburn was in Alabama country six times during the game.

The second time was in the second quarter when Tucker Frederickson scored from the three. Then in the fourth quarter Jimmy Sidle raced in with a 16-yard pass from Tom Bryan.

The hyped-up Alabama defenders killed Tiger drives at the two, 24, 26 and 46.

The Crimson Tide gave up its first touchdown as the result of a bad snap on a punting situation back at the 29 and Auburn scored four plays later.

Frederickson carried on three plays for 25 yards and scored by leaping three yards over right guard. Sidle picked up the other four. Don Lewis kicked the extra point and Auburn was out front, 7-6, when the half ended.

Ogden changed the complexion of things in only 15 seconds after Ben McDavid's toe touched the football to open the second half.

A 6-2, 217-pound senior from Jesup, Ga., Ogden took the kick seven yards deep in the end zone and blasted right up the middle for a touchdown. He was in the clear before reaching midfield and outran a couple of Auburn defenders to the goal line.

Sloan dropped back in an attempt to pass for a two point conversion, couldn't find a receiver open, and plunged into the end zone.

Later in the third quarter Auburn lost the ball on downs at the two; and early in the fourth quarter a fumble at the Tide 23 killed still another Tiger march.

Bowman blasted 53 yards up the middle on a draw; Hudson Harris gained two yards and then Namath passed to Perkins, in the clear, at the five. He stepped in for the winning touchdown.

Auburn's other six-pointer came in the last two minutes of play on a 16-yard pass from Bryan to Sidle. Lewis had ignited the drive by recovering a Wayne Trimble fumble at the 43. Four straight passes by Bryan moved the Tigers in for the score. Lewis again kicked the extra point, making it 21-14 with 1:10 left.

Namath killed the clock in two plays.

-30-

Sidebar

Auburn's Big Tuck added the spice

(Original version published in The Gadsden Times, Friday, November 27, 1964)

BIRMINGHAM – Alabama won the football game, but it was Big Boy Tucker Frederickson from Auburn who added the spice to the huge serving of gridiron at Legion Field on yesterday's Thanksgiving Day.

Auburn's 6-2, 215-pound fullback put on a one-man display of football talent second to none. And after the knocking was over several members of the National Broadcasting Company crew agreed with what the coach, Ralph Jordan, has said all along – that "Frederickson is perhaps the most complete football player in the country."

He was the choice of many sports people for the Heisman Award this fall. And had the voting taken place after yesterday's game, it is very likely he'd have won.

Frederickson, who has already made several All-America selections, lived the part yesterday. He ran the ball 22 times, gained 117 yards and scored Auburn's go-ahead touchdown in the second quarter.

Not once was he stopped for minus yardage and only once did Alabama halt him at the line of scrimmage. That was in the third quarter when the Tigers had a fourth and goal at the two.

Tucker's day's work was only seven yards short of the entire net rushing for Alabama.

He was just as good on defense, moving up from his safety position to make numerous tackles near the line of scrimmage. It was during one of the few times he left the game that Alabama's Steve Bowman burst up the middle for 52 yards to set up the Tide's only rushing touchdown.

Alabama's coach, Paul Bryant, praised Frederickson after the game for both his offensive and defensive play. In fact, the short punt formation the Tide ran a couple of times was put in because of his defensive play.

"We were so worried about Tucker that we put French (Buddy, the Tide punter) about eight or nine yards back of center. If Tucker came up, we were going to pass; if he stayed back it was to be a punt," Bryant explained after the game.

Peahead Walker of the New York Giants, on hand to scout Frederickson as well as the Tide's Joe Namath, was also greatly impressed with what he saw.

-30-

The author interviews Coach Ralph Jordan at a lake cabin near Auburn.

THE GAME - 1966

By Jimmy Smothers, written in 2011

The Auburn vs. Alabama game of 1966 isn't listed among the "Notable Games" by Wikipedia, the free encyclopedia that can be found with Google Search on the Internet. Nor does it have a title, such as the 1967 game the following year, which fans remember simply as "The Run in the Mud" game.

However, that doesn't lessen the way Alabama fans have come to look back at that year's team and its accomplishments with great respect. Actually, the word "respect" doesn't do full justice to the affection Alabama followers have developed for that team, coupled with their everlasting and growing despair for its being denied Alabama's third straight national championship.

Actually, much of that season was one of controversy over the football polls, particularly the more popular one conducted by The Associated Press among some 63 members of the media, although usually only 50 voted. Even the UPI poll, with a lot more college coaches casting their votes, was in for a share of attention.

Alabama had won two straight national titles and had a combined record of 19-2-1 in 1964 and 1965, and was ranked No. 1 in the 1966 pre-season poll. But by the time the Tide opened its season on Sept. 24, other contenders for the title had already played games, and Alabama was No. 3, behind No. 1 Michigan State and No. 2 UCLA, and ahead of No. 4 Notre Dame and No. 5 Southern Cal.

Alabama was never ranked any higher and actually dropped to No. 4 during four weeks of the season, but was back at No. 3 the last three games of the year.

The controversy started on Nov. 19 when the two top-ranked teams, Notre Dame and Michigan State, played to a 10-10 tie. Two weeks later, Alabama, now the only unbeaten-untied team in the nation, dominated Auburn. But neither of the top major polls changed.

No. 1 Notre Dame and No. 2 Michigan State were 9-0-1; No. 3 Alabama was 10-0-0 and No. 4 Georgia was 9-1-0. After the regular season, No. 3 Alabama defeated No. 6 Nebraska 34-7 in the Orange Bowl. But neither Notre Dame nor Michigan State played in a bowl game that year; so if the bowl games had counted in the polls, Alabama might have moved to No. 1.

After Alabama had lost to Texas in the 1964 Orange Bowl, after being named national champion, the AP elected to wait until after the bowl games to pick a No. 1 in 1965. But it had returned to a final No. 1 poll after the regular season for the 1966 season. Because of these changes in voting timing, Alabama won championships '64 and '65; then missed out in '66 for the same reason.

Tide end Ray Perkins (left) and quarterback Kenny Stabler, in an imagined 1960s conversation concerning Tide receiver Dennis Homan: "Ray, if you could catch my passes without that bushel basket, I wouldn't have to throw so many to Dennis."

* * * * *

Bryant said a few days after the win over Auburn that year that his current Alabama team, which was not elected national champion, was "probably a sounder, better all-around club than those which won the coveted honor the past two seasons".

That '66 team held six opponents scoreless; allowed three opponents seven or fewer points; and gave up only 44 all season. Only Mississippi State scored two touchdowns, coming in a game Alabama won, 27-14. The closest game was over Tennessee, an 11-10 win.

In 2006 Keith Dunnavant wrote a book about the 1966 team entitled "The Missing Ring," and that phrase has come to symbolize not only THE GAME of 1966 but the entire season among Alabama fans. There wasn't much to the game against Auburn, which Alabama won 31-0, using third and fourth teamers in the second half.

After Dunnavant's book came out, it created a revived interest in the 1966 team, and a couple of years after that the University of Alabama presented members of that team with rings.

Although 1966 was a huge year for Alabama, and Tide fans were making a big deal about the "injustice" of not being named No. 1 in the polls, it was just the opposite for Auburn and its coach, Ralph Jordan. Auburn wound up 4-6, its first losing season in 14 years.

After the game that year I remember someone mentioning something about Alabama going for a third straight national championship to Coach Jordan. In reply he said, "I'm for any team in the SEC being No.1. Alabama has the best football team that we played. But what about an Alabama-Georgia match? There are four million people in Georgia who claim they have the best team. Such a game would be one helluva match. But I'm just expressing an opinion."

Others must have had similar opinions because not only was Alabama denied the national championship, but its coach, Paul Bryant, was denied SEC Coach of the Year honors. That went to Vince Dooley of the Georgia Bulldogs, although the 'dawgs wound up 10-1-0 and ranked No. 4 behind Alabama in both polls. Surprisingly, Tom Cahill, Army, was named the national college football Coach of the Year. His Black Knights wound up 8-2 that year.

-30-

Pre-game column

Bryant says Auburn now a strong club

(Original version published in The Gadsden Times on Thursday, December 1, 1966)

TUSCALOOSA – Undefeated Alabama puts all its marbles in the same basket Saturday afternoon by playing Auburn's Tigers in a nationally-televised game at Birmingham's Legion Field. Kickoff time is 1:15 p.m.

The only unbeaten and untied major college football team in the nation, the Crimson Tide of coach Paul "Bear" Bryant will be seeking to extend its consecutive winning streak to 16 games and run its "without-defeat" streak to 20 games against the resurgent Tigers from Auburn.

"Auburn probably has more football players than any team in the Southeastern Conference at this stage," Bryant said. "I say this because Auburn lost a lot of good players early in the year due to injuries and they had to get others ready to play. Now their injured boys are back healthy and that gives them a lot of outstanding players."

Auburn will be a much tougher foe than the 4-5 record might indicate. Coach Ralph "Shug" Jordan's team developed into a strong outfit in the final stretch drive and gave both Florida and Georgia rugged games before falling in the final minutes.

Auburn also will have the benefit of having three weeks in which to prepare for Alabama. The Tigers last played on November 12 against Georgia.

Alabama will be seeking to finish the season 10-0 and has aspirations of copping its third straight national championship.

"We certainly think we deserve the national championship – that is, if we can whip Auburn," Bryant says forcefully.

"After all, we were voted the No. 1 team in the pre-season poll and our players felt that meant the voters expected us to win. Well, we've won and yet the only time we were ranked No. 1 was in the pre-season poll.

"No team has ever defeated Tennessee, Mississippi and LSU in the same season before – but our boys did. We led the SEC in total defense and have the highest scoring offense. This is a rugged conference and not many teams have led it in both categories before," Bryant added.

ABC-TV will carry the game nationwide and some 30 million viewers are likely to be watching. Included will be the 50 voters on the Associated Press poll and the members of the United Press International Coaches Board.

Alabama will be out to make a splash in order to renew its bid for the national title.

The Crimson Tide can possibly win two national statistical titles in the finale, also. Southern Mississippi still ranks first in total defense, but Bama rolled up 348 yards last week in whipping the Southerners 34-0. Bama trails Southern 163.7 to 174.1 in defense. That means the Tide will have to limit Auburn to 69 yards or less in total offense – something no team has done all year.

Bama also could win the defensive crown against scoring, but only by shutting out Auburn. The Tide has allowed 37 points in nine games while Notre Dame has given up 38 in 10 games. A whitewash would be the sixth of the year for Alabama and would give it the title in the category.

Bryant's Tide has averaged 312.6 yards on offense this season, getting 181.4 on the ground and 131.2 through the air. Quarterback Kenny "Snake" Stabler leads the Tide in both rushing and passing, having gained 345 yards running and 787 in the air. His total offense mark of 1,132 yards puts him eighth in the all-time Alabama total offense category for a single season.

The only injury of significance that Alabama suffered against Southern Mississippi was to offensive tackle Johnny Duncan, who sprained a knee. Duncan, though, should be ready to play by Saturday although he has missed most of the work this week.

-30-

Game

Stabler, passing game give Tide 31-0 win

(Original version published in The Gadsden Times, Sunday, December 4, 1966)

BIRMINGHAM – Lightning speed, popping defense and a No. 12 quarterback. That was Alabama football at its finest yesterday and they added up to a 31-0 victory over Auburn before a capacity crowd of 67,786 at Legion Field.

The triumph, in turn, polished off a perfect 10-0 regular season for the Crimson Tide, only such record in the nation this time among major college ranks.

The game will have little bearing on Bama's bid for a third straight National Championship, but it clamped the lid on a share (with Georgia) of the Southeastern Conference crown. Bama and the Bulldogs are each 6-0 in conference play.

The three-way combination of defense and the running and passing game employed by Bryant to defeat the school's in-state rival was no real stranger to Auburnites. They saw about the same thing a year ago as the Tide romped, 30-3. Only this time, Bama's defense is tougher, its passing game is still strong, but its ground game a little weaker.

There is also a new face wearing the No. 12 red jersey made famous by Joe Namath.

Coach Bryant refused to compare junior southpaw Kenny Stabler with either Namath or Steve Sloan. But there was no doubt that Stabler was the difference in this game, just as was Sloan a year ago.

Stabler broke the game open with his passing in the second quarter after the Tigers had dominated play the first quarter, but failed to score when they had an opportunity.

Stabler completed 11 of 16 passes for 169 yards and a touchdown. His passing ability made him a dangerous runner and he gained 51 yards to lead the Tide in individual rushing.

Wayne Trimble also passed for a touchdown, throwing to Donnie Sutton. Les Kelley ran for two touchdowns, and Steve Davis kicked a field goal and four extra points to round out the Tide scoring. It could have been more.

"We certainly don't tell our boys not to score, but when we feel we have a game won we let everyone play. The reserves practice just as hard and want to play just as badly as anyone else," Bryant said after the game was over.

"We could have left Stabler out there and scored two or three more times, but how would Trimble and (Joe) Kelley have felt? The only reason I played any first-teamers in the fourth quarter was because they were seniors."

Auburn rammed the ball straight at Alabama with great success in the first quarter, moving to the eight-yard line on its second series. But a busted signal and a couple of big defensive plays by Bob Childs and John Sullivan threw up a roadblock and Jimmy Jones missed a 25-yard field goal.

Auburn fullback Tom Bryan was injured as the quarter ended, causing the Tigers to make adjustments. And this, both Bryant and Jordan said, was perhaps the big thing leading to the turning point of the game.

"They really surprised me by running straight at us in the first quarter. And Bryan was doing a great job, both catching passes and running the draw. They were also putting (Freddie) Hyatt at different places. When you have to double-team him on every down this presents quite a problem," Bryant said.

Bryant didn't want to single out any of his players until he'd graded the film. But he did say that Ray Perkins and Dennis Homan are the greatest and "that is the only way we gained any (yardage) at all."

Perkins grabbed a long pass and scored with 6:18 left in the second quarter. But Stabler's ability to get away from Auburn's hard-charging Robert Miller was what made the play. When the passer appeared to be trapped, the Tiger defense relaxed; but not Perkins, who kept digging it down field. And he was wide open when the ball was thrown right into his arms.

The score sparked the Tide's rugged defense and Auburn punted back three plays following the kick.

Two straight passes, Stabler to Perkins, then to Homan, put the ball in scoring position. This led to a 17-yard draw play by David Chatwood, which Bryant called the "most important play of the game".

It was third and 10 on the Auburn 28. The Fairhope junior took the ball on the draw and ripped up the middle to the 11 for a first down. Then Kelley slanted over right tackle for the second Bama touchdown four plays later.

Richard Cole came up with an Auburn fumble when Mike Ford nailed Loran Carter, who was trying to pass. Bama took over at the 42 and a 19-yard pass interference call at the 10 gave Steve Davis an opportunity to try a second field goal. This time his kick was good and Alabama led, 17-0 at the half.

Alabama took over on downs at the 44 and moved 56 yards in five plays for its third touchdown, which Kelley scored from the 12.

Next time the Tide had the ball Trimble threw 41 yards to Sutton, alone in the end zone.

-30-

Sidebar

Jordan said Tide had no weakness

(Original version published in The Gadsden Times, Sunday, December 4, 1966)

BIRMINGHAM – The game was a mismatch from the beginning, the Iron Bowl game of 1966. Alabama was 9-0, the nation's only unbeaten major college team, but still ranked No. 3 in both the AP and UPI polls. The Tide had won national championships the past two seasons and had 18 wins and a tie since losing its opening game to Georgia in 1965.

Auburn had a 4-5 record, and only one of those wins was against an SEC team. If Tiger fans had any hopes of pulling an upset, they were put asunder by an avalanche of Crimson jerseys early in the game.

Even Auburn coach Ralph Jordan said as much. When he met with reporters after the 31-0 loss his first comment was: "I thought we had a good start there in the first quarter, but in the second quarter we went to sleep in the secondary on that forward pass and that was all they needed."

He was right. By shutting out the Tigers, Alabama would have won the game with that lone touchdown – a 63-yard pass from Kenny Stabler to Ray Perkins with 6:18 left in the second quarter.

"I guess that the defensive halfback thought that Stabler was trapped and he just relaxed," Jordan explained. "Then those additional 10 points in the last minute and a half of the first half killed us. It's a lot different being seven points behind rather than 17."

Auburn's game plan has been to run straight at Alabama, which Jordan said was the most effective thing his team did. And in the first quarter, Auburn even had an opportunity to score and take an early lead. The drive stalled and Jimmy Jones missed a field goal from the 25. In addition, star running back Tom Bryan was injured as the first quarter ended and the Tigers had to change their game plans at halftime.

"In fact, we were up with them until that bomb," Jordan said of the long pass to Perkins.

Tide coach Paul Bryant said, "They really surprised me by running straight at us in the first quarter. And Bryan was doing a great job, both catching passes and running the draw. They were also putting (Freddie) Hyatt at different places. And when you have to double-team him on every down, this presents quite a problem."

But winning the game would still have been a long shot. Even Jordan said that in preparing for the game his staff could find no apparent weakness. "They have a fine secondary, fine linebackers, fine ends. You might term their defense as invulnerable. It's difficult to penetrate, as one would think."

Alabama's coach Paul Bryant used 56 different players in the game and said that everyone who played did as well as they could. He used three different quarterbacks, Kenny Stabler, Wayne Trimble and Joe Kelley.

"I think Stabler probably played his greatest game; he had several big plays for us," Bryant said. "In the second half we used Stabler very little although I really didn't feel safe until 30 seconds before the end and we had a 31-0 lead."

Bryant said the only reason he played any first-teamers in the second half was because they were seniors. He did put Ray Perkins back in the game in the fourth quarter when he got word from the press box that Perkins had tied Tommy Tolleson's record for career catches (at 63) earlier in the game.

Bryant didn't tell Perkins about the record, only Kelley, the third-team quarterback, who was in the game at that time. He was instructed to throw the ball to Perkins.

"Ray played the rest of the game but we were unable to get the ball to him," Bryant said. "The only thing we accomplished was getting him knocked out".

Although Perkins tied the record for career catches (three years), he only had four receptions. Dennis Homan was the leading receiver with six, for 68 yards. Stabler was the leading rusher with 51 yards.

-30-

Auburn coach Ralph Jordan with No. 35 Doc Griffith (1962-64) and No. 31 John Cochran (1963-65).

THE GAME - 1967

By Jimmy Smothers, written in 2011

There is a lot of talk about this game having been played in the worst of playing conditions. Paul Bryant and Ralph Jordan said as much at the time, so did some visiting coaches, such as Harry Mehre, a former head coach at both Georgia and Ole Miss.

I won't say the weather conditions were THE worst I've seen, because I've covered other games played in adverse weather conditions such as freezing wind and rain, ice, sleet and snow; and once during a heavy thunderstorm and high winds when a tornado touched down in another part of the city. But even at those games, I don't recall the playing surface being as bad as it was on this day.

Legion Field wasn't covered with sod that day, but with water and mud. And the rain kept pouring down, causing play to be halted at times while raincoats and other wet-weather apparel that had been blown onto the field were removed.

I was certainly thankful I was in the press box that day and stayed dry. When writers went down to the field to be on hand for post-game interviews, I didn't go on the sideline and stand in the mud, but went under the north end zone stands and stood outside the locker room with other writers until the game ended and school officials let us in to interview the players and coaches.

The game is nicknamed "Run in the Mud" in reference to Alabama quarterback Kenny Stabler's 47-yard run for the game's only touchdown that gave Alabama a come-from-behind 7-3 win. It was the third straight year that Auburn had failed to score a touchdown against the Tide. Alabama had won 30-3 in 1965, 31-0 in 1966, then 7-3 in 1967.

Two other things stand out to me.

The next day on his TV show, Auburn coach Ralph Jordan said that Alabama was holding on the touchdown play and it should have been called back.

The other thing is that Stabler was famous as a passing quarterback, yet in that game he threw only five passes, completing three for 12 yards. Bryant said after the game that the weather was just too bad to employ the passing game.

However, Auburn's quarterback, Loran Carter, a passer of some renown in his own right, threw 19 passes, completing 10 of them for 117 yards. I don't remember

Jordan saying anything about not being able to pass in that weather; although he may have mentioned it.

Both Stabler and Carter are still listed among their team's career passing leaders in various categories; a good indication of just how good they were back then. Stabler moved on to the pros, leading the Oakland Raiders to their first Super Bowl.

The mention of Carter brings to mind that the next year, 1968, center Tom Banks and Carter had a terrible time on snaps during the season. This resulted in several lost fumbles. So I suggested in one of my columns that perhaps Carter should start signaling for a fair catch on snaps from center.

-30-

Pre-game column

Auburn has edge, Tide will win

(Original version published in The Gadsden Times, Friday, December 1, 1967)

It all started way back before the turn of the 20th century, this Auburn-Alabama feuding. 'Twas 1892 to be exact. Auburn won, 32-22.

Since then the two have gone at one another so fiercely that the series was once stopped; that was in 1907, following a 6-6 tie. It took an act of the State Legislature to get the two back on the same field at the same time and place again.

The series was finally resumed in 1948 at Legion Field in Birmingham. Before Alabama was finished whipping the Tigers 55-0, Auburn folk were wishing the politicians at Montgomery had kept their noses at lawmaking and left the football scheduling up to the coaches.

There was revenge of a sort a year later as Auburn slipped in with a 14-13 victory. But it was almost 10 years and a national championship team later before the Tigers could really pour it on. That year was 1957 and Auburn won 40-0, marking the fourth straight time the Tigers had bested the Elephants.

Alabama yelled so loud at that licking that Papa Bear heard the cry all the way out at Texas A&M. He thought it was his mama calling and before another year rolled around Bryant was commander at Alabama.

Auburn welcomed Bryant to the rivalry that fall with a 14-8 smacking. But since then it has been an all-Alabama show on Tide-Tiger day in Legion Field. Only once since has Auburn managed a triumph. That was 10-8 in 1963. But it was something.

That second win over Alabama made Tiger coach Ralph Jordan one of only two coaches to manage two wins against a Bryant-coached Alabama team. The other is Bowden Wyatt, one-time coach at Tennessee.

Coaches such as Vince Dooley, Bobby Dodd, Doug Dickey, Johnny Vaught or Charlie McClendon have not done as much. Some have even quit trying.

Auburn folk feel this is the year – tomorrow is the day – for Coach Jordan and his Tigers to chalk up No. 3 against the Bear.

When the two teams collide at 1:30 no holds will be barred. They never are when these two meet, whether it's at football or ping pong.

Alabama has a Kenny Stabler and a Dennis Homan. Auburn's fearsome twosome features Loran Carter and Freddie Hyatt. But this doesn't mean these will decide the outcome of the game.

Not by a long shot.

The air may be filled with passes and both quarterbacks have sore arms when the game ends. But the battle will be fought in the line where the bruising melee will be no example for the weak at heart.

A rumble, one any self-respecting ruffian would pride himself with, will be the order of the day.

Our David Muskett, young, able and with a heart tuned for adventure, has asked to cover from the sideline. He wants to get a firsthand view of the battle; wants to be up close where he can hear the knocks and groans.

We're satisfied with our seat up on high – front row of the glassed-in press box.

Auburn will outweigh Alabama 18 pounds (216 to 198) per man on offense. The Crimson Tide will enjoy a narrow two-pound (197-195) advantage on defense.

Auburn has averaged 26 points a game this year while Alabama has a 20.1 scoring mean.

In scoring defenses, Alabama has allowed 12 points per outing to 19.9 by the Tigers.

Auburn's rushing offense is 131.3 yards per game to 129.0 yards for Alabama. Total offense also favors Auburn, 311.3 to 276.2.

However, in total defense Alabama is the leader, having surrendered 229.9 per game to 246.3 for its rival.

Alabama's coach, Paul Bryant, was quoted by Charles Land earlier in the week in The Tuscaloosa News as saying that Auburn keeps the pressure on in all phases of the kicking game.

"They have a fine passer and terrific receivers at every position," Bryant added. "They have more football players than they have been having. They've got more than we've got, too. But so what? They just play 11 at a time.

"We're just going to have to go out and play a lot better than they do. And better than we've played at any time this year, if we are to win."

A prediction?

We'll go along with Bryant. Auburn has a better football team, man for man, all the way down the line. And the Tigers will give Alabama a scrap. Probably beat the Tide in statistics. But when it comes time to figure the score, we'll take Alabama – 21-17.

-30-

Game

Snake upstages the Bear

(Original version published in The Gadsden Times, Sunday, December 3, 1967)

BIRMINGHAM – Bear Bryant may not be able to walk on water … really? But Snake Stabler can!

Ask any of the 71,200 die-hards who sat through a wind and rain storm here yesterday afternoon at Legion Field Bay to witness the annual Tide-Tiger tussle.

Alabama won, 7-3, and it was Stabler who turned the trick, but not the way most had expected.

This time, with the field ankle deep in water and mud with gusts of wind up to 25 miles per hour, Alabama's highly publicized passing quarterback elected to stay on the ground and ran the Tide to victory.

The lone Alabama touchdown – the one which won for muddy-shirted, once white-jerseyed Tiders – came with 11:29 showing on the fourth quarter clock.

Stabler did it.

Coming up with a third and three at the Auburn 47, the Snake swam out around right end on an option, elected to keep and was sprung loose with a key block by David Chatwood.

Stabler picked his way over the mucky, slippery turf (?) all the way to the Auburn end zone.

Steve Davis tacked on the extra point and Alabama had it wrapped up, 7-3.

This was only the third time in the game Alabama had been across midfield and it was set up on a bad snap as Tommy Lunceford was attempting to punt from Alabama's 31.

He grabbed the ball but was tackled for a 15-yard loss back on the 46. Tommy Wade ran twice, getting five and two yards, setting the stage for Stabler's heroics.

Auburn tried to come back, but twice, after completing long passes to Tim Christian, Loran Carter had tosses intercepted by Bama linebacker Bob Childs. The first of those king punches came with 4:10 left as Childs picked off what was supposed to be a short lob over the middle to the Auburn 36. Alabama couldn't advance and Auburn was given another shot from its 20 with 2:26 remaining.

On first down Carter passed to Christian for 31 yards to the Tide 49. Then he went for another long gainer, but Childs was there, at the 36, taking the ball out of Freddie Hyatt's arms.

Auburn's three points had come with 10:33 left in the third quarter on a 38-yard field goal by John Riley.

Riley had missed a 35-yard attempt in the second quarter and wanted to try one from the 29 later in the third. But a bad snap prevented this.

Auburn had also missed two scoring opportunities in the first half, losing the ball on downs at the two (1:51 before the first quarter expired) and coming back to the seven without scoring with 2:27 left in the half.

Alabama won the toss to start the game and took the wind. But it did not pay off as the Tiders only had the ball four times, couldn't get a first or get outside its 23 yard line.

Lunceford's punting had done the trick, giving Bama the ball first on the one and later at the six.

A bad snap to Davis resulted in only a 29-yard boot and Auburn set sail from the 41, getting the first, first down of the game on an 11-yard blast by Dwight Hurston to the Tide 30.

Hurston and Al Giffin ran the ball to the 17 and Carter lofted a 12-yard pass to Christian at the five.

Here Alabama's finest – the goal line defense – stood up. Mike Hall, Brownie Sides, Stan Moss and Alvin Samples stopped Carter three times for a total two yards gain. On fourth and three, Richard Plagge attempted to turn the corner, slipped and Dickey Thompson was on him.

Mike Currier put Auburn back knocking late in the second quarter, getting 26 yards to the 15 in two carries. But four plays later the Tigers were still two yards short of a first at the seven. Hall had made three of the four tackles to kill the drive with Eddie Propst getting the other.

Auburn didn't get a chance in the second half, getting only to the 21 (Riley's field goal) and the 23 (field goal attempt failed on bad snap).

Alabama got no closer than the 27, except for the score, and that came on the last play of the game when Stabler ran 14 yards on a fake punt.

-30-

Sidebar

The day wasn't fit for man or passing

(Original version published in The Gadsden Times, Sunday, December 3, 1967)

BIRMINGHAM – "The day wasn't fit for man or beast … or the passing game," former coach Harry Mehre said on his way to the airport after THE GAME.

Paul Bryant had said about the same thing minutes earlier as he looked back on Alabama's 7-3 triumph over Auburn.

"I expect the weather today gave us the worst conditions under which we've played a game since I've been back at Alabama," said the Crimson Tide coach.

It had rained almost continuously throughout the game and Bryant had donned rain pants and jacket in addition to his old un-shined plow shoes and a new, solid red cap with a big white "A" which he was wearing for the first time.

"It would have been stupid to throw under the circumstances," Bryant said in reply to a question. His quarterback, Kenny Stabler, noted as a passer, had put the ball in the air only five times. Only one fell into the mud as his teammates caught three and an Auburn player grabbed the other as it bounced out of a Tider's arms.

Bryant had been asked why he ran so much when the Tide had not been very successful on the ground during the year.

The Tide coach was overly pleased with the blocking of David Chatwood, David Reitz, Dennis Dixon and Bruce Stephens. This was especially so on one play. That play was the big one – "prettiest one I saw all day" Bryant said.

The play was the one on which Stabler ran 47 yards for the winning touchdown.

Bryant said he played the percentages, punting often on third down and waiting for a break. And when it came the Tide turned it into a win.

"We really had our backs to the wall in the first half. I thought we got a couple of good breaks. The good play on that punt late in the game really helped out.

"It is the understatement of the year, of course, but I'm mighty proud of them, particularly today," Bryant said.

-30-

Sidebar

Auburn dominated but Alabama won

(Original version published in The Gadsden Times, Sunday, December 3, 1967)

BIRMINGHAM – Auburn dominated the game statistically, that game in the rain yesterday at Legion Field. But when it came time to write who had won or lost it was the Crimson Tide that stepped forward. Seven to three, it was. Or 3-7 if you were on the other side of the field.

The first half, especially, was an all Auburn showing – 130 yards total offense to 36; eight first downs to one; and through the air it was 43 to 5.

Alabama fought back for a bit of respectability in the last half, outrushing the Tigers 133 to 12. But the air still belonged to Auburn, 74 yards to seven.

Total offense was 216 to 176, Auburn; first downs it was 13 to four.

Kenny Stabler, famous for making passes – on the field and off – showed he can also play the running game.

When the rain grounded his air attack, the southpaw from Foley turned runner, picking up a net 75 yards in 14 attempts to outpace all others in the rush department.

Stabler also scored the only, and game-winning, touchdown on a 47-yard fourth-quarter scamper. That was the longest play from scrimmage and the longest play of the game for either team.

Teammate Tommy Wade carried the ball one less time but netted only 38 yards. Gene Raburn ran four times for 22 yards and Ed Morgan gained 18 in nine attempts.

For Auburn Richard Plagge was best, lugging 17 times for 58 yards. Mike Currier had 28 in six carries. Al Giffin was clocked at 22 in 11 rips and Dwight Hurston was called upon seven times for 27 yards.

Loran Carter completed 10 of 19 passes for 117 yards; two of his passes were intercepted. Stabler had one pass intercepted and completed three of five for 12 yards.

Tim Christian was the game's top receiver with six for 89 yards. Hyatt caught two for 30 and Currier and Plagge caught one each. Dennis Homan caught two of Stabler's passes for 11 yards and Pete Jilleba one for one yard.

-30-

Alabama running back (1969-71) Johnny Musso. He was drafted in the third round by the Chicago Bears.

Auburn quarterback Pat Sullivan (1969-71) was drafted by the Atlanta Falcons in the second round. He was the recipient of the 1971 Heisman Trophy.

THE GAME - 1971

By Jimmy Smothers, written in 2011

Maybe this year THE GAME should have been called THE BIG GAME because it was just that and more. Alabama and Auburn were undefeated, nationally ranked and playing for the Southeastern Conference championship and a shot at the National Championship against No. 1 Nebraska in the Orange Bowl.

This was the first time that unbeaten teams had met for the SEC title, and with a spot in the national picture awaiting the winner, the game was drawing attention from outside the state.

Alabama (10-0) was ranked No. 3 and No. 4 by the two wire service polls, the Associated Press and United Press International; Auburn (9-0) was ranked No. 5 and No. 3. Alabama went into the game with a 10-0 record, Auburn was 9-0.

Oddsmakers rated the game a near toss-up, fans were divided along partisan lines, each thinking their favorite team would win. But no one expected what happened – a 31-7 victory by Alabama.

A big factor in the outcome was hardly mentioned before the game, but got a lot of talk afterwards. It may have been the first time that Brother Bill Oliver moved into the national spotlight as one of the top defensive coaches in the nation.

Oliver had been an assistant coach at Auburn since 1966, working with the defense. His players had practiced against the passing duo of Sullivan to Beasley every day for three years. Although he had accepted a similar job at Alabama before their senior season, he knew what they could do, and how best to defend them, better than anyone else.

The 1971 season had been one of a tremendous passing game for Auburn. Quarterback Pat Sullivan had wound up winning the Heisman Trophy with a brilliant performance in a 35-20 win over Georgia. Fans felt like Terry Beasley should have shared the honor, because the two were a combination of brilliance.

But against Alabama in the next game, Auburn's great air attack could never get airborne. Many fans thought it was because the team was flat after that electrifying game at Athens, Ga., perhaps the most exciting game environment I have ever experienced. Some fans pointed out that all the ballyhoo over the Heisman had taken something off Auburn's preparation and enthusiasm.

Some of that may have played a role; but I think it all comes down to the defensive game plan that Brother Bill Oliver came up with. It was brilliant.

Sullivan, who had already won the Heisman Trophy that year after a brilliant game two weeks earlier against Georgia, was limited to 14 completions in 27 passing attempts. He was intercepted twice. He had one 40-yard completion, but most of them were short yardage; and his total passing yardage was 121. Overall, his performance was far below par for him.

The win snapped Auburn's two-year winning streak in that game, but the momentum didn't carry over for the Crimson Tide, which lost to Nebraska, 6-38, in the Orange Bowl, thus failing to earn another national title. However, except for a loss in 1972 when Auburn went 10-1, the Crimson Tide had started a string of 10 wins in 11 games. There was the 1971 win, then nine in a row beginning in 1973.

Auburn wasn't able to bounce back from its loss to Alabama, losing 22-40 to Oklahoma in the Sugar Bowl.

Despite its big loss to Nebraska, Alabama wound up 4th in the AP poll, 2nd in the UPI poll; Auburn was 12th in the final AP poll, 5th in the UPI poll.

-30-

Pre-game column

No lineup changes, Shug's Tigers ready

(Original version published in The Gadsden Times, Friday, November 26, 1971)

AUBURN -- Tomorrow Auburn and Alabama meet in Birmingham's Legion Field which Ralph Jordan refers to as the "Iron Bowl". It's a history making classic in that it's the first time unbeaten teams have clashed for this championship in the season finale.

Kickoff time is 3:05 p.m. as the game will be the second half of a television doubleheader. Army and Navy meet in the first half of the TV grid viewing.

This biggest of the big Southern games has received more publicity than any previous game. Every word was deserved. Hardly anything has been left unsaid. With only a night of waiting before the outcome will be decided on the playing field, here's a brief recap of the situation from the Plain.

Coach Jordan says, "Alabama has a big, strong physical team and is truly one of the top three or four teams in the nation. They have a great kicking game, just as we have. They have a fiery defense and run the Wishbone as well as Texas. I'd say that based on what's gone on in past games this season I suspect it will be a scoring battle. But sometimes I've seen two great offensive teams play a 7-6 game."

It will end the careers of Auburn's celebrated stars Pat Sullivan and Terry Beasley, who will leave their names in practically every record for which they are eligible. But there are many others on both teams that will ultimately determine the outcome. Both teams are sound here, but one error in any phase of it could determine the winner.

Judging by past performances you can expect a thrilling windup. Since 1958, seven games have been settled by eight points or less. Last year Alabama led 17-0 after the first quarter, 17-10 at half. Auburn finally won it, 33-28 on a fourth quarter touchdown after the two teams accounted for 970 yards total offense. The Tide leads the series 18-16-1.

The Tigers are one of the few top teams still surviving on a pass-oriented offense, but then few schools own a passing combination like Sullivan to Beasley. Sullivan not only has a strong and accurate arm but can run the option well enough to spring his backs. Auburn will trap and use delays, but the big weapon is the bomb to Beasley or a long pass to Dick Schmaltz. If Bama tries to double cover both, Tommy Lowry and Terry Henley, each averaging five yards a carry, can work inside the tackles effectively.

Defensively, Auburn uses a four-man front with a rover.

Statistically, Auburn is the SEC's best in passing, eighth in rushing, and first in total offense. The Tigers are fourth in rushing defense, fifth in passing defense and fifth in total defense.

Sullivan, the 1971 Heisman Trophy winner, has never lost to Alabama. His career statistics against Bama are impressive: 70 yards rushing in 20 attempts, 35 of 64 passes for 509 yards and four touchdowns (he's been intercepted three times). That's an average gain per play of 7.3 yards.

To move the ball Auburn will have to get off on the snap, block the right man on every play, have no fumbles or interceptions, put forth extra effort, make at least five yards on first down, make a first down on third-and-short-yardage situations, score when opportunity arises, limit mistakes, be alert for stunts.

Lineups for Auburn will be the same as the last four games, both offensively and defensively. The running game has been jelling since Lowry and Henley have been regulars at fullback and tailback respectively. Everyone is reportedly in good physical shape.

The winner? Anybody's guess. Sports editors from across the state have their predictions elsewhere on these pages.

The AP article with the predictions has nine writers picking Alabama, seven Auburn. In that piece, Smothers is quoted: "For Alabama to win, it will have to put a pass rush on Sullivan. If he can throw the football, he can complete it. I think it will be a high-scoring game with probably the team that gets the breaks winning. I don't think the Auburn defense can stop Alabama's Wishbone if Musso is healthy. I don't think Alabama's defense can stop Auburn's passing if the line gives Sullivan time to throw. I go with Auburn to win by less than a touchdown. It could boil down to the team that has a shot at the national championship in a bowl game having enough added incentive to win."

-30-

Game

Tide controls football to win game, 31-7

(Original version published in The Gadsden Times, Sunday, November 28, 1971)

BIRMINGHAM -- Johnny Musso paced an awesome Alabama offense that refused to let Auburn have the football. And the defensive gang did its thing by keeping the Tigers from advancing with the pigskin the few times they had it. By putting the two together you come up with a 31-7 Crimson Tide victory that could hardly have been more convincing.

Musso, playing for the first time in three weeks, turned in one of his finest games of the season, running the football 33 times for 167 yards and scoring two fourth-quarter touchdowns.

But it wasn't his show alone. Terry Davis did a good job of running the Wishbone option; getting a two-touchdown lead for the Tide the first two times it had the football.

Defense was also a big thing in the game of unbeatens with the SEC championship riding with the winner. A combination pass rush by the front four and a tight secondary with the corner men turning in a superb performance limited Auburn's running attack and prevented Heisman Trophy winner Pat Sullivan from establishing any sort of passing attack. He was held to only one bomb, a 40-yard toss to Terry Beasley. Most of his tosses were thrown short and quick and picked up few yards, although he was able to complete 14 of his 27 attempts.

"We took away those easy things they've been getting against everybody, including us last year," Coach Paul Bryant said after the victory.

"I felt like to keep from losing we would have to have a sound kicking game, and defensively, we would have to keep from giving them anything cheap. If we did that, we'd have a chance of winning by controlling the ball and putting some points on the board. And we did just that. I didn't know if we could hold them to seven points, but I sure knew that if they just scored seven we would win."

While Alabama was taking the "little things" away from Auburn, the Tiders were adding a wrinkle to their attack that threw their cross-state rivals off guard. First, Alabama would shift from the Wishbone formation to the split formation, using it both as a running and passing set. Secondly, Davis threw 11 passes after having tossed only 55 all season. He completed nine of these for 105 yards. Musso passed once for 17 yards.

Auburn took the opening kick, missed a first down by inches on a third-and-seven as Sullivan passed to Tommy Lowry, and lost the ball as David Beverly fumbled the snap on an attempted punt. John Mitchell was on top of the play and the Tide got that break it was counting on much sooner than anyone expected. The Tide drove the 20 yards for a touchdown in only five plays, with Terry Davis going the final six around left end for the touchdown.

Despite the blitzing Alabama defense, Sullivan managed to complete a 17-yard pass to Dick Schmaltz for his first, first down. But a third-down pass to Beasley came up inches short and Beverly punted into the end zone.

With Musso carrying five of 13 plays, The Tide punched back 80 yards for a second touchdown. Outside of a 17-yard pass, Davis to Joe LaBue, and a 14-yard gallop by Musso to the 13, the drive consisted of the time-eating short-yardage plays for which Alabama and the Wishbone are famous.

Davis was again the man of the hour, running eight yards around left end for the touchdown. Bill Davis toed it to 14-0, 58 seconds before the first quarter ended.

Auburn got back in the game in the second quarter as Sullivan, noted for sparking the Tigers to comeback victories; hit Terry Beasley with the 40-yard pass on the first play. But the drive bogged down again. However, an exchange of fumbles gave Auburn the ball back at the 31 and on the first play, Sullivan pitched out to Harry Unger who passed to Beasley in the end zone.

That was the scoring until the fourth quarter, when Bill Davis kicked a 41-yard field goal to up the score to 17-7 with 13:03 remaining.

Auburn, which had gotten the ball at the one in the third quarter, put it into play at the 20 in the fourth. Sullivan was intercepted on first down by Chuck Strickland, who returned 21 yards to the 12. Musso scored on the next play, running round right end and lunging the final three yards into the end zone.

Alabama again used over five minutes in driving 61 yards to the one where Musso fumbled (for only the third time in his career) as he leaped over the line.

Auburn got a touchback and put the ball in play at the 20. Two plays netted 16 yards but again a pass bounced off the fingertips of the intended receiver into the waiting arms of Jeff Rouzie, who rumbled 34 yards to the six. Musso scored on the next play.

The defeat ended Auburn's 11-game winning streak which began with a 33-28 win over Alabama last year. It gave Alabama the SEC championship and an 11-0 record thus far this year.

Musso said Nebraska, the team which Alabama will play in the Orange Bowl, deserved a little credit for the win.

"We were pulling for Nebraska against Oklahoma Thanksgiving. Their victory probably had a psychological effect on us. It sure couldn't have hurt." Alabama, ranked third nationally, will be national champion if it can whip the No.1 Cornhuskers.

Auburn, ranked fifth going into the game, will play Oklahoma in the Sugar Bowl. All four teams were undefeated going into this week's games.

-30-

The author and Coach Paul Bryant, taken in the spring of 1981.

Sidebar

It Was Just That Kind of a Day

(Original version published in The Gadsden Times, Sunday, November 28, 1971)

BIRMINGHAM -- It was a day for the Crimson and White. A day like so many others in the life of Paul Bryant . . . like Alabama fans of a decade ago remember so well.

The game, before nearly 70,000 in Legion Field and with a national TV audience peeping in, wasn't what it was expected to be. True, it was for the SEC championship -- 10th for Alabama, 5th for Bryant. And it was for the state crown. A battle of unbeatens, it was, between two teams that so much deserved unblemished records for this amazing run on the gridiron. A win was also the final stepping stone for a shot at a national title in a bowl game.

The game wasn't the offensive battle expected. It wasn't the exciting, nail-biting, heart-stopper as Turkey Day tube-watching had often produced. Auburn didn't play as it had played against Georgia last time out two weeks ago.

Yesterday the packed house called Legion Field belonged to Alabama -- white-shirted Alabama -- that got the breaks and the bounce, played the kind of defense it takes to win games and conference titles and get a shot at national championships.

Alabama defused the Auburn bomb with a tremendous pass rush that kept Heisman Trophy winner Pat Sullivan from lighting the fuse. He was under tremendous pressure all day and while he was not sacked, four of his attempts were slapped down at the line, two were broken up in the secondary, and two were intercepted.

And just for good measure, the Alabama defense threw up a running defense like Auburn hadn't faced all fall. The Tiger runners were limited to a grand total of 27 net yards.

Alabama's offense complemented its defense by keeping the football. Alabama, which was to win 31-7, a score which no one would have believed possible before the kickoff, scored the first two times it had the football and controlled the pigskin the rest of the way.

For the game Alabama ran 83 plays, Auburn 44. Alabama had the football 41:49 and Auburn 18:11. Auburn, missing third-down plays by inches, couldn't stop the Wishbone or Johnny Musso. Bama rolled for 278 yards. Musso had 167 of that.

Sullivan, who had managed to rally Auburn from behind and to victory over Alabama during three previous years, couldn't get anything going against this ready Bama outfit only an Orange's throw away for that coveted No. 1. (In the freshman game in 1968 Sullivan led Auburn back from a 0-27 deficit to a 36-27 win.)

After Alabama had jumped on a fumbled snap and scored early in the game, then drove 89 yards to pay dirt next time it had the football, Auburn got back in the game with a touchdown of its own.

It was 14-7 at the half. Still anybody's ball game.

Auburn was remembering last year when Alabama led 17-10 at intermission. Auburn had roared back to a victory.

Alabama, too, remembered. And the Davises, Mussos, and Bisceglias decided the best way to keep the lead was to keep the football. That they did. And in a style befitting a victory in any championship game.

The third quarter Alabama got the kickoff, kept the ball six minutes, 30 seconds. Auburn ran 10 plays, taking just over five minutes, then punted. Alabama killed the rest of that frame while marching to Bill Davis' 41-yard field goal which came on the fourth play of the fourth quarter.

Alabama, leading 17-7, refused to give the Tigers a chance or the football. The final 15 minutes of play the men from the Plains had the ball but 13 plays. Two of those were punts, two were pass interceptions.

It was a day Musso had waited three years to come. It was his first victory ever against Auburn. He showed his joy, dancing with joy each time he scored Bama's two final touchdowns making it a runaway score.

It was a victory Bama fans had long awaited. And long after the lights of this giant arena went out yells were echoing from the darkened corners . . . from cars, backed up for blocks in the massive traffic jam . . . from parents and friends who waited outside the dressing room.

Disheartened Auburn rooters were silent. They filed out without a word, heads bowed. Their solemn march began with 3:39 left in the game. That was when a Sullivan pass bounced off the hands of intended receiver Robby Robinett and into the waiting arms of Jeff Rouzie. He returned it 34 yards to the six. That was the final blow. Sullivan walked off the field a beaten man. Musso scored on the next play.

It was that kind of a day.

-30-

Post-game column

Pat, Tigers ran out of magic

(Original version published in The Gadsden Times, Monday, November 29, 1971)

Hindsight on a game that has everyone mentioning this Alabama team in the same breath with greatness. Maybe the best of the Bama greats of by-gone years. Another game . . . Another Tide victory . . . then 1971 Crimson Tide will have arrived in all its glory . . . bigger, better, best so far.

But that can wait ... that New Year National Championship showdown with Nebraska in the Orange Bowl.

Memories linger still. Memories of a late Saturday afternoon and early evening. A cool, clear evening in Legion Field which was the scene of a duel between a couple of football giants. The expected battle royal never materialized. Auburn never had a chance. Heisman Trophy winner Pat Sullivan wasn't allowed to get his throwing arm loosened. Alabama played control football like it's never been played. Crimson Tiders turned in such an airtight defense that they should have passed out oxygen masks.

When it was over and Bama had kept its unbeaten record with a 31-7 victory, about the only question which remained was whether offense or defense had been the sternest test for an Auburn team which also came to fight with a perfect slate and title hopes.

Alabama's ball-hogging offense had the ball over two-thirds of the game, ran 83 plays to 44. Alabama's defense kept Sullivan pinned in and his playmates pinned back.

The question was put to an Alabama coach hours after the game had ended. Was it offense, led by slick-operating Terry Davis and hard-running Johnny Musso? Or was it the Tide defense that limited the SEC's most explosive offense to a single second-period touchdown? Which one was it that did in Auburn, the coach was asked.

"It was a combination of the two plus a sound kicking game," the Bama coach said. "We got the early break, turned it into a touchdown and played ball control the rest of the day. Our defense prevented them from ever having the ball in good field position. And the secondary played them airtight. They were going for the ball and not giving them a thing."

Alabama lineman John Hannah (1970-72) was the No. 4 pick in the 1973 National Football League draft. He was later designated by *Sports Illustrated* in 1981 as "Best Offensive Lineman of All Time".

* * * * *

Alabama knew that to beat Auburn Sullivan must be stopped. So they blitzed him with the strong safety. The defensive ends and tackles went in high. It paid off with three passes being batted down at the line. And while he completed 14 of 27 tosses, none were for touchdowns.

Auburn's longest series of the day came in the third quarter, beginning on the one-yard line. Sullivan picked up two first downs, moving out to the 32 in 10 plays. The drive took four minutes, 33 seconds.

In the first quarter Alabama's defense gave Auburn the ball at the 20, 27, and 30. The Tigers crossed the 50 once, getting to the 41 before punting.

In the second quarter Auburn had its best field position of the game, driving to the Alabama 26, fumbling, getting it back at the 31 on a Tide fumble, then scoring. Later the Tigers got the ball at their 42, then at Bama's 43, drove to the 38 and punted.

After the one series in the third quarter Auburn got the ball four times in the fourth, three times at its 20, once at the 27. Sullivan was intercepted twice, which set up touchdowns, Beverly punted twice.

Alabama's defense also got the Tide in position to score its first touchdown, forcing a bad snap on a punting situation and getting the ball at the Auburn 20.

Alabama's only scoring drive came the second time it had the football and covered 80 yards in 13 plays.

Meanwhile, Auburn's defense had trouble with Alabama's Wishbone, covering the two pitchmen and letting Davis cut inside. And when they went to Davis, he'd pitch around them. Finally when they had it solved, Davis would go to the split formation with three wide men; one was usually open and he completed nine of 11 passes. One was thrown out of bounds to stop the clock. It was his best passing day and proved that Alabama can, and will, put the football in the air when it has to.

The turning point of the game, if there was one, had to be the bad snap on the fourth play of the game. That enabled Alabama to get the early easy touchdown and force Auburn to play catch-up football. And that is about impossible against this Alabama team. Coming from behind has been Sullivan's magic touch during most of his Auburn career. But somewhere along the line his magic had to play out. Winning the Heisman only two days before may have been his limit of glory for one week.

Realistically, that had nothing to do with the game. Alabama played a near perfect game. Even Coach Jordan and his players admitted that.

Alabama's defense was so strong that the front four just about ignored Auburn's running game which netted but 27 yards. That left seven men to roam the passing zone, with the exception of an occasional red-dog. One writer said Alabama's three deep men played so far back defending against the bomb Bryant should have given them end zone tickets. It seemed Alabama had a man listening in on Auburn's huddle because the Tide knew, or guessed correctly, just about every play Auburn called.

Auburn's defense, which played most of the game, did well by keeping it close for three quarters (14-7). The offense was never really in the ball game.

-30-

Running back Terry Henley, known as the 'Shining Spirit' of Auburn's 1972 football team. It is said, with only slight exaggeration, that year the Auburn Tigers had only three plays - Henley right, Henley left, Henley up the middle.

THE GAME - 1972

By Jimmy Smothers, written in 2011

As was customary at the time, sports writers would go to Auburn and Alabama on Monday and Tuesday before a Saturday game. It was not unusual to spend the night in one town, and then drive over to the other the next morning before returning home. When Terry Henley was playing at Auburn George Smith (Anniston Star) and I often spent the night in Auburn. Henley would come to our room and give us good quotes for our stories. Some of the tales he told were actually true. In addition, he'd suggest questions that we might want to ask his teammates when we talked to them the next day.

That year (1972) when we talked to Auburn's head coach, Ralph Jordan, he told us the kicking game loomed large in the upcoming game against Alabama. I doubt he knew just how large it would be, but looking back I wonder if he had an omen that something would happen in the kicking game that would decide the outcome.

It did. A blocked extra point and two blocked punts. They resulted in a 17-16 upset victory for Auburn.

The Crimson Tide was undefeated and ranked No. 2 before the game. Henley told a few of the writers, "We're going to beat the No. 2 out of Alabama." No. 2 has a double entendre and Henley wasn't referring to the ranking. After the game, Auburn students celebrated at Toomer's Corner. This year they reflected on Henley's prediction by tossing rolls of toilet paper in the branches of the big oak trees, thus adding to the tradition on the Plain. Former Athletic Director David Housel said, "It morphed into what it is today."

I remember one day that week sitting in the sports information office with two or three other writers waiting for practice to begin. Henley walked in and said: "I think it is lowdown for a coach who is 60 years old to stoop and call our school a cow college. I'm not saying this to go on Alabama's dressing room wall or anything like that; I'm just speaking up for Auburn."

Next day the headline in The Birmingham News read: "Don't say cow college around Auburn's Henley"

After the upset win, Hee-Haw Henley said, "Our cows actually kick awful hard." He also said, "We took them like a capsule", although Alabama dominated the game statistically and would have won easily except for those two blocked punts.

That game became legendary and has become known as the "Punt, Bama, Punt" game. For years afterwards, before each game against Alabama, Auburn fans would set up loudspeakers in the parking lot and broadcast replays of Gary Sanders' call of those ensuing touchdowns.

That year's Auburn team wasn't expected to be very good. It was the year following the Pat Sullivan – Terry Beasley era of the passing offense. In '72 Jordan had gone back to the running game with a new inexperienced quarterback named Randy Walls. But amazingly, the team just kept on winning, and its only loss was 7-35 to LSU.

The team, led by running back Henley, became known as "The Amazin's" which was another phrase coined by Coach Jordan, just as was "Iron Bowl" a few years earlier. He also liked to use the term "bell cow" when referring to a team leader. Henley fit into that role, claiming it just fit an Auburn player.

THE GAME of '72 suddenly jumped to the front of the many exciting and legendary games in this series. And it has stood the test of time. Even more than 30 years later, even after all those great games in the '80s, and since then, this game stands out. This game, the "Punt, Bama, Punt" game, which underdog Auburn managed to win by 17-16, tops the list. Bill Cromartie, in his book "Braggin' Rights", lists it first among his five greatest games.

I doubt that is a consensus opinion, just as people might disagree about the biggest pre-game build-up. Was it the 1971 game, when both teams were undefeated and looking at a national title; was it when Bryant was going for the record 315th win; was it the first time the two teams played in Auburn?

I will not say 1972 was THE best game, not when looking at the overall play of the two teams. But the way Auburn won the game in the fourth quarter was a shocker, making the outcome of that game among the best in this series. But so are some later games, such games now known merely as "Bo Over the Top", "Wrong Way, Bo", "The Kick", "The Thumb", "The Drive" and "Cam's Comeback".

When it comes to THE GAME, and when the Tide and Tigers go on the field, something unusual almost always happens. In fact, you might say it was unusual if something didn't occur that made the game stand out in some way or fashion. But not since 1972 has there been anything such as "Punt, Bama, Punt" occurring as the deciding factor in the outcome. In fact, it may never happen again.

-30-

Pre-game column

Terry Henley on facing Alabama

(Original version published in The Gadsden Times, Thursday, November 30, 1972)

AUBURN – Terry Henley still had the floor when Randy Walls entered the room. Auburn's senior running back was at ease. He's as good at talking to reporters as he is at running with a football. And he's the best of any football player in the SEC this season – on both counts.

"I'm a senior so lots more ride on this game for me than in previous seasons. I've played against Alabama twice. We won one and lost one. Saturday I'll get to line up against Alabama for the last time so it is something special. I'd like to go out a winner," Henley said.

"Last year and this year are entirely different. This year we're a tougher ball club. Last year they knew we were going to pass. Last year they defended against the pass, then would get the football and keep it for seven and eight minutes at a time. This year we can do that, too. We've got a ball control offense and a tough defense."

One difference between the two ball clubs is Auburn plays a lot on determination and inspiration while Alabama is more of a mechanical club, performing a la Dallas Cowboys.

Henley said he couldn't have a better friend than John Hannah, All-Star guard for the Crimson Tide. He explained it thusly: "John Hannah and I are good friends. The other day we were talking on the phone and he said he'd like to ask me just one question about our football team. He wanted to know how we could drive 80 yards on Tennessee. I told him we were only able to do it because we wanted to.

"Determination. That's been the key to this Auburn football team; wanting to do something so badly we refused to accept defeat."

Meanwhile, Auburn's quarterback, Walls, was pacing the floor. He wasn't as confident with reporters as Henley. He'd been called an "ugly duckling" in the papers and didn't appreciate it. He has had to face a battery of reporters all fall and it has created added pressure for a sophomore from a small town who was stepping into the vacancy left by Heisman Trophy winner Pat Sullivan, the most popular quarterback in school history.

Besides, Walls had a girlfriend outside waiting for him to take her shopping, and practice time was drawing nigh.

A couple of scribes called Randy over to the side and asked how he ever got to call a play when Henley was in the game?

The tough and talented quarterback loosened up, actually laughing with the writers. "You know, the only time I ever get to say a word is when we're in the huddle. The huddle belongs to me and it's the only place I know of where Terry never says a word. He even talks during the plays."

Walls said the plays he planned to call during Saturday's game against Alabama were the ones he called all fall.

"We only have three plays," he explained. "That's Henley right, Henley left and Henley up the middle. I guess that's the reason why he never talks in the huddle. He listens to see where he is to run the football." The quarterback said Alabama has the biggest team Auburn has played this fall and in his opinion has the best athletes in the nation.

"I guess they want to beat us as badly as we want to whip them. And I don't think what's been in the papers makes any difference. That stuff gets fans excited, but the players are going to do the best they can, regardless of what has or hasn't been said. I know I'm going to."

Walls has trouble sleeping before games and said since this was Alabama; he probably wouldn't catch a wink after Wednesday night.

Meanwhile, Henley was still rapping as other writers joined in, some asking questions he had answered earlier. But that's part of the game. Athletes face this chore almost daily. Sometimes they get to sounding like a broken record. But Henley doesn't mind. He's always patient and will take as much time as required to talk with any and all reporters.

"It's a privilege to be selected to the All-SEC team," he said. "I didn't believe I could make it, but it was one of my personal goals. Others were to make 1,000 yards, to beat Alabama and to play in the Senior Bowl."

On each of these goals, Henley said:

On making the All-SEC: "I would not even have made the team if Harry Unger hadn't gotten hurt. He was first team and has more talent and ability than I have."

On nearing 1,000 yards: "I don't have size or speed, but I have a great line. I don't consider myself good, but I do want to win for Auburn."

On beating Alabama: "We'll take them like a capsule."

On the Senior Bowl: "The pros have a lot to do with who plays in it. So I don't know what kind of chance I have. I think I'm good for Canadian ball, but I doubt I can play in the NFL."

Henley never misses an opportunity to praise the offensive line, and he didn't this week either. Here are his comments, four days before playing THE GAME:

"A lot has been said about Jim Krapf and other Alabama linemen; and about our own Mac Lorendo, Bill Emendorfer and Don Leathers. But Jay Casey (Auburn) is the most underrated lineman in the SEC. He is just great. He comes back to the huddle moaning and groaning, but he always goes right back to the line and blocks like a champion again. You notice I didn't mention my friend, John Hannah. That's because he is fabulous. He's the best there is and is so far above everyone else he's in a class by himself."

The interview was ended and as reporters filed out the always cheerful Henley chirped gleefully: "Hey, you all come back to see me again sometime, hear?"

Auburn's Hee-Haw. Some ball player. Some talker. We hate to see him graduate.

-30-

Pre-game column

Bryant pulled an Ara trick

(Original version published in The Gadsden Times, Friday, December 1, 1972)

Would you believe that Coach Bryant has gone and pulled one of Ara Parseghian's tricks? You know all about the stir Ara caused with Bama people by popping off at a Columbus, Ohio, Quarterback Club meeting about the Tide's choice of bowl opponent?

Well now, Bryant, speaking in a similar jovial mood at a Birmingham QB meeting, done went and stuck his hand in his mouth by referring to Auburn as a cow college.

Naturally, it got a lot of laughs, made for good newspaper copy and has Auburn fans boiling mad. The fact that both Parseghian and Bryant were jesting has made little difference in the reaction of those with opposing views. But what was said by the coaches will not play a part in the outcome of the Alabama vs. Auburn game

Saturday afternoon in the All-American City; nor will it help or hinder anyone in winning the national championship.

What it has done is kindle anew the rivalry so prevalent each year the week before the battle for football championship of this state.

There is no better climax to a season than for two state rivals to clash. Any game after this (except for bowls) would have to be anti-climatic.

Shug happy with situation
Ralph Jordan, dean of SEC coaches, says regardless of what happens Saturday this is the most fitting time for Alabama and Auburn to play.

"I've never been for a state rivalry being played in the middle of the season," he said, leaning back and lighting up a big cigar with a holder on the end. This is a rarity for Jordan. So was the interview, which he had begun by explaining, "I'm dry. You are going to have to pull it out of me."

Usually, Auburn's football coach is a ready talker and one of the best interviews in the country.

Jordan said Auburn's practices had been spirited and his players realized what a tremendous task awaits them in Alabama. "But, of course, we've had to get in the ring and go 15 rounds with every opponent we've played this year. We're respectful of Alabama's strength and overall performances, but we are not in awe of them. I think I speak for the entire football team when I say that."

Depth big factor in outcome
Depth is expected to be a major factor in the game and the coach explained that Alabama's schedule had been conducive in developing such. Auburn games have mostly gone to the wire, thus few reserve players have gotten experience.

"Right now we feel we have more depth than at any other time, thanks largely to the injuries of Terry Henley, James Owens and Bill Newton. We were able to give Chris Linderman, Rusty Fuller, David Williams and Miles Jones playing time. Henley will start. We could have used him against Georgia. I don't know about Owens," the coach said.

Kicking game looms large
What about the kicking game?

"It looms large in this game. Up until now we have faced teams with only average kicking games. But Alabama is as good, if not better, than we are on this part of the game," said Jordan.

The Wishbone?

"We feel like the Wishbone offense has gone to the called plays rather than the quarterback reading. I'm not belittling the Wishbone. It's very formidable and has certainly caused problems for defensive coaches. But Oklahoma didn't beat Nebraska with it. They won with pitching and catching and a freshman named Tinker Owens," said Jordan.

The coach added that LSU stopped Alabama's Wishbone, but by doing so left itself vulnerable to the pass.

"Terry Davis (Alabama) is the most spectacular and the most underrated quarterback in the country. He is a master at the Wishbone and can pick you to pieces with his passing. He is truly an All-America," Jordan added.

The coach said he expected it to be a good ball game but that he had never been any good at predicting whether it would be a high-scoring or low-scoring game.

Wants to know the odds

Pulling a "Kickoff" from his pocket he viewed it a moment and noted Alabama was rated a 13-point favorite. He asked what Jimmy the Greek had to say.

Jimmy says 14, Jordan was told.

"Well, what I really want to know is what the gut bookies, the alley guys, think about it?" he asked.

A friend from Birmingham answered, "Somewhere around 15 and 16 points."

"Doesn't look like anyone gives us a chance, does it?" Jordan asked.

No one had given Auburn a chance to win over two previous opponents that fall; no one but the Auburn coaches and players. Now Auburn was 8-1 and rated ninth in the nation.

-30-

Game

Auburn Pulls 17-16 Upset Of Alabama

(Original version published in The Gadsden Times, Sunday, December 3, 1972)

LEGION FIELD, BIRMINGHAM – That "Cow College" on the Plain changed into a "Castle fit for a King" here yesterday afternoon when time ran out in a game that will go down as the biggest football upset in Southern history – maybe in all of the grid kingdom.

It was 17-16, Auburn. Those are magic numbers that War Eagle fans will forever remember.

Not only do they spell out a tremendous victory, unbelievable victory, for the 16-point underdog Tigers; they established the means by which royal subjects were created to occupy the afore-mentioned castle.

King of that castle has to be Ralph Jordan, who most surely sealed his bid as "Coach of the Year". But reigning with him in the Loveliest Village of the Plain are members of an Auburn defensive unit that rose up and won a game against overwhelming odds.

Auburn may have been a "cow college" as dawn broke on Dec. 2, but it was capital of the football champions in this state before the sun sank slowly in the West.

Bill Newton made it so. David Langner made it so. Auburn's team, Cinderella team of the Southeastern Conference, made it so. Thus it will remain. The clock struck midnight yesterday as Auburn ended its regular season, but the team did not turn into mice or a pumpkin. This team, 9-1, and solidly entrenched among the Top 10, is for real. Ask any of the 72,386 people on hand.

Newton, a junior linebacker from Fayette, blocked two Alabama punts in the fourth quarter that Langner, junior defensive back from Birmingham, caught on the bounce and cashed in for touchdowns.

Gardner Jett, who had finally put points on the scoreboard for Auburn with a 42-yard field goal with just over nine minutes to play, was also cool-headed and sure-footed with extra points late in the game. Both of his kicks split the uprights.

The last one – the one that won the game for Auburn when hardly anyone in the world of college football gave it as much chance as a frog in a snake pit – came with the score tied at 16-16 and only 1:34 remaining in the game.

Langner, who said Alabama had considered him too small and too slow for college football, capped the victory that wasn't to be by intercepting a Terry Davis pass at the 36 yard line with 36 ticks of life left on the stadium clock.

Even then, when the final horn had sounded, fans were stunned. It was so unbelievable.

Mighty Alabama, unbeaten, untied and No. 2 in all the land had been humbled. Hopes of another National Championship were smashed. The SEC Championship, won on that very soil in the finest of fashion just weeks before, suddenly became tarnished.

Alabama had so completely dominated the game, statistically, that there was no way Auburn could have won. But it did, just as it had all fall, beginning with a 10-6 upset of Tennessee on Legion Field's sod back in September.

Looking back at the first half Alabama had 7 first downs, Auburn 1; Alabama 112 yards total offense, Auburn 8; Alabama led, 9-0.

Auburn had gotten a break with hardly 10 minutes elapsed in a scoreless game as that boy Langner intercepted Terry Davis' only pass of the first half at the 34. He returned it to the 10, but an Auburn penalty put the ball back on the 25.

Auburn was forced to go for a field goal but a bad snap killed the play. Holder Dave Beck grabbed the ball and tried to run, but was chased down and tackled by John Croyle.

Auburn had gotten its break and failed to tack up points. Most fans, including Auburn officials in the press box, felt that was the ball game as Alabama roared back in the second quarter, like the dam had broken, and scored nine points for a 9-0 lead at halftime.

Actually, the referees had spotted the ball at the 29 after Croyle had run down Beck. Alabama didn't give it up until it reached the end zone 14 plays later. Steve Bisceglia, who would dominate the rushing scene with 102 yards on 24 carries, got 48 of them on nine carries during that 71-yard drive. He bulled over right guard for three yards and the touchdown with 11:16 remaining in the first half.

All his yardage, including the touchdown, came behind John Hannah's blocking.

Bill Davis's PAT attempt was blocked by Roger Mitchell, which would provide a margin for victory before this day of miracles ended.

Auburn quarterback Randy Walls passed for the first time with 2:41 left in the half and Lanny Norris intercepted at the 40, returning it to the 13. Auburn's defense held, as had Alabama's earlier. Headed by Beck and Danny Sanspree, Auburn halted the Tide with a fourth and four at the seven. Bill Davis came on and kicked a 19-yard field goal for a 9-0 lead.

The third quarter saw the Tide continue to rise, just as it had done all season during second-half play. First time Alabama got the football it was goal line bound. This time it marched 77 yards in 12 plays (including a pass interference call). The fine for interfering with Wayne Wheeler was 22 yards. Two plays later Davis connected with Joe LaBue for 16 yards to the 20. It was his only completion in seven attempts during the game.

Terry Davis later ran 16 yards to the one. After a five yard penalty Wilbur Jackson scored from the six behind the blocking of Hannah. Bill Davis kicked the extra point and Alabama led, 16-0, which was to be the high Tide for the game.

Alabama's Greg Gantt just missed a 50-yard field goal as the third quarter came to an end.

Auburn took over at the 20 and put together its longest drive of the game, 55 yards to the 25. Gardner Jett kicked a 42 yard field goal with 9:21 to play; which didn't worry the Tide, which was content to allow them that.

Tide fans felt it was sort of a consolation prize for the Tigers' determination. They settled back to await the end, then it would be on to Dallas, the Cotton Bowl and hopes of yet another National Championship.

That would not be, not on this day. The mighty Big Red Tide was about to be in for the shock of its life.

What Auburn's offense couldn't do against the strong Bama defense, its defense did. With Terry Henley, James Owens and Chris Linderman all ailing; and Walls unable to get anything going, Newton, Ken Bernich and the defense took over, scoring two touchdowns.

The first came with 5:30 to play when it was all over but the shouting. Alabama misread Auburn's punt rush and allowed Bill Newton to break through untouched. He blocked Greg Gantt's punt; Langner caught it on the first bounce at the 25 and dashed into the end zone for a touchdown. Jett kicked it to 16-10. Auburn was back in the game.

Alabama wasn't going to play that game, taking the ensuing kick and beginning to eat up the clock. Using the long count and ball controlling Wishbone, Terry Davis had a first down in three plays. Bisceglia and Jackson made five yards each and it was still Alabama's ball.

The Tide was running and so was the clock. Just over three minutes remained and Alabama could sew up the victory with two more first downs. But Auburn's defense stepped up in the persons of Newton and Bernich, nailing Bisceglia after only a yard gain. Terry Davis rolled out at left end for five before Newton smacked him to the ground.

On a big third-and-five Neel broke through on a blitz, slamming Davis for a five-yard loss. That brought up a punting down and Alabama would have to give up the ball with just over a minute to play.

A good kick would have sealed the victory, but lightning was to strike twice in the same spot. Newton, much to his surprise, again charged through Alabama's line untouched (inside the tackle) and blocked Gantt's punt a second time. And again Langner was David on the spot; the ball bounced right into his arms and he raced 20 yards for a tying touchdown.

Jett's placement gave Auburn a 17-16 lead. There was 1:34 left, time for Alabama to score.

Davis calmly set up shop at the 20, fed the ball to Jackson for nine and ran for four and a first down, stopping the clock. A minute and four seconds remained, still time to score, but he threw short incomplete, and then went long to Wheeler. But the pass was too long, going over the receiver's head and right into the arms of Auburn's defender, Langner, who made the catch on his knees. He just sat there, with his body wrapped around the ball.

Auburn's players stormed onto the field, although 49 seconds remained. Walls ran out the clock in three plays and the game was officially over. Auburn had won. Unbelievable.

No one in the country had given Auburn a chance to win many football games this year; no one but Jordan, his staff and players. No one in the country gave Auburn a chance to defeat Alabama in this game; no one but Jordan, his staff and players. But they did, and they wound up 9-1. Amazing.

-30-

Post-game column

Playbacks had the same score

(Original version published in The Gadsden Times, Monday, December 4, 1972)

Two days past football's biggest upset since the Jets downed the Colts in Super Bowl III football fans in this state remained stunned. Playbacks yesterday still ended with Auburn 17, Alabama 16, just as had the game.

Alabama's unbeaten season was smashed and its National Championship hopes are no more. Auburn not only won its biggest rival game but has avenged, in a way, its only defeat of the season. The Tigers defeated the only team (Alabama) that defeated the only team (LSU) that defeated them.

Nothing said or done will change the outcome. And there will be no attempt here to make it anything but what it was – a heartbreaking defeat for the second-ranked Tide; a tremendous triumph for the ninth-rated Tigers.

The game had such an abrupt turnabout that words are not equal to the shock of the moment. But such a victory, which Ralph Jordan called the greatest in his 22 years as a head coach, deserves another look. And from this distance it would appear there was more to the Auburn accomplishment than two strikes of lightning.

Manner of win a fairy tale
True, Alabama dominated the game and lost it in a fashion so unbelievable that Ripley would even turn it down. A Hollywood script writer wouldn't dare create such a climax. But there was more. Let's look back at the two series that forced Alabama into punting situations at such crucial times when it was so important to hang onto the football.

Up until Auburn finally got a field goal in the fourth quarter Alabama had converted seven of 11 third downs; Auburn had made four of 14. Then in the fourth quarter, the quarter that Alabama likes to claim as its own, something went wrong. Alabama couldn't come up with the big play so necessary to win a football game.

Auburn used up 5:45 of the fourth quarter to complete a 14-play, 56-yard drive that climaxed with a 42-yard field goal. At the time the score was 16-3 with 9:15 to play. And Auburn would not run another play until only 49 seconds remained and it was clock-killing time.

Auburn makes the big plays
The three points, which would provide the margin of victory, apparently had done no damage as Alabama took the ensuing kick at the 23 and moved 22 yards for

two first downs in four plays. Then the movement slowed and third down rolled around with five yards to go from the 50.

Big play!

It belonged to Auburn. Terry Davis fumbled the snap and it was recovered by Buddy Brown (according to the official play-by-play) for no gain. That mistake brought on a punting situation which brought on Bill Newton. Auburn was back within striking distance at 10-16 with 5:30 to play.

Alabama put the ensuing kick in play at its 20 and appeared to have regained its touch. Davis ran for five, Steve Bisceglia for three and Davis converted the third down with four. The clock was running and so was the Tide, running up another first down in two plays.

Then again Bill Newton and Ken Bernich met the challenge and Alabama faced the most crucial third down of the game. Four yards were needed from the Bama 48. Less than two minutes remained to play. A first down was essential if the Tide was to run out the clock. Davis took the snap and started to roll out, but Mike Neel was on him.

That man Newton again
Bigger play!

Again, it belonged to Auburn as Neel sacked Davis for a five-yard loss.

Punting situation from the 43 and Tide kicker Greg Gantt went back to take the snap. Newton again shot through to block the punt. It was only the second time in two years Alabama had allowed a blocked punt; and now Newton had blocked two back-to-back. For the second straight time, David Langner caught the ball on a bounce and scored a touchdown. This time it tied the score. Gardner Jett went in to kick the winning point.

Alabama coach Paul Bryant said big games are won on a few big plays. He said there were five in Saturday's game and that Auburn had won four of them.

In addition to the two blocked punts, Langner also intercepted two Davis passes. Once Alabama drew a five-yard penalty as it was lining up to attempt a field goal.

Auburn set the pattern on Alabama's first punt by getting a hand on the ball. The Tigers later blocked a placement, slapped down one pass and tipped up another.

Auburn has been the reverse of Alabama this year as it has been weak in the fourth quarter, having scored but 27 points against 47. Outscoring Alabama in the fourth quarter last Saturday was another big thing that shocked fans.

Bryant said there was a difference in losing a game and in being beaten. He said Alabama wasn't beaten, but lost the game by mistakes. Jordan said a good team makes its breaks.

Take your choice. But the fact remains, 17-16. That will be remembered long after all else is forgotten.

-30-

Wilbur Jackson (1971-73) was an outstanding running back for the Alabama Crimson Tide. He was a No. 1 draft pick by the San Francisco 49ers in 1974.

THE GAME - 1973

By Jimmy Smothers, written in 2011

It was a game of revenge for Alabama, whose faithful had grown tired of hearing about the Punt, Bama, Punt, game for a year. The Alabama players really wanted to block two punts. They came close the first time Auburn punted, but didn't even come close after that. Auburn's Roger Pruett punted seven times in the game for a 37.3 yard average. His longest punt was for 54 yards.

Sophomore Ray Maxwell was beginning to play for Alabama that year as a reserve offensive lineman and on the kicking team. He tells this story about the first day the players reported in the fall of 1973.

The routine was for the players to line up military style and go from doctor to doctor taking a physical. They would then draw equipment and go out and run the mile, a few 440 dashes and whatever the coaches asked them to do. Afterwards, head coach Paul Bryant would meet with the players. Two-a-day practice would begin early the following morning.

"That year Coach Bryant came in while we were still taking physicals and announced there would be a team meeting as soon as we got on the field," recalls Maxwell. "When we got out there he told us he had a couple of unusual schedule dates that fall, that we were to play Miami on a Saturday (Nov. 22) and five days later play LSU in Baton Rouge. He explained it would be on Thanksgiving night and be the first college game ever televised at night."

Alabama normally had seven days between games, so the five-day turn-around was unusual; especially since LSU had a really good team that year and wound up second to Alabama in the SEC standings.

Maxwell recalls that Coach Bryant told the players that LSU Coach Charlie McClendon (he had played for Bryant at Kentucky) had phoned him and said Roone Arledge (ABC Network) was asking that the game be changed to Thanksgiving night so they could broadcast it.

"Coach told us one reason he agreed to do it was because all that summer he had heard that Punt, Bama, Punt stuff and he'd had a gut full of it," Maxwell said. "Back then, a team could only be on TV three times a year, so having a game televised was a really big deal. Coach said he agreed to change the game date if the network would agree to also televise the Alabama vs. Auburn game.

"He said he wanted the world to see just what kind of team Auburn had, using some words that I'm not going to repeat," Maxwell said. "He told us that day that it would be a long, long time before Auburn beat him again. And I think it was 10 years before that happened."

Maxwell said to his knowledge, Bryant never mentioned the Punt, Bama, Punt game again, but that when game week rolled around he didn't have to, the players all remembered what had happened the year before; and they all wanted their revenge.

"We should have won that 1972 game, and if we had, we'd have won the national championship," Maxwell said.

In 1973 Alabama got its revenge, beating Auburn 35-0, and finished the regular season at 11-0. UPI named Alabama its national champions.

As SEC champions Alabama went to the Sugar Bowl and played Notre Dame for the Associated Press national title. The Irish won that game, 24-23, and the Tide wound up 11-1 overall and ranked No. 4 in the AP poll.

Auburn went to the Sun Bowl, lost to Missouri 17-34 and finished the year at 6-6.

At the end of the 1973 season no one was mentioning Punt, Bama, Punt. But that 1972 game is still regarded as one of the tops in this storied series.

-30-

Pre-game column

Langner, Newton pictures go up

(Original version published in The Gadsden Times, Thursday, November 29, 1973)

The bulletin board just to the left of the scales in the hallway across from Alabama's training room had a hand-printed sign of commendation and encouragement.

"You have disciplined and trained yourself to do the job at hand. Let no obstacle stand in your way," it read.

Down the hall a little way, outside the locker room was another bulletin board. This one was across from huge pictures of former Tide All-Americas Tarzan White, Lee Roy Jordan, Ed Salem, Pat Trammell and Fred Sington. But the pictures on this board were not of wearers of the Crimson and White.

There was an 8x10 glossy of David Langner crossing the goal line for a touchdown in the 1972 game. The inscription across the bottom read: "I want your ring." It was signed, "Stud".

Langner assured me the signature had been forged.

There was a large poster which carried two pictures of Bill Newton blocking punts. Between the two pictures are the words, "Punt, Bama, Punt".

The bulletin board also had a poster paste-up of newspaper headlines and clippings from last year's game. Underneath was a hand-printed sign which read, "Remember and Hate!"

Wayne Hall and John Croyle stopped to gaze as they passed. These two were among the leaders in the team's Fellowship of Christian Athletes Huddle.

"Can you actually hate anyone?" someone asked Croyle. The big 6-6 senior replied with a big toothy grin. Neither boy said a word.

-30-

Game

No blocked punts, no sweat, easy win

(Original version published in The Gadsden Times, Sunday, December 2, 1973)

BIRMINGHAM -- There were no blocked punts, no miracles and no doubters to Alabama's claim to No. 1. The Crimson Tide saw to that by taking the 11th step in their bid toward a fourth National Championship under Coach Paul Bryant.

The Tide football team took this step in the same manner as it had taken the first 10. That is, white-shirted Alabama displayed both offensive and defensive might, a herd of running backs and enough power to solve the energy shortage within this state.

The only thing remaining in Alabama's 12-part journey to the collegiate football crown room is a Sugar Bowl victory over fourth-ranked Notre Dame on New Year's Eve. But Coach Paul Bryant didn't want to talk about that at this time.

"We'll take this week off and announce our plans next week," he said. "I want our players to forget about football for a while. It's been a long, hard season."

It's doubtful they'll forget the 1973 game for a week ... or forever. The 35-0 victory over Auburn was a "sweet game to win" according to Tide quarterback Gary Rutledge, who admitted the final score was somewhat of a surprise.

Wilbur Jackson, the game's most valuable player, called it the "most satisfying win in my career". He carried the ball 15 times for 89 yards and a touchdown.

"This wasn't my best effort," Jackson, a native of Ozark, confessed. "But I couldn't be happier. I've had to live with my most disappointing loss for 365 days."

Jackson and his teammates were not the only ones happy the Auburn domination within the state had ended.

"I was just sitting here trying to remember that little tune," said Coach Bryant as writers greeted him after the game. "How'd it go? Something like Punt, Bama, Punt, wasn't it?"

Actually, Alabama punted four times for a 34-yard average with Greg Gantt toeing one for 41 yards and Richard Todd three times for a 31.7 average. He got off his longest punt of the year, a 34-yarder, the last time he kicked.

Auburn's Roger Pruett kicked seven times for a 37.3 yard average with a 54-yard long kick. First time he toed leather Alabama put on a mighty rush with Mike Washington almost getting a hand on the ball.

Alabama's big offensive show which totaled 405 yards broke two team and conference records – most touchdowns in a season (59) and most first downs rushing in a season (192). This display of might impressed the foe as well as home folk, if one can consider Auburn as such.

"Well, Alabama is just as good as we thought and all of the writers who voted and predicted," said Auburn's coach, Ralph Jordan. Alabama was favored to win by 28 points and beat that by a touchdown and extra point.

Alabama followed the same pattern it had employed all year by substituting freely throughout the game. Second teams were in the game in the first quarter and third teamers by halftime.

Overall, the Tide used 11 different ball carriers that ran the ball 61 times for 352 yards total. All five TDs were on the ground with Rutledge getting two – on one- and three-yard runs.

Randy Billingsley and Jackson scored one each (seven and 14 yards) and James Taylor the last one on an eight-yard scamper.

Behind Jackson's 89 came Billingsley with 66 yards, Rutledge 37, Taylor 34 and Paul Spivey 30. High for Auburn was Secedrick McIntyre with 59. Rusty Fuller had 29.

Alabama used 63 players, Auburn 53.

-30-

Post-game article

Bama vs. Irish; best of century
(Source: The Gadsden Times, Monday, December 3, 1973)

Following its 35-0 win over Auburn, No. 1 Alabama turns its attention to playing No. 3 Notre Dame in the Sugar Bowl on New Year's Eve night. Both teams have perfect records and the game is already being billed as "The Game of the Century" although, in actuality, it is just one of numerous games that have been billed as such in recent years.

During his TV show Sunday Auburn's coach, Ralph Jordan, extended well wishes to the Crimson Tide. "I don't want to put them on the spot, but I think they'll win," Jordan said, referring to Alabama's Sugar Bowl game. Alabama's coach, Paul Bryant, made no mention of the bowl game on his Sunday TV show.

Jordan said, "Alabama, in my opinion, is the No. 1 team and probably one of the greatest teams I've ever seen. They impressed me with their kicking game, which is superb, and their specialty teams. And, of course, they have fine defensive and offensive personnel. Beyond that, they have great coaching by Paul Bryant and his staff."

On his TV show Jordan singled out Tide quarterback Gary Rutledge and halfback Wilbur Jackson were singled out for outstanding play in the win over Auburn. On Bryant's show, he said, "We're thankful for our people, and thankful to their parents for letting us have them."

Jordan pointed out that "one thing Alabama didn't do was block a kick." Bryant said, "We tried awfully hard to block a punt." Reference was to the 17-16 game of the previous year when Auburn won by blocking two punts and scoring touchdowns on the plays.

While Alabama will be playing Notre Dame in the Sugar Bowl, seeking a fourth national title, Auburn 6-5) will play Missouri in the Sun Bowl on Dec. 29.

-30-

THE GAME - 1979

By Jimmy Smothers, written in 2011

No one realized it at the time, but as I look back on it, this season was kind of like the calm before a storm. It was the last National Championship season for Coach Paul Bryant at Alabama. He had only two more years to coach before he retired; then he died a month later.

Each of those last two years was kind of downhill by Bryant standards; especially coming on the heels of the '79 season. And what a year that was.

Alabama had been co-champions the year before, sharing the honor with Southern Cal. Each team ended up with impressive bowl wins and 11-1 records. The AP poll had Alabama No. 1; the UPI poll had Southern Cal No. 1, probably because the Trojans had beaten Alabama earlier in the season. Southern Cal's only loss had been two weeks later to Arizona State.

Alabama had gone 6-0 in the SEC and won the conference title in 1978, and repeated that feat in 1979.

In addition, the 1979 Crimson Tide went 12-0 for the first time in school history; and was the unanimous selection as National Champions. It was the sixth time that Alabama, under Bryant, had either won outright, or shared, the National Championship.

According to the Alabama record book, Alabama was ranked No. 2 before its first five games that year, No. 1 before its last six. But despite a 25-18 win over Auburn in the final game of the regular season the Tide dropped to No. 2 before its Sugar Bowl game against No. 6 Arkansas.

Ohio State, which had been ranked below Alabama all year, had suddenly jumped to No. 2 before facing Michigan the same week No. 1 Alabama faced Auburn. Ohio State won 18-15 and moved ahead of Alabama.

Alabama fans were in an uproar, thinking the Tide was going to be deprived of another championship as it had been in 1966 and 1977. No. 2 Alabama was to play No. 6 Arkansas in the Sugar Bowl; No. 1 Ohio State was to face No. 3 Southern Cal in the Rose Bowl.

Alabama and Ohio State were both undefeated with 11-0 records; Southern Cal had no losses but one tie. Arkansas was 10-1.

Pre-game column

Bryant knows how to beat the Tigers

(Original version published in The Gadsden Times, Thursday, November 29, 1979)

TUSCALOOSA – What will it take for the Crimson Tide to defeat Auburn's Tigers Saturday in Birmingham?

The question was put to Paul Bryant Wednesday; and the Alabama football coach had an answer.

"First of all, we'll have to have a perfect kicking game. That's where you always start," Bryant said. "And we'll have to control the ball some. We'll have to be able to move the football some and use up the clock.

"Defensively, we'll have to hold Auburn's great backs (James Brooks and Joe Cribs) down – not let them get a lot of big runs.

"That way we'll have a chance. Otherwise, we don't have a chance."

Alabama, the No. 1 ranked team in the nation, is a 17-point favorite over the 14th ranked Tigers. And the pressure is on the Tide to win. By doing so, Bama will not only win another SEC championship and another trip to the Sugar Bowl, but will also have a second straight National Championship.

Bryant likes this kind of situation – a pressure situation.

"I'd rather be playing for first place and a championship rather than playing for last place," he said. "A bowl game is important for the players because they enjoy it and they deserve it. I'd just as soon be playing for a National Championship."

The game is important in this state as well; even if Alabama wasn't a national football power – a defending National Champion playing for a legendary coach.

"When you lose this one, you have to listen to it all year," said Bryant, whose teams have lost to Auburn but five times in 21 years – and not at all in the past six years.

And when Alabama wins?

"Well, I think it helps when we start recruiting," the coach said.

Bryant said he remembers most the 10-0 win over Auburn in 1959.

"It was the first one we won over them and I guess it stands out more than the others because it was the first. But some of the others stand out, the ones we blew because of poor coaching, like the two blocked punts thing."

Bryant was referring to the 17-16 Auburn win in 1972. That was the last time an Auburn team has beaten an Alabama team.

Alabama people don't like to talk about that game. But they will hear replays of it over loudspeakers in the parking lot at Legion field Saturday. Auburn people have had the radio description of announcer Gary Sanders' call recorded and take pride in playing it back loud and clear, refusing to let Alabama fans forget about beating the Tide on two blocked punts.

Bryant had rather talk about this week, which he says has been exciting and busy, one that he will be glad to see end.

"Auburn has more material down there than I've seen since I've been here," he said, turning his thoughts to the game. "And by far, they are the best team we'll play this fall. They have the most explosive football team that I've seen in a long time.

"First of all, Auburn has a great quarterback (Charlie Trotman). And I don't think I've ever seen two as great running backs on any one team. I mean backs with that much speed – capable of breaking a game open at any time."

Brooks has rushed for 1,153 yards and 10 touchdowns this fall; Cribbs for 1,027 yards and 14 touchdowns. And no two backs on any one team have ever done that before in the Southeastern Conference.

And where there are great backs, there are usually great linemen. So is the case at Auburn and Bryant has been impressed.

"I noticed the offensive line comes off the ball quick and tries to tie people up down around the ankles," Bryant says of the Auburn linemen. "They are well coached. Doug Barfield is a fine football coach and has a fine staff, too.

"I saw them on TV (Sunday playback) early in the season and both the offensive and defensive line are greatly improved. Early, they were not too well organized on defense when they had a lot of people injured. But they are getting their people back now and no one has scored much on them the last three games. That's for sure. They have really improved in all aspects of the game."

Auburn's defense seemed to peak in the second half of the last game when it shut out the Georgia Bulldogs the last two quarters, limiting them to 37 yards rushing after the half. Auburn won that game, 33-13, and is on a three-game winning streak. Previously, Auburn defeated Mississippi State 14-3 and Florida 19-13. The three wins followed the upset loss at Wake Forest (38-42).

This is the second time this season that Auburn (8-2) has been on a three-game winning streak. But during Barfield's four years at Auburn, the Tigers have not won four games in a row.

Alabama (10-0) has now won 19 games in a row, the nation's longest winning streak. The last Bama defeat was Sept. 23 of last year, a 14-24 loss to Southern Cal in Birmingham.

Auburn people feel the Tigers have their best chance in years of beating Alabama. The Tigers rely on the long-range running of Brooks and Cribbs. Alabama, meanwhile, prefers the more time-consuming offense and has used 18 different backs this fall in its Wishbone attack.

-30-

Pre-game column

Time to give scoop on Tide, Tigers

(Original version published in The Gadsden Times, Friday, November 30, 1979)

It is time for another great revelation.

Today is the day – that day which comes each year at this time when astonishing disclosures are supposed to be made.

Today I am writing my final story before the annual Alabama vs. Auburn football game at Legion Field. I am expected to be enlightening. I am supposed to tell people what is going to happen; who is going to win, and why.

Sports writers talk a lot to coaches and players. They ask a lot of intelligent questions. They get a lot of intelligent answers, straight from the horses' mouths. ("Horses," here, means star football players.)

One question that a writer always asks a player is if he is going to be up for the game on Saturday.

Such a thought-provoking question deserves an equally deep-rooted answer. So the player will appear to give it some thought before asking. It is always yes. He and his teammates will be real high for the game because it is the biggest game of the year. And it's the biggest game of the year because it is the next game.

I always ask the players if they are going to win; bring it right out in the open. I want to know, my readers want to know.

People are always asking me about THE GAME. Neighbors, people I meet uptown and in stores. Even the wife asks so she can pass on inside information to her friends.

A collector dropped by the office, but he was more interested in finding out who is going to win this football game, and by how much, than he was at collecting the premium due.

"Who is going to win?" he asked, as I made out the check.

Alabama, I told him. (An Alabama player had told me so.)

"I thought so. By how much?"

A touchdown or two, probably.

He smiled as he started to put the check in his wallet without even looking at it.

Want me to sign that?

This time I grinned, as he handed it back.

The boss dropped by to find out what kind of a game to expect. I had to really come up with some smarts. You know, try to say something that sounded as if I actually knew what I was talking about. Try to impress upon him that I had been working and that the earlier trips to Auburn and Tuscaloosa (on expense accounts) had been worth the money.

I told him that Coach Barfield had told me that Auburn's defense would have to be alert to the inside traps, the power-sweeps and the triple options. That Steadman Shealy would have to be stopped from cutting back inside the tackles if they took away his outside pitch.

I talked about Alabama playing odd and even man fronts, stack defenses, zones and man coverage in the secondary. I mentioned every term I could remember hearing Dandy Don talk about on Monday night TV. I even started to throw in something about cheating, but I couldn't remember if that was used in reference to the players' activity on the field or what the coaches did in their card games in the locker room. So I left that part out.

The most remarkable thing is that one coach said his team would have a hard time scoring without the football. And the other coach said if his team had a chance to win, it would have to control the football.

Sports writers get a lot of inside information like that when they talk to the coaches.

Other things I found out, that I'm happy to pass on now that the teams have concluded their pregame practices, are:
- --- The team that gets the breaks will win.
- --- It's a big game for Auburn. It's a big game for Alabama, too.
- --- If Alabama worries too much about Brooks and Cribbs, Trotman can hurt it.
- --- Brooks has got a burst of speed that can beat a team anytime.
- --- Cribbs is more of a tough, inside runner, but he can break away, too.
- --- Auburn runs the option more than any team Alabama has faced except Mississippi State.
- --- Auburn's offense will cause Alabama's defense some problems.
- --- To win, a team will have to have a perfect kicking game.
- --- Auburn will have to play its best game of the year to win.
- --- Alabama will have to play its best game of the year to win.
- --- To win, a team will have to force some things to happen.
- --- The team that makes the fewest mistakes will win.

Isn't it amazing, the things a writer can learn from talking to the coaches?

-30-

Game

Tide, Tigers give crowd 60 minutes of thrills

(Original version published in The Gadsden Times, Sunday, December 2, 1979)

BIRMINGHAM – What might have been an easy chore turned out to be an all-day job for the Crimson Tide of Alabama. Twice in the early minutes of Saturday's annual game between football teams from the University of Alabama and Auburn University the favored Tide had the ball in four-down territory – had great opportunities to jump on top by a couple of touchdowns. But it didn't happen.

Auburn, playing its best defensive game of the year, turned the Tide back both times it came knocking in the first quarter.

Auburn, surprising Bama and its coach, hit so hard it caused four turnovers via fumbles in the third quarter alone.

Auburn, playing its usual brand of explosive offense, took a 3-0 lead in the first quarter; and an 18-17 lead in the fourth.

It was the first time all year that Alabama had trailed in the last half. In 10 previous games the Crimson Tide's defense had given up but 13 points during the final two quarters; and here was Auburn, scoring 15.

Auburn was moving mountains; putting the Tide fans in a state of shock.

Auburn scored nine points to Alabama's three in the third; and got six more in the fourth to go out front.

Excitement mounted. Tension hung heavy over the stadium with its standing-room-only crowd of 77,918. Upset was on everyone's mind.

Time and again Alabama was blowing opportunities on offense. And suddenly, as everyone expected sooner or later, Joe Cribbs hauled in a Charlie Trotman pass and rambled 16 yards for a touchdown.

Auburn was back in the game, down by five, 12-17. Another bolt of lightning and the Tigers would be in control.

Momentum had suddenly shifted. With a James Brooks or a Joe Cribbs, Auburn could now win this most important ball game on any one play.

It didn't happen.

What did was that Steadman Shealy directed Alabama in what he called the greatest drive of his career as the Tide came from behind in the fourth quarter to regain the lead.

It was an 82-yard, seven-play drive which Alabama fans will not forget. Shealy had runs of 10 and 15 yards before scoring later from the eight. The touchdown was set up on a 20-yard rip by fullback Steve Whitman, charging straight ahead like a bull, behind the blocking of Jim Bunch.

Alabama was back out front, 25-18, with just over eight minutes to play. But the game was not decided until the final play. Auburn refused to give up and was in good field position at the Alabama 37 before losing the ball on downs with just over three minutes to play.

Alabama tried to run out the clock, but finally had to punt with seconds left. And Auburn quarterback Charley Trotman had time to put the ball in the air twice more before time ran out.

It was a game that neither team should have lost. It was the kind of game that Auburn and Alabama are expected to play at the end of every regular season. It was the kind of game where every player from both teams can hold his head high.

The Alabama-Auburn game of 1979 was not one where Tide fans were concerned with "We're No. 1" or with making plans for a bowl trip.

The game played here Saturday was one in which the most important thing on the minds of players and spectators alike was winning.

Both teams gave fans a thrill, not only in the nail-biting fourth quarter, but from the opening minutes of play when Alabama got the ball when Auburn fumbled the opening kickoff. Roll Tide!

Auburn's defense, with Ken Hardy, Freddie Smith and Frank Warren, threw Shealy for 12 yards in losses, turned the Bama break the other way. War Eagle!

Next time Bama got the ball it turned Major Ogilvie loose for 19, one, one, 13 and four yards as the Tide rolled to the six. Roll Tide!

A fumble in the backfield brought on the field goal team. Alan McElroy's kick, from 32-yards out, was wide. War Eagle!

Auburn fans got an eyeful of what they came to see on the next down as Cribbs broke through tackle for 35 yards to the Tide 24. A penalty carried to the 12. First down. War Eagle!

Bama's pride and joy, its defense, headed by E.J. Junior, David Hannah, Robbie Jones and Randy Scott, rose up like a mighty fortress and threw the Tigers back. Roll Tide!

Now it was Auburn's turn at field goal kicking. Jorge Portela did things up right from 47 yards away and Auburn was on top, 3-0. War Eagle!

Once the ice had been broken Alabama warmed to the task of ball-control offense, driving 80 yards in 11 plays for a go-ahead touchdown. The scoring play came on third down and hit Auburn where Auburn is weakest – in the secondary. Shealy passed 28 yards to Keith Pugh, who broke a tackle at the 15 and ran in for the touchdown. Alabama, 7-3. Roll Tide!

The second quarter belonged to Alabama, which was making a show of breaking the game open. But things didn't click for the Tide in the third. On three of its first four plays, Alabama lost the ball on fumbles. Auburn got a field goal. Bama drove to the Auburn 12 on the ensuing kick but fumbled again. War Eagle!

Finally, just before the quarter ended, McElroy kicked a field goal. But Auburn bounced back with a touchdown. The quarter ended, 12-17 and excitement was beginning to mount. Auburn was within striking distance – Auburn was in upset territory.

Then it happened. Trotman hit the Tide with a 55-yard pass to Byron Franklin, then completed an 11-yard pass to Mark Robbins in the end zone. Auburn was back on top, 18-17, and had the momentum.

Now it was time for Alabama to prove itself worthy of its No. 1 rating. Championship teams are not teams that fold, but teams that keep their poise when things go wrong. They come from behind to win late in the game.

This was the mark of Bryant's Alabama teams, and it's what this team did. With Shealy at the throttle, with 10 good men shoveling coal, the Tide Express rambled 82 yards in seven plays; it rambled into the end zone; it rambled to a 25-18 victory. Roll Tide!

This Tide Express will now ramble to New Orleans and the Sugar Bowl where, if it can ramble to a victory over Arkansas, it will have its second straight National Championship.

-30-

Post-game column

Bama won big one, has yet to peak

(Original version published in The Gadsden Times, Monday, December 3, 1979)

Legion Field, Saturday, packed with people yelling and screaming as they looked down on the field of battle could readily have been a coliseum. And the athletes, decked in their red and white, and orange and blue, might have been gladiators.

Seventeen strong, brave young men in white uniforms, lined up on one side; fourteen wearing blue filed in on the other. Then they marched toward center field, as if to war.

Bands played. Fans shouted.

Charlie Trotman stepped up front as spokesman for one group, Curtis McGriff and Wiley Barnes did likewise for the other.

It was the peace before the storm. The toss of the coin, they call it. Auburn won the call, elected to receive. And as the formal ceremonies ended, all hell broke loose. In the stands, on the sidelines. There is hardly a moment in any sporting event as exciting – or as suspenseful – as the start of a football game. The coin toss, lining up for the opening kick, the first play from scrimmage.

SATURDAY IT DIDN'T end there. It carried on down to the end of the game.

I felt the course of the game change for the last time with 3:28 left on the clock. It was fourth and 11 for Auburn at the Alabama 38. A deafening shout, rising from the West stands like one mighty voice, was urging the Tigers to victory. Trotman took the snap, faded back and threw. Fans held their breaths. And as the ball fell incomplete, the sound of the masses seemed to shift, like the mighty wind. It began to hush in the West and to rise in the East.

The stands where Alabama's student body was seated burst forth, vocally.

Alabama got the ball on its 38 with 3:22 to play. And the Crimson Tide, which needed to control the football the rest of the game to preserve a 25-13 win, just about did that.

Auburn finally got the ball back with nine seconds left and managed to get off two passes. But the Tide had the win, the SEC championship, the Sugar Bowl berth and retained its No 2 national rating.

THE GAME WENT down to the wire with Auburn having a shot to pull the upset of the year. James Brooks came within one man of breaking a kickoff return for a touchdown after Alabama's final score. Four plays later a pass to Mike Locklear would have been a touchdown if he'd held onto the football.

Ken Simon made a big play on Brooks' 65 yard return, forcing him to cut to the left and allowing Don McNeal to tackle him from behind. And Jim Bob Harris managed to block Locklear's vision a split second on the pass.

It's things like this that make the difference in winning and losing in close games.

Alabama halfback Major Ogilvie, looking back, said it should have been a short day for the Crimson Tide but that they turned it into a long day.

"We had the opportunity early to make it a short day," he said. "We should have cashed in our first two possessions, but we didn't. And I'd like to credit Auburn for that. They kept us from doing it."

THE ALABAMA running back said it wasn't because Auburn did anything different or caught Alabama off guard.

"We were well prepared for what Auburn did. But they had a good scheme of things, kept mixing it up. Auburn has some great players and had a chance there at the end the way things turned out."

Ogilvie said, "We're not an emotional team. No rah-rah stuff. We kept our minds on what we were doing and proved we were a championship football team. If we'd panicked when we got behind, we'd never have scored."

He called the 82-yard, fourth-quarter drive, Alabama's "most crucial drive, but maybe not the best, of the season."

Considering Auburn has been weak against the pass this fall, it seemed surprising that Alabama threw little – eight times, but for 80 yards and a touchdown.

OGILVIE SAID HE thought Auburn was prepared for the pass but didn't think the Tigers were daring the Tide to throw.

"I think we still have some improving to do," said quarterback Steadman Shealy. "I think we can get better. There are some little things that keep happening that keep us from really exploding offensively."

Shealy and his teammates think that will happen in the bowl game.

-30-

Defensive back David Langner is listed in the Top 10 defensive records at Auburn in both career and single season categories for pass interceptions. He is tied for fifth (with 12) for a career and tied for second (with 8) in one season. However, he is most remembered for returning two blocked punts for touchdowns in the fourth quarter in the 1972 game against Alabama, which Auburn won, 17-16. In that game he also intercepted a pass to stop an Alabama drive.

Photo courtesy Auburn Athletic Department

The Final Whistle for Coach Jordan

Sept. 25, 1910 ◻ July 17, 1980

By Jimmy Smothers, written in 2011

Coach Ralph Jordan retired after the 1975 season and Doug Barfield became head coach of the Auburn Tigers. So the death of Coach Jordan, while shocking since he had only been ill four months, wasn't the same as if he had been coaching at the time.

I drove down to Auburn and attended the funeral and burial, which drew a capacity crowd that included a lot of big-name coaches, former players, newsmen and friends. It was a sad occasion, just as had been his farewell speech to his players in the locker room at Legion Field after his final game against Alabama – a 28-0 loss. It was the third straight loss to the Tide, which would extend to nine in a row before another coach, Pat Dye, defeated Alabama 23-22 in 1982 in Coach Bryant's final game against Auburn.

I mention in a column later in this chapter that my final visit with Coach Jordan was when he spoke at a meeting in Gadsden a little while before he became ill. That is the visit I like most to remember. But I did "see" him one other time. Well, actually, I didn't really see him.

John Pruett and I went to his home one final time, but the coach was too ill to have visitors. Pruett recalls that Ralph, Jr., (Pee Wee) was home but not Mrs. Jordan. We asked if we could see his dad and he said something like, "Let me go check. He hasn't been seeing any visitors for quite a while."

He went into the bedroom and came out a few minutes later and said, "Daddy said he really appreciates the two of you coming by and wishes you the best, but that he just doesn't want you to see him like this."

Pee Wee handed each of us a little cross with an inspirational saying written on the back. "Dad said to give these to you as a remembrance," the son said. We both still have them.

I'm not real sure, but it seems as if we got a glimpse into the bedroom as Pee Wee was either going in or coming out but only saw a "lump" on the bed. That was probably good, because I now remember him last from that final speech at the club when he was so full of life; not on his death bed.

I remember once, when I was a young sports writer and didn't know any better that I wrote him a letter, criticizing him about something I thought he did wrong. He wrote back and apologized; admitting that he'd made a mistake, and sent me an autographed picture. That never came up during any of the many conversations we had over the years.

-30-

Jordan to be buried today on the Plain

(Original version published in The Gadsden Times, Thursday July 17, 1979)

AUBURN – Ralph "Shug" Jordan, football coach for Auburn University who became one of Dixie's football legends, was to be buried here this afternoon. Laid to rest forever in the Loveliest Village which he loved – and where he spent a lifetime making others happy through athletics.

He died Thursday at his home, a victim of acute leukemia. He was 69 years old and had been retired from coaching for four years after serving as head coach of the Tigers for a quarter-century with tremendous success.

His family, which was with him at his death, requested that memorial gifts be sent to the Auburn Foundation, Shug Jordan Fund, in lieu of flowers.

Burial was at Memorial Park following 2 p.m. services at Holy Trinity Episcopal Church.

Jordan, who retired in 1975, had been in failing health due to leukemia for about four months. Heart difficulties had occurred during that time, also.

"While the death of Coach Jordan was not unexpected, it leaves us all very much saddened," said Harry Philpott, who recently retired as president of Auburn University. "A great coach, a great Auburnite and a great gentleman has passed away.

"He will be held eternally in the memory of those who know Auburn as one who made tremendous contributions to its advancement in all areas."

Tributes poured in from athletes, coaches, and friends. Among them was Governor Fob James, who was a star running back for Jordan in 1953-55, and from longtime cross-state rival Paul "Bear" Bryant of the University of Alabama.

Jordan was remembered as an always-tough competitor on the field but a courtly, colorful, warm and generous man away from the gridiron.

He was a gentleman, a man who was like a father to his players, polite to everyone. He wasn't uneasy in the limelight, yet he didn't seek it, happy to live in peace and harmony with neighbors and friends. He was a history buff and liked to talk about World War II, in which he fought.

He compiled a record of 175-83-7 during his 25 campaigns as head coach and in 1957 led his Tigers to the Associated Press' National Championship.

A native of Selma, he was a three-sport star at Auburn when he graduated in 1932.

He stayed on the next year – the year the Southeastern Conference was formed – working as an athletic assistant. He held that post for 12 years, serving for a time as Auburn's basketball coach. During that time he also worked with the football teams as an assistant.

Kentucky basketball coach Adolph Rupp, upon hearing that Jordan was considering giving up basketball coaching, advised him against it. "I don't know why you keep fooling around with football. Your future is as a basketball coach," Rupp told Jordan back then.

Auburn people were glad Jordan didn't listen to Rupp. While Jordan was successful in basketball, his football career proved to be the greatest in Auburn history.

After a tour with the military during World War II and a brief stint back at Auburn, he joined the staff at the University of Georgia, where he served for four years.

Then, in 1951, the call came from his alma mater. He was named head football coach.

A measure of Jordan's success is that he made Auburn one of the South's most formidable clubs even though, for his last 19 seasons, he had to contend with his rugged cross-state counterpart, Bryant, a dominating force who might have destroyed any lesser rival.

Jordan refused to be awed by Bryant and his teams although they beat him more than any others during the times they competed. And it was the Bryant-Jordan rivalry, more than anything else, which has made football what it is in the state of Alabama today.

There were numerous highlights in the Jordan era. Among them: The unbeaten AP National Championship team in 1957; the team led by Heisman Trophy winner Pat Sullivan in 1969-70-71 which defeated Bama two of those three years; and the incredible 1972 team which turned two blocked punts into fourth-quarter touchdowns for Auburn's memorable upset victory – a 17-16 win which has come to be known as the "Punt, Bama, Punt" game; an Auburn triumph that killed Alabama's National Championship hopes.

In 1973, two years before Jordan retired; Auburn University renamed its football stadium — Jordan-Hare Stadium — so fans would always remember this great coach. The dedication was at the October 6 game with Ole Miss, which Auburn won, 14-7.

-30-

Shug could make others feel 10 feet tall

(Original version published in The Gadsden Times, Friday, July 18, 1979)

It was years ago, back when Auburn's athletic offices were located in that old brick building behind the north end zone of the football stadium. The end with the grassy slopes where fans used to sit when the stadium was filled to capacity.

That happened often back then.

I was a young sports writer – had traveled to the Loveliest Village on the Plain for an interview which proved to sell me on the school and the man.

I'd met Ralph Jordan before, the day he drove up to Crossville to sign John Cochran to a football scholarship. And I'd staffed several Auburn football games; attended several press conferences with him. But this was different.

I'd made an appointment with "The Man". I was going to sit down in his office, face to face, and talk with the head football coach of the Auburn Tigers.

Even then, with much of his 25-year coaching career still ahead of him, he was a legend. He had already turned the Auburn program into a major powerhouse – had won the school's only National Championship.

I'll never forget that visit. The Blue and Orange telephone on his desk; the pictures on his wall of War Eagles and Tigers.

I was scared when I walked into his small office in the basement. But the portly man behind the desk immediately put me at ease. Ralph Jordan was that kind of a man – warm and personable. He was an outgoing man who understood his fellow man.

Gentleman, that's what he was; and friendly. He knew when a reporter walked in that he wanted a story. And the fact that I was from a small daily paper didn't seem to matter. Jordan had a knack of always coming up with something special for anyone with enough interest to visit him in Auburn.

That day Jordan gave me an exclusive story about Scotty Long – even got him out of class to talk with me and pose for a picture.

Ralph Jordan made me feel like I was 10 feet tall – like I was sports editor of the nation's biggest newspaper. I'll never forget it. I left Auburn that day floating on air.

I sensed that day that he was sincere. There was nothing phony about this man they called Shug. He wasn't just putting on the dog; certainly not for me. During the years since I have made hundreds of trips to Auburn – and gone with the Auburn team to big games and on bowl trips. I've visited with Jordan in his home – and with him after he moved into large, plush offices in the new Memorial Coliseum.

He never changed. Coach Jordan never imagined himself anything other than what he was – an old country boy from Selma who enjoyed eating sugar cane – thus the nickname, Shug. That was Auburn's head football coach – a humanitarian – a man with a feeling for young men and for the game of football.

Deceit would have been a burden too heavy for Coach Jordan to bear – big a man as he was. And firm as he could be. Hard-headed, maybe, at times. But his toughness wasn't the kicking and shouting or physical kind which is so familiar to many football coaches on the practice field. He believed in respect for a leader rather than fear for a man. Jordan would take a player into the privacy of his office and sit down with him. And without any doubt, he could sure make himself understood.

His coaching philosophy – his philosophy in life – was based on honesty. "Be honest with yourself," he'd say. Diogenes, the Greek philosopher who spent a lifetime looking for "the honest man" would have liked Shug.

I remember Jordan letting writers ride the team bus from the motel to the stadium that year in Athens, Ga., when Pat Sullivan won the Heisman Trophy. That was an experience few non-players have ever had. And in 1974, after the Gator Bowl win over Texas, Jordan let reporters in the locker room to hear his farewell speech to his players. Only he didn't retire, but returned for one more year.

That led to another experience that stands out because he again let writers into the locker room after the game to hear his farewell speech after his final game against Alabama. This time, he meant it. The Jordan era was over.

I remember prospects saying that the highlight of their visit to Auburn was not the entertainment, but meeting Coach Jordan personally. I understand that. Visiting with "The Man" was always the highlight of every trip I ever made to Auburn when he was the coach.

I remember the last time I visited with Coach Jordan. It was at a Quarterback Club meeting. He was keen of wit behind the lectern; and always a master with words.

On that final visit he was the perfect gentleman as he greeted former players, Auburn fans and old friends.

-30-

THE GAME - 1981

By Jimmy Smothers, written in 2011

When Alabama defeated Auburn 28-17 that 28th day of November in 1981 it gave Coach Paul Bryant his 315th career win; it broke Amos Alonzo Stagg's record and made Bryant the winningest coach (at that time) in NCAA 1-A football.

To say the Alabama football faithful were extremely high is putting it mildly. The setting was perfect for this record-setting game and Legion Field was filled to overflowing. Alabama wore its white uniform, signifying it was the "home" team, although at that time the tickets were equally split 50-50 between Alabama and Auburn fans. But Alabama clearly had more fans, probably in anticipation of Bryant passing Stagg's record.

Alabama went into the game ranked No. 4 with an 8-1-1 record; Auburn was 5-5, unranked, and was expected to lose to the Tide for the ninth straight year. This was Pat Dye's first year as the Auburn coach and he was already showing signs of turning the program around. But it didn't take a miracle to find Auburn fans willing to sell their tickets.

The press box was also running over as a large number of national media had come into Birmingham to cover that game. Although no cheering is allowed in a "working press box" there was plenty of excitement.

The game is remembered as the "315 Game", especially by Alabama fans. But for Auburn it was the beginning of a new era in the rivalry. Although the Crimson Tide was a heavy favorite, the Tigers gave a good preview of what was to come in the Dye régime. He had Auburn on the pad ready to launch his era of dominance in football.

Even Bryant told Dye, who had once been an assistant coach under him, that he (Bryant) was proud of him (Dye) and the way his team had played – taking the fight to Alabama all the way to the final second.

Amid all the excitement and news coverage of Bryant's 315th win, no one suspected that it would be the coach's final win over Auburn; or that in 14 months he would be dead. Or that Auburn was on the verge of winning four SEC titles and six bowl games plus a tie during the next nine years. During that span Auburn also defeated Alabama six times.

Alabama Coach Paul "Bear" Bryant and Auburn Coach Pat Dye, prior to THE GAME of 1981 (the 315 game) at Birmingham's Legion Field. This was Dye's first year at Auburn, and Bryant's penultimate year at Alabama. Dye had been Bryant's assistant at Alabama for nine years. Bryant's win in 1981 would break Amos Alonzo Stagg's record of 314 wins in American collegiate football.

Pre-game column

Bryant's one-track mind – Beat Auburn!

(Original version published in The Gadsden Times, Wednesday, November 25, 1981)

TUSCALOOSA -- Forget the record; forget Texas and the Cotton Bowl. There is only one thing on Paul Bryant's mind – beating the Auburn University football team Saturday in Legion Field.

He's trying his best to keep all other things from distracting his players as they go about preparing for their last regular season game of the year.

"If we don't beat Auburn, none of those things will mean very much," said Bryant. "It won't be much fun going to a bowl if we don't win this week."

A win over Auburn will give Alabama a share (with Georgia) of the SEC championship. And a win, coming on the heels of a rousing 31-16 victory over Penn State would send the Tide into the Cotton Bowl at its highest peak of the year.

"We played well against Penn State," said Bryant. "Actually, we may have played over our heads. We soundly defeated a pretty good football team. But that is behind us. We have to forget Penn State. In football, nothing matters except next week."

Bryant pointed out that football is a game of concentration, meditation and preparation.

"There are excellent teams losing to inferior teams every week," he added. "If a team, college or pro, does not concentrate on its business, it can be upset."

The Alabama coach said Auburn wants to beat Alabama Saturday worse than Alabama has wanted to beat any team it has played.

"We've come a long way this year, in my opinion, but we have a long way to go before we are a great team," he said. "We have to get our injured people well, get a little better every day, and concentrate on executing."

Bryant said he has seen Auburn on film and was impressed, particularly with its kicking game and defense. But, as usual, he added, "I am more concerned about our team than theirs."

The game is getting national attention because a win will give Bryant his 315th career coaching victory, making him the winningest college coach of all time. And while the Alabama players want to be on the team that enables him to break that record, they are hearing nothing about it from Bryant.

"I don't think our players will be worried about any record except their record against Auburn," said the coach. "That's the only record they should be worried about."

Alabama's seniors have never lost to Auburn – were only in grade school the last time an Alabama team did. That was in 1972 – 17-16 – the "Punt, Bama, Punt" game which probably prevented the Tide from winning a national championship.

Overall, Alabama holds a 27-17-1 advantage in the series. Bryant teams are 18-5 against Auburn.

The win over Penn State gave Bryant 314 career wins, tying him with Amos Alonzo Staff. So the record chase, which has been on all fall, will come to an end with the Tide's next win.

"I'll be glad when it's over, "said Bryant, who is more concerned with trying to beat Auburn, win the conference championship and getting a chance at bigger things in the Cotton Bowl.

-30-

Game

Tide sinks Tigers, 28-17

(Source, The Gadsden Times, Friday, November 29, 1981)

BIRMINGHAM – The countdown had ended the week before when Alabama went on the road and defeated Penn State. That win moved Coach Paul (Bear) Bryant into a tie with Amos Alonzo Staggs for most career wins.

The count was now 314 and the next opponent was cross-state rival Auburn before a capacity home crowd at Legion Field, Football Capitol of the South. What better setting could be found?

When the Tide came back from Pennsylvania with that win, it was common knowledge that it was only a matter of time before Bryant would be the winningest college coach in 1-A college football. As the Crimson Tide stepped onto the field it was common knowledge that time had run out.

Tide split end Jesse Bendross said even after Auburn took an early lead that he never doubted but that the game belonged to the men in Crimson and White.

"Coach Bryant always tells us to keep the faith and things will turn out right," Bendross told John Alred, who helped with the game coverage for The Gadsden Times. "He told us if we wanted to win the game bad enough we couldn't get beat no matter what happened."

What happened was that Bendross, a sophomore split end, was one of the game heroes. He had two pass receptions for touchdowns that proved to be the difference in the Tide's 28-17 win.

He scored Alabama's second touchdown on a 26-yard "X-whoopee" pass from Ken Coley in the third quarter. Then in the fourth quarter, after Auburn had regained the lead, he scored again, this time on a 38-yard pass from Walter Lewis. This gave the Tide a 21-17 lead

On the first touchdown Joey Jones made the key block that sprung Bendross.

"We really caught Auburn by surprise on that play," Bendross said. "I couldn't believe I was that wide open. It was a wonderful call by Mal Moore (offensive coordinator under Bryant).

In that game Alabama, which was still running basically the Wishbone offense, completed only four passes (for 80 yards), and three of them were to Bendross for 76 yards.

"Those two that went for touchdowns were the greatest of my career because this was the record game for Coach Bryant; and they were big because it was against Auburn."

Auburn's fullback, George Peoples, was the game's leading rusher with 155 yards on 26 carries, scoring a touchdown on a 63-yard run that tied the game at 7-7 in the second quarter. Tailback Lionel James scored Auburn's other touchdown.

Alabama's leading rusher was quarterback Alan Gray with 68 yards on nine carries. He had a 62-yard run that set-up Alabama first touchdown, which he scored from the one. Linnie Patrick scored one touchdown.

The game was Pat Dye's debut in the "Iron Bowl" and the first time he had fielded a team against his former boss. Dye had been an assistant coach under Bryant for nine years, and his Tigers gave the No. 4-ranked Tide a struggle, although they had won only five games that year.

With the win, Alabama moved to 9-1-1 overall and 7-0 in the SEC. The win also earned the Tide a berth in the Cotton Bowl against Texas; and a tie (with Georgia) for the conference championship.

(Gadsden Times assistant sports editor John Alred contributed to this article)

-30-

Post-game column

Tigers a winner in defeat

(Original version published in The Gadsden Times, Monday, November 30, 1981)

"The old gray Bear is doomed to Dye"

Those were the words printed on one banner Auburn University students displayed at Legion Field Saturday.

Another said: "All Bear gets today is a Pat on his back"

Both are indications of the confidence Auburn supporters had in their football team. And for three-and-a-half quarters it looked like that confidence was going to be rewarded.

Auburn, 5-5 going into the game against fourth-ranked Alabama, outplayed the Crimson Tide. The Tigers were a winner, even in defeat.

Auburn twice fought back from a touchdown deficit to tie the game at 7-7 and 14-14; then took the lead at 17-14 in the fourth quarter.

The Tigers had momentum. And when Alabama twice fumbled punts – setting up Auburn's second tying touchdown and the go-ahead field goal – it appeared to be the day of the Tigers rather than one for the Bear. But as has happened so often in the past 24 years with Bryant-coached teams, the Tide roared back to pull out a late fourth-quarter victory.

Alabama gave Bryant his record-breaking 315th career win, despite being beaten in just about every statistic. Auburn had more first downs, more total offensive plays and more total yardage.

"I told you we were gonna get after your tail, but it just wasn't quite good enough," Auburn's Pat Dye told Alabama's Paul Bryant after the game.

"We whipped your tail in statistics and I wish they counted," Dye added.

Bryant told Dye, who once was an Alabama assistant, he was proud of him.

"You did a great job this year," Bryant said. "If I didn't mean that, I'd say something else."

Bryant also said Alabama had better personnel than Auburn, yet had to play hard to win.
"Auburn players fought their hearts out. They will get better and better. But I don't want them to get much better for the next few years."

This indicates that Bryant, although 68 years of age and having broken Stagg's all-time winning record, still is not considering retirement anytime soon.

Stagg head-coached 57 years and was still an assistant in his 80s. Bryant has been a head coach for 37 years.

"Pat told me before the game his team had come to play," Bryant said. "He didn't have to tell me, I knew it anyway."

Dye told writers after the game that Auburn's kicking game was what killed the Tigers.

True, Auburn missed two field goal attempts and failed to get another off. But even if it had made all three, that would still have been only nine points and Alabama won by 11.

I thought that Auburn's kicking game was what kept the Tigers in the game.

Alabama was minus 35 yards on punt returns, Auburn plus 83.

Two fumbled punts by Alabama set up 10 of Auburn's 17 points. And a 44-yard punt return by Chuck Clayton to the Alabama 13 gave the Tigers another scoring opportunity, which they missed.

Each team punted seven times. The punting average favored Alabama but Auburn had more overall return yardage.

Despite the loss, Auburn has reason to be proud. The team played well enough to have won – gave a good account of itself – and ended the season better than had been expected.

Although the record was a loser – 5 wins, 6 losses – many people had felt the team would win only three and maybe four games. Five wins is a tremendous accomplishment for the Tigers. And they could, with a few breaks, have won three or four more.

"No question but we've made a lot of progress with our program," said Dye. "Nobody likes to lose, but our football players have accepted our way and I think they believe in our way. That is really what I tried to get across. I had rather have that than a few more wins and have to live with something less in the future."

Ironically, a 5-6 record and a few plays short of three or four more wins are identical to what the team did a year ago.

A year ago Auburn also led Alabama once by three points, but the Tide scored twice in the fourth quarter to win.

A year ago Auburn was going about firing Doug Barfield.

This year, Auburn people are talking about the great job Pat Dye has done and are looking forward to good things in the future.

I believe they are right. I believe that once Bryant retires, the dominant team in this state will be Dye and the Auburn Tigers.

-30-

Auburn was the home team in 1981 when it faced Alabama in Legion Field, so it was in charge of printing the game program and tickets for the game. This was the game when Alabama coach Paul Bryant was going for his record-setting 315th win and was getting national attention. Auburn officials, including Sports Information Director David Housel, realizing the importance of the game, put Bryant's picture on the cover beside Auburn head coach Pat Dye (in his first game against Bryant) and made note that the Bear was going for the record. Alabama won that game 28-17. It was the final time a Bryant team defeated Auburn. Amos Alonzo Stagg, with 314 wins, was shown in inset.

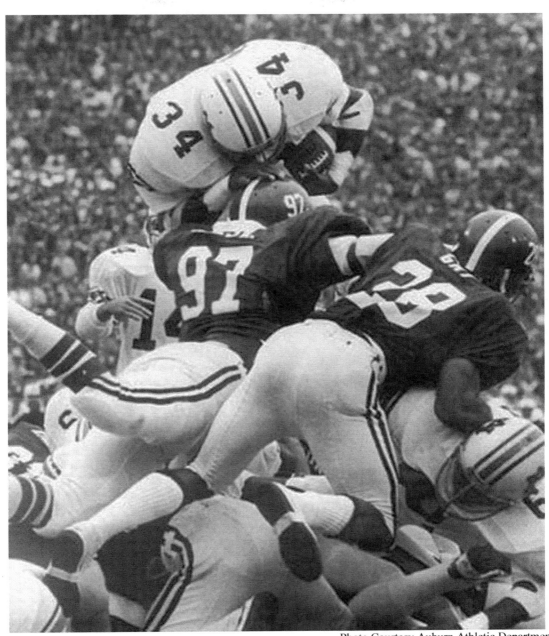

Photo Courtesy Auburn Athletic Department

Bo Jackson goes "Over the Top" for winning touchdown in the 1982 game.

THE GAME - 1982

By Jimmy Smothers, written in 2011

This game just may be the biggest in a series that is filled with big games. More than a quarter-century later memories of this game are yet vivid in my memory. A lot of times a reporter has to search for the story line, but not when looking back at this game. There were so many angles the problem was selecting which one to follow.

Briefly, here are just a few:

This was Paul Bryant's final game against Auburn; it was Pat Dye's first win against Bryant, his former boss; and Auburn's first win against Alabama in the Dye era. It was the game that broke Alabama's nine-game winning streak over Auburn, longest in the series; and it was the first time in Bryant's 25 years at Alabama that his team lost three games in a row.

After opening the year with a 7-1 record (the loss was to Tennessee, Bryant's biggest foe), the Crimson Tide did not win a game in November – losing to LSU, Southern Mississippi and then Auburn. The regular season ended at 7-4. That's not bad for a lot of teams, but it was below par for Bryant and the Tide.

This game was also the first time that Bo Jackson played against Alabama; a team that he wanted most to beat. An Alabama assistant coach had told Jackson when he was being recruited the year before that if he signed with Auburn, he would never beat Alabama. Jackson had something to prove. Late in the game he dived over the line for the winning touchdown, giving Auburn a 23-22 win.

Jackson had been the driving force late in the game as Auburn drove almost the entire length of the field to the one-yard line. Two minutes remained when he dived over a pile of linemen into the end zone for the winning touchdown.

Ever since, the game has been remembered for that one play, and fans refer to this as the "Bo over the top" game.

After nine years of losing to their biggest rival, Auburn fans went wild, celebrating long and loud. Dye brought his players back onto the field to join in the celebrating. And the school's sports information director, David Housel, even joined in by dancing in the north end zone as the Auburn band played.

The Bryant era was ending, and Dye was beginning his reign at Auburn. In the decade of the '80s, Alabama would beat the Tigers only two other times. Ray Perkins, who replaced Bryant, whipped Auburn in 1984 and 1985; but Bill Curry, who replaced Perkins, never defeated the Tigers.

There is no cheering in the press box and reporters don't pull for either team. Their job is to cover the game and write stories about what happens. Going in, they know their assignment, and what stories they have to write, regardless of which team wins; and this doesn't change because there will always be a winner and a loser. Still, this game produced a kind of bitter-sweet emotion.

It was sad to see Bryant, now old and ill, lose this game in the fading minutes. There was no question that his football magic had faded and his dynasty had fallen apart.

It was delightful to see Auburn celebrating, many shedding tears of joy at finally winning against the Crimson Tide. There was no mistake, Pat Dye had turned the program around and was about to take over as the football power in the state.

Yet, even he, tough as he was, said he'd rather have beaten anyone than Bryant.

-30-

Game

Turnovers did Bama in

(Original version published in The Gadsden Times, Sunday, November 28, 1982)

BIRMINGHAM – Auburn people told Pat Dye they wanted most to beat Alabama when he was hired 22 months ago as Tiger head coach. Saturday he gave them what they asked for – a victory over the rival Tide.

Although he has fulfilled their demands in short order, Dye took no personal credit. Instead, he said the greatest of Auburn victories in his era was the result of others, even the fans.

"First, I'm mighty proud of our coaching staff and our people," he said, meeting the media first following the 23-22 win that will be proclaimed long and loud throughout the state during the next 12 months.

"We've had so much support from our fans; they're so hungry for victory. I think they pulled us out at the end."

Dye even praised Alabama for a tremendous job.

"They have tremendous athletes and I ain't figured out yet how we won. I guess their turnovers, and our not having any until the end, had something to do with it," he said.

The Auburn coach also said he thought Alabama played its best game of the year, but that Auburn won the fourth quarter, which is a step in the right direction.

Auburn's effort wasn't that good for the first three quarters, but two Alabama turnovers kept the Tigers in the game until the fourth quarter. Then they came from behind to win – something they just missed doing twice earlier in close games against Florida and Georgia.

"Coach Bryant is still the greatest coach in the business. He always has been and always will be," said Dye. "If he wasn't they (Alabama's players) wouldn't have had the kind of effort they had."

Auburn, basically a Wishbone team, went with the I formation a lot in the game because Dye said he had been concerned about having just two running backs.

"I figured if Lionel (James) and Bo (Jackson) got hurt, we could still run the "I" offense with two tight ends or two flankers."

Dye also said he is satisfied with the progress Auburn has made during his two years as Auburn's head coach, but he pointed out that the team missed going to the Sugar Bowl by only seven points.

"I'd like to be going down there," he said.

Instead, he is taking the Tigers to the Tangerine Bowl and rewarding them by giving them a week in Florida before the game.

After Dye had his say, Alabama's head coach, Paul Bryant, took the floor and congratulated the Auburn coach and his team.

"I'm proud of our team. They played real hard and had great effort," Bryant said, showing no outward emotion of the defeat, which must have been hurting him inside.

The loss was the third regular season defeat in a row for Alabama, something no other Bryant-coached Tide team has suffered in his 25 years there. It was the fourth defeat this season.

"We may lose five," Bryant said, grinning, when asked his feelings on this rare deal. Last time an Alabama team lost this many games was in 1970, going 6-5-1. The tie was in a bowl game. Alabama has a bowl date remaining, which could produce the fifth defeat he said was possible.

"It would have gone the other way with a break or two or not having a couple of assignments missed," he said. "But that's part of it. You're supposed to teach them well enough not to do those things. And the other team forced some of those breaks."

Bryant said from where he stood, it was a fine game – an entertaining game – for the fans.

"I can't say I was entertained. I'm happy for Pat (Dye) but I'm not glad for him.

"Throw out a couple of coaching errors and it was the best game, or as good as any, we've played this year."

Bryant refused to comment on the pass interference call late in the game that gave Auburn the ball first and goal inside the 10, setting up the winning touchdown. Jeremiah Castille intercepted the pass, but a 21-yard penalty was called and Auburn kept the ball.

"I'm no official," Bryant said. "I just saw the man come from the other side of the field and throw the flag. My heart dropped when he did it."

Bryant also refused to comment on his future as the Alabama coach; and what, if any, the loss would have upon any decision he might make regarding retirement.

"I'm not going to talk about the future. I'll think about that on the way home. I think we need to see what the university thinks about my future plans," he said.

-30-

Auburn fans tore the goal post down celebrating a 23-22 win over Alabama at Legion Field on November 27, 1982. It snapped Alabama's 9-game winning streak over the Tigers. This was Bryant's final game against Auburn, and Pat Dye's first win over Alabama.

Sidebar

Dye would rather beat anyone but Bryant

(Original version published in The Gadsden Times, Sunday, November 28, 1982)

BIRMINGHAM –Pat Dye was hired as head football coach at Auburn University with one particular goal in mind – to build a football team capable of beating the Alabama Crimson Tide.

Fans wanted it then, that first year. But he wasn't given any timetables and he didn't make any promises. However, accomplishing that goal in his second year at Auburn has surely put his program ahead of schedule.

Saturday, after Auburn defeated Alabama for the first time since 1972, Tiger fans were ecstatic. They began jumping the fence in front of the stands and rushing onto Legion Field's playing surface before the final seconds had ticked off the clock.

They tore down the goal post in the south end zone. They cried, they yelled, they hugged one another.

They wouldn't go home. Even after the Auburn football players, who had gone back out on the field, left a second time for the locker room, the fans still lingered.

Fans crowded around the locker room under the north end zone stands where the players were dressing. They surrounded a nearby interview trailer where coaches Pat Dye and Paul Bryant were meeting with newsmen.

There were so many media people inside that the trailer's foundation fell with a bang, then some fans tried to climb on top.

The din of the crowd outside sometimes drowned out the words of the coaches inside, especially when some fans tried to climb on top of the trailer.

"There were cries of "War Eagle" and "We're proud to be a Tiger".

Coach Dye heard it all, and I'm sure he felt proud. This had to be his biggest moment as a head football coach. But this man, who has been criticized for being such a tough disciplinarian, for an apparent lack of emotion or regard, showed a different side – a compassionate side. He was not only modest in victory, but viewed the results with mixed emotions.

After the interview had ended and he was leaving someone asked another question. He stopped, pushed his cap back and spread his arms, palms out, in a humble fashion.

"To tell you the truth, I'd rather beat anyone in the world than Coach Bryant," Pat Dye said. "He's done so much for me there's no way I can ever repay him.

"It's kind of sad for me, but I've got to love my people and our team. Coach Bryant has been to the arena lots of times though, and he understands."

I'm sure he did because Bryant congratulated Dye on the win, said his former assistant had done a real fine job all year and an excellent one that day.

But it was Bryant's team that dominated play for three quarters.

At the half Auburn led 14-13, scoring on two Alabama turnovers. But the Tide had almost a two-to-one margin in the statistics.

But in the clutch, when it came down to making the plays that decided the winner or loser in the waning minutes of play, it was Auburn, not Alabama, that came through.

Alabama failed to move the ball on its first two possessions of the fourth quarter and each time Auburn took over and scored points. At first it was a field goal, then the winning touchdown.

In the end it came down to a field goal Alabama didn't attempt, and a two-point conversion it tried, but failed to make, that proved fatal.

With the score tied at 7-7 Alabama had the ball at the 19, fourth and one. Craig Turner was stopped for no gain and Auburn got the football.

Bryant said after the game he went for a first down because he thought they could make it. But that looking back, he should have called for a field goal.

"Even if we'd made a first, we would not have been sure of a touchdown, but we'll make 95 out of 100 field goals from inside the 20," said the Tide coach.

Alabama went for two after scoring in the third quarter, taking a 19-14 lead. Two points would have given Alabama a seven point lead, which it needed at that point in the game. That's what the book called for. But missing it left the door open for Auburn to win by the narrowest of margins, which it did, 23-22.

A one point win was as good as a hundred for Auburn – maybe better.

Coaches say losing by one or two points is always tougher because there are so many "what ifs" involved.

Such was the case here.

Alabama fans will be talking for years about what might have been. What would have happened if Alabama had kicked that field goal or had kicked the extra point? What would have happened if the officials had allowed the Alabama interception on a pass during Auburn's winning touchdown drive rather than calling interference?

None of that happened and Auburn fans will be celebrating this win for a long, long time.

It is Dye's first win over his old coach. It was a day, a game, a win that will live long in the minds of Auburn people.

-30-

Post-game column

Frustration ends for Bellew, AU

(Original version published in The Gadsden Times, Monday, November 29, 1982)

For Ronny Bellew four years seemed like a lifetime. That's how long he's been a member of the football team at Auburn University. But that time vanished in the wink of a tiger's eye Saturday at Legion Field.

When Auburn defeated Alabama 23-22 everything was made perfect. The slate was wiped clean. The heartaches of losing three previous seasons, of hearing all the talk about Alabama beating Auburn since he was a youngster in grade school, of the boasts that Auburn would never, ever, beat Alabama as long as Paul Bryant was coaching, all that was over.

Saturday was Bellew's last chance to be on a winning team against Alabama. It was the last regular-season game of his career. And this native of Attalla wanted to make good a team goal, a personal goal, to end the nine-year losing streak to that cross-state rival here and now.

Ronny and his teammates did just that. And their feelings afterwards in the locker room almost defied description.
"There is no other kind of love than the love I have for this team," he said. "There ain't nothing else like it. It's been four years for me, but now I feel great."

Bellew said he couldn't believe it was happening. He refused to let himself believe Auburn had the game won until right at the end.

"I first felt like we were going to win when we got the interception (by Bob Harris at the Auburn 31 with 1:45 remaining). But then doubts started creeping back in when Bo fumbled four plays later."

There was 1:09 remaining and Alabama had the ball at its 21.

Walter Lewis completed two passes to Jesse Bendross for 15- and 11-yards to the 47. One more such completion and the ball would be in Peter Kim's field goal range. But on the next play Auburn caught Lewis behind the line and he was called for grounding the ball, resulting in a 22-yard penalty.

"That's when I knew we had it won, after we sacked the quarterback there," said Bellew.

That they did, and won the game. Alabama turned the ball over on downs and Auburn's Randy Campbell ran out the remaining 13 seconds.

Alabama took charge early, dominating the game. In first downs, rushing, passing and total offense the Tide led about three to one. Had it not been for two turnovers Alabama would possibly have been on top 17-0 at halftime. But Auburn, alert and playing heads up, cashed both turnovers into touchdowns and was on top, 14-13, at intermission.

"We didn't move the ball at all but things just fell together for us and we won," said Campbell.

"We started slow, but got stronger as the game went along. They (Alabama) were running inside and outside in the first half and third quarter," said Bellew. "But in the fourth quarter, we sucked it up and took it to them."

This senior quarterback said Alabama did nothing unexpectedly -- that Auburn had prepared for everything the Tide did including using two wideouts and throwing on first down.

"Normally, they run the option on first down, but we were prepared for the first down pass. We expected that's what they would do," Bellew added.

"They hurt us early but, again, whoever wins, wins. It don't matter how you do it. And we won.

"We didn't do anything different, defensively, in the fourth quarter except play harder. We knew they were gonna run the short passes and try to get out of bounds late. And we expected the draw.

"We kinda messed up on their curl routes, but they didn't do anything we didn't expect, nothing we weren't prepared for."

After the game the Auburn players went in the locker room, said a prayer and sang the Auburn fight song, "War Eagle!" Then they went back out on the field where thousands of Auburn fans were waiting.

"Our fans, whether we win or lose, are behind us," said Campbell. "We got beat by Georgia and they stayed out on the field for 30 minutes chanting, 'It's great to be an Auburn Tiger'."

-30-

The Final Whistle for Coach Bryant

Sept. 11, 1913 □ Jan. 26, 1983

By Jimmy Smothers, written in 2011

As I write this Coach Bryant has been dead for exactly 28 years. But as I read what I wrote when he died, memories of him become very much alive. It seems just yesterday, or last month, when Greg Bailey and I were in Memphis covering his final game – a Liberty Bowl win over Illinois.

I remember the day before the game when he invited a few of the Alabama writers to his room, which was his custom at bowl games. But that year it was different; and the attitude of everyone was somber. This was the end of an era and everyone knew it.

Bryant looked old and sick, sitting in a big cushioned chair smoking Chesterfield cigarettes as I snapped pictures of him. There was cheese and crackers on a little table beside the chair. He looked longingly out the window at a bridge across the Mississippi River and talked about when he was a boy back in Arkansas how he'd sometimes come to Memphis and walk across that bridge into town. He said he had crackers and cheese in a brown paper sack for his lunch.

"I wonder where you all will be a year from now," Bryant said. "I wonder where I will be."

In years past, on bowl occasions, Bryant talked about the past season and previewed the next season. That year he did neither. The past year no longer mattered, and there would be no next year for him. Ray Perkins had already been hired as the next coach at the University of Alabama. The old coach mostly reminisced about the past and wondered about the future.

Bryant was to remain as athletic director for the time being. He was planning to take a little time off and maybe do a little teaching at some point. He had already been given an honorary doctor of laws degree by the university. I had forgotten about that until I recently found a news release and photo of him dated May 11, 1981. It pictured him in cap and gown, tipping his mortarboard to fans. It had been sent by the University of Alabama news department and referred to the coach as Dr. Paul "Bear" Bryant.

I covered Alabama football for 24 more years after Bryant died, but I never went to Tuscaloosa without thinking of him. I miss seeing him on the sidelines, I miss going to his office and sitting on the red leather couch that sank low so you had to look up at him.

I'm filled with memories of Coach Bryant, having covered him and the Tide for 23 years. There were big games, locker room scenes, days at his cabin, during bowl trips and on the golf course. One vivid memory is from one year in Knoxville when it rained all morning and during pre-game warm-ups. Bryant stayed in the locker room.

He came out with the team to start the game, and just as he stepped out from under the stands the rain stopped, the clouds parted and a ray of sunshine beamed down on him. I can close my eyes and still see him standing there.

Exactly a month after that game in Memphis Bryant was dead, and the nation mourned. The scene of cars and trucks stopping on I-59 as the funeral procession traveled from Tuscaloosa to Birmingham was very moving; People stood with caps in hands, bidding him farewell, holding "We Love you, Bear" and other signs. Banners were strung on crossover bridges.

Many of today's fans were not even born back then, so they never knew the man. Many of today's old fans remember that day, but refused to let the man die. It almost seems as if he's as much alive today as he ever was – at least with Alabama followers.

-30-

Bear: ... It's the little things

(Original version published in The Gadsden Times, Thursday, January 27, 1983)

TUSCALOOSA – Bear Bryant joked about it.

For the past 10 or 12 years, whenever someone would ask him if he was planning to retire, he'd chuckle and say no, that "If I were to retire I'd croak in a week."

Even Mrs. Bryant has told me the same thing, in different words. She said that football was Paul's life and he'd never be able to live without it. And she'd giggle, that little girl laugh that has stayed with her all these years.

Wednesday afternoon about 2:15 when John Alred walked into my office and said that Coach Bryant was dead I thought he was pulling a joke on me. Less than two hours before the wire services had moved a story saying he was relaxing in the hospital, joking with nurses, showing neither pain nor signs of serious illness.

It was no joke. Paul William Bryant had died. And it hit like a ton of bricks. It's been hours now and I'm still numb, drained of energy, lacking emotion, at a loss for words and almost in a state of shock.

It has less than a month ago that I sat in a suite on the 11th floor of a Memphis hotel and listened to Coach Bryant say a man should have a plan for everything. A coach should have a plan for winning and a plan for losing.

I'd heard him say many times, that a man should consider every option and be prepared to react to each one.

When he retired four weeks ago following a win in the Liberty Bowl, it became evident that even Bryant realized that life doesn't go on forever.

No, I don't believe he had a premonition about dying. But I do believe he realized, that at age 69, he couldn't maintain the pace that had made him the winningest football coach of all time.

Bryant told us that day he'd had a physical recently and the doctors said they found nothing wrong that would keep him from continuing his coaching career. That didn't prove to be the case.

Regardless, he could not have gone back to coaching like he had 20 years ago.

Bryant didn't want anything less than the best for his team. So, he felt it was in the best interest of his school to step down. And he did.

Some people are saying that his uncanny sense of timing, something fellow coaches have said was what set him apart, had stayed with him to his death.

Dexter Wood, who played at Alabama and is now coaching at Gadsden High School, said he was afraid when Bryant retired that this would happen.

I didn't. I guess I thought Coach Bryant would always be there. That he would stand like a mighty oak against the wind and weather whatever the storm.

I was not prepared when it happened. I doubt that even the most dedicated of the "Bear Boys" – those who lived by his strictest standard – were prepared.

As a newsman, one who has covered Bryant and Alabama for more than 20 years, I should have been. I knew the end would come someday and I would be faced with writing that the Bear was no more.

I remember the first time I walked into his office at Alabama. It was in the basement of the old athletic building. I'd phoned ahead and made the appointment. I was scared to death, but Coach Bryant quickly put me at ease. Naturally, he was better prepared for the interview than I.

He opened the conversation by asking about my wife and son, calling them both by their names. He'd cared enough to somehow find out something about my family before the interview and it made a lasting impression on me.

Then there was the first time I was invited to join a dozen or so other writers at Bryant's summer hide-away at Kowaliga Beach on the shores of Lake Martin down below Alexander City. After a fish supper the first night, as we were leaving the café, Coach said, "Jimmy, you come back to the house and sleep with mother (Mary Harmon) and me. If you go with the drinkers and card players you won't get any rest."

It's strange, how at times like this, little things come back to mind.

There have been hundreds of similar incidents over the years. All the football games, bowl trips, summer golf tournaments, visits to his home and office, phone calls and press conferences.

As I think of them, Bryant is alive, grinning, laughing, telling a story. That's the way I want to remember him.

-30-

State mourns death of Bryant

Sunny sky turns dark

(Original version published in The Gadsden Times, Thursday, January 27, 1983)

TUSCALOOSA – As athletes left their dorm, Paul Bryant Hall, for classes Wednesday morning the sky was blue, the sun shining.

It was a beautiful, almost spring-like morning. It reminded many of the Crimson Tide football players of daybreaks back on the farm where life was free, living relaxed, work was hard.

It reminded them of times much different from college life on the University of Alabama campus.

It was the kind of clear morning Paul Bryant had seen many times as a lad back on the farm in Arkansas.

Defensive back Sammy Hood, sophomore from Ider, said he'd heard that Coach Bryant had been admitted to the hospital the night before with chest pains. But reports that morning said he had not suffered a heart attack and was resting comfortably. He was to undergo tests during the day.

The players expected him to be released in a few days. Maybe sooner. After all, how could an old farm boy be expected to stay in bed on a beautiful day like that?

Shortly after noon the skies began to darken. Clouds hid the sun. There was a threat of rain as the athletes, Bear's Boys, as they had been called before a new coach took over less than a month before, headed to Memorial Coliseum.

This time of the year football players spend the afternoon in the weight room building muscles and strength for the upcoming season.

In the midst of the workouts Alabama trainer Jim Goostree walked in. He had an announcement. It was bad news – Coach Bryant had suddenly died.

The word hit like a bombshell. A sickening silence filled the room.

The family had asked, Goostree said, that athletic activities be continued. That Bryant would want that. After all, these were the things he had devoted his life to.

Suddenly, it started to rain.

"It was ironic," said Hood. "It gave me an eerie sort of feeling. Only this morning everything was so pretty and bright. Now this."

It seemed, in a way, that the weather had taken a turn for the worse just as had Coach Bryant. And when he died, the skies opened and wept.

It was fitting; just as it was when it rained the day he announced his retirement a month previously. But then the rain would stop and the sun would shine. That will happen here one day, just as it did before, and it will again be the magic of the Bear.

This became part of the legend of this man who they said not only could control the weather but could also walk on water. Some said he once took a bag of Golden Flake potato chips and a Coca-Cola and fed 50,000 Alabama fans in the Superdome one year at a Sugar Bowl game.

Bryant will be remembered for those things. And the legends will grow with time.

He will be remembered for his many victories, the championship years, the fourth-quarter rallies which were once a way of life for his team.

Most of all, to boys who played for him, he will be remembered as a teacher, a maker of men.

"That was his main goal in life – to help people," said Danny Ford, Clemson head coach, who once played for and coached under Bryant. "And he helped so many. He taught all his players something about life. He related football to life and everybody who was under his teachings had to come out a better person.

"He is going to be missed by so many people because he helped so many. It is going to be difficult not seeing him on the sideline next fall, but his death is going to leave a void in so many other places as well."

Charley Pell, Florida head coach, who played on Bryant's 1961 National Championship team and also served as an assistant coach, said he was shocked.

"I talked with Coach Bryant yesterday (Tuesday) morning and he was in good spirits and laughed often. It was the best talk we've had since I've known him. I got to express many of my strong feelings for him.

"He was the greatest coach that has ever been," Pell added.

Toughness was part of Bryant's makeup. He drove himself hard and he drove his players hard.

He seemed to be afraid of failure. He talked about a fear of having to go back to the poor-dirt farm and hard times of his youth.

If it ever came to that, he once said, "If I had to go back and plow, I'd plow the straightest furrows in Arkansas."

-30-

HALFTIME

At this point, if you're proceeding through this book game-by-game, you have now reviewed 10 of the 20 games treated in the book. So it's time for the halftime show, a collection of short features related to the history of THE GAME:

Getting THE GAME Restarted   112

James Owens, 1970   113

Sand Mountain to the SEC   116

Jersey Colors   117

A Favorite Story and Coach   119

Covering THE GAME via TV   121

Getting THE GAME Restarted

By Jimmy Smothers, written in 2011

It took a while, 41 years and an act of the Alabama State Legislature, to be exact, but the Alabama vs. Auburn football series was finally restarted in 1948. The last time the two teams had played had been in 1907, a game that ended in a 6-6 tie. Auburn led the series at that time 7-4-1.

Harry Butler, former sportscaster for a Gadsden radio station, gave me five newspaper articles from October and November 1932 editions of The Gadsden Times with articles about Alabama Governor B.M. Miller trying to get the teams to resume the series that year to raise funds for Birmingham charities.

That was during the Great Depression era and the two institutions were also badly in need of funds. Their presidents, Dr. L. N. Duncan and Dr. George Denny, said they would confer with their athletic directors and head coaches on the Governor's proposal. They were in favor of resumption of athletic relations between their two schools, but felt the game should not be played under the auspices of the American Legion or under auspices of any Community Chest.

The teams did not play that year, or for another 16 years. Finally, the State Legislature succeeded in getting a game arranged in 1948. Alabama won, 55-0. Auburn would have preferred to have waited another year, when it won 14-13, in what was said at the time to be a tremendous upset.

The two teams have played annually since, and the rivalry has grown; it has yet to reach the proportions of 1907 when brawls between the followers of the two teams resulted in the series being canceled.

According to one of the old newspaper articles, based on interviews with one former player from each team, the game was clean and hard fought.

"Auburn was a prime favorite in the contest and led at the half, 6-0," the article said. "The military shift was introduced by 'Bama in the 2nd half and before the bewildered Auburn team recovered, the Crimsons had scored."

After the game students downtown engaged in fights and the series was canceled, according to that 1932 article.

With the renewal of the series, two games were played in the decade of the 1940s.

In the 1950s Ralph Jordan built Auburn into a national power, defeated Alabama five years in a row and won a national championship. Former Auburn players M. L. Brackett and Jackie Burkett said Alabama was not very good at that time; and the rivalry didn't really get started until late in the decade after Paul Bryant took the Alabama job. "Georgia Tech and Tennessee were our biggest rivals at the time," the players said. "Alabama was just another game." Still, the teams split, 5-5, during those 10 years.

Bryant began to make his mark at Alabama in the 1960s, dominating Auburn 8-2 and winning three national championships.

Bryant survived a mid-career crisis in 1969 and 1970 and enjoyed his greatest success during the 1970s. He again dominated the Auburn series 8-2 and won three more national championships. Jordan retired in 1975 after 25 years at Auburn.

In the 1980s Pat Dye took over the Auburn team; defeated Alabama in Bryant's final game in the series, and took the Tigers to their greatest heights in years. Auburn defeated Alabama six times in those 10 games.

Bebes Stallings had Alabama back among the national elite in the early '90s, winning a national title in '92. NCAA investigations hit both teams, who wound up with new coaches. Terry Bowden replaced Dye at Auburn and had a perfect season his first year and went 20-1-1 his first two years. But Alabama dominated the series, 7-3, as Auburn was hit hard with NCAA probations.

In the first decade of the new century Alabama suffered a similar impact with NCAA probations. Tommy Tuberville had Auburn ruling the state, one season going 13-0, beating Alabama six times in a row and 7-3 overall.

Nick Saban was named Tide coach in 2007, beat Auburn in 2008 and won every game in 2009, including the BCS national championship.

In 2010 Auburn's Gene Chizik matched Saban's feat, winning every game and the BCS national championship.

-30-

Owens Integrates THE GAME, 1970

By Jimmy Smothers, written in 2011

Here's a trivia question that rarely comes up among Tide and Tiger fans who take great pride in their knowledge of every player and every play in every game in this storied series.

Who was the first black player to participate in this great in-state football rivalry?

It was Auburn's James Owens. He was the first black football player on the Plain and he was the man who broke the color barrier in the Auburn-Alabama series. The year was 1970 and Owens was a sophomore. He played in one series as a linebacker and says he made one tackle and got in on another, although he was credited with just one assist on the tackle chart.

It was the close review of that ancient tackle chart by my trusty research assistant Ben Barnes that led us to suspect that James Owens had indeed played in THE GAME in 1970, a suspicion later verified by Owens himself.

The first black Alabama players were Wilbur Jackson and John Mitchell, who both played in THE GAME in 1971.

Owens grew up in Fairfield, and had been the first black athlete to play for that high school. So breaking color barriers was nothing new for him when he signed with Auburn. The Auburn-Alabama rivalry was.

"I didn't know much about those two teams," he recalls. "Back then I was keeping up with Grambling and Southern and the big rivalry between those two teams. And I followed Miles College, which was right there near home.

"The first Auburn-Alabama game that I saw was at Legion Field when I was being recruited as a high school senior. I couldn't believe the number of people at that game. It was about 60,000 or so and I'd never seen that many people at a football game.

"Then after I went to Auburn, and we got down to that game on the schedule, I just couldn't believe the rivalry. I couldn't believe that people cared that much about a football game. I was aware of the rivalry between Grambling and Southern, but I quickly found out that it was nothing compared to Auburn and Alabama. You talk about rivalry, that rivalry was unbelievable," he added.

His first year he played on the freshman team that beat Alabama. Then he played on the varsity team the next three years, seeing action in winning games against the Tide as a sophomore and senior. His junior year Alabama beat Auburn.

"Because I didn't know anything about the Alabama-Auburn tradition, it was extremely hard for me to get caught up with the spirit that the others had going into the game," he recalled. "Actually, it wasn't much more to me that first year or so than just another big game that we wanted very much to win. Another thing that made it hard for me that first year on the varsity was because I wasn't getting much playing time. I was mostly just another cheerleader standing on the sideline cheering for my teammates."

But when the game ended, and Auburn won 33-28, Owens got so excited that he started jumping up and down on the bleachers and broke one of them.

That year (1970) his position coach had been Paul Davis, who told Owens, "You are the worst linebacker I've ever seen." Owens had also played defensive back earlier in the season and even returned a punt for a touchdown against Florida.

The next year (1971) he was switched from linebacker and tight end to the backfield and saw a lot more playing time at both fullback and halfback.

"I still didn't start against Alabama, but I played a lot in the game," he said. "We lost that year and it was a big disappointment. We had gone into the game undefeated and we wanted to see our seniors go out on a victory note," Owens says. The indication was that the seniors not ending their careers with an unbeaten season were a bigger hurt than the loss to Alabama.

Although he had been at Auburn for three seasons, there was still a lack of knowledge about the rivalry. Even as a junior, the Alabama game was just another big football game to Owens. But things were beginning to change for him.

As a senior in 1972, he was the starting fullback until he suffered a knee injury against Florida State the seventh game of the year. It was decided to wait until after the season to have surgery, so the trainers would tape the knee and let him play.

Against Alabama that year, he'd play a while, and then let the knee rest while sharing the fullback position with Rusty Fuller.

Owens remembers that throughout his college career he and his teammates always worked extra hard in practice, preparing for the game against Alabama.

"It would be an exciting week for everyone, not just the players and coaches. It was one of those games where the coaches didn't have to do anything to fire you up; it was one of those games that you automatically got excited about. Everything we did, we did with great enthusiasm and the belief that we would win," Owens recalls.

When Owens was a junior, the team was winning every game behind Sullivan and Beasley. The players were expecting to go undefeated and there was great camaraderie among the players. Owens, although not a starter, was seeing a lot of playing time and feeling like a part of the team.

As the Alabama game approached in 1971, Owens was beginning to feel some of the tradition and the game was becoming more of a rivalry than just another big game. It had been an exciting year up to the end. Then there was the loss to Alabama, followed by a loss to Oklahoma in a bowl game.

"My senior year we just had a bunch of guys that believed in each other," Owens recalls. "We didn't have any superstars, no big name players; actually, no one that was really known by the fans. We were just a bunch of guys that came together, lived together and played together. We were just one group, not a bunch of individuals. I often tell people that we were more afraid of the coaches, and what they would do to us after a game if we lost, than we were afraid of the people we were playing. So we knew we had to find a way to win, somehow, someway."

Owens says the team, which came to be known as the Amazin's, felt like they had the kind of defense that could win if the offense could score a touchdown or two.

"It was an exciting year because I was getting a chance to play a lot, until I got hurt. But even then I wasn't just standing on the sideline watching; not even in that 'Punt, Bama, Punt' game. I was a part of it all – of Auburn, the tradition, and that game. It was the most exciting thing that anyone could ever want to be a part of," Owens said of his senior year.

That is the tradition that makes this series, this rivalry, what it is. It's THE GAME in the state.

-30-

From Sand Mountain to the SEC

By Jimmy Smothers, written in 2011

At the beginning of my career with The Gadsden Times my biggest assignment may have been covering the unbeaten football season at Crossville High School in 1961. Two of the team's best players were lineman Richard Cole, who later became an All-America player at the University of Alabama; and "Big Bad" John Cochran, who signed with Auburn, stayed there and became Dr. Cochran, head professor of the aerospace engineering department.

It was natural, that shortly after I joined The Times and started covering Alabama and Auburn, that some of my first articles would be about local guys whom I knew and had covered in high school. Here is one of those articles that I wrote about Big John.

Cochran making it big at Auburn

(Original version published in The Gadsden Times, 1962)

A former All-State player who is making the grade on the college scene is Crossville's John Cochran.

A recent trip to the "Loveliest Village on the Plain" afforded an opportunity to talk with the War Eagle drum-beater, Norm Carlson. And what we heard about our favorite "Big Bad John" was music to our ears.

John started out as the No. 3 fullback on the freshman squad. But it was an unfamiliar role for Cochran, who had never been a reserve. He went to work, and by the time the first of three games came up he was the second choice. In that game, with Georgia, he scored a touchdown without seeing much action.

By the time the battle with the Crimson Tide frosh rolled around, John was the No. 1 offensive power-driver and a linebacker on the first defensive unit. The Tide's defense was rugged and he gained only 11 yards in five carries. On defense he was tops. It was a different story at Florida. John was the top ground-gainer that day with 51 yards, also starring at linebacker.

"He was eager at first," said Carlson. "And, naturally, this caused him to make mistakes. Starting out in the third slot kinda knocked him off his feet. But since, he has regained his form, and has rolled past two great fullbacks, and is living up to every expectation we had when he was signed last spring.

"There is no doubt in anyone's mind here at Auburn that Cochran will be a great ballplayer before he leaves."

What more could you say?

This column in The Gadsden Times that Sunday also mentioned two other players I had covered in high school and who were then playing collegiate ball. They were Bobby Bethune of Mississippi State and Johnny Holtzclaw of Memphis State. Bethune had family ties in Tenbroeck, Holtzclaw was from Fort Payne. -JS

-30-

Jersey Colors

By Jimmy Smothers, written in 2011

Once upon a time, in the days of yore, college football games were a much more colorful experience. The teams wore uniforms sporting their school's colors. For example, Alabama wore crimson and white; Auburn was decked out in orange and navy blue.

I don't remember what colors the teams were wearing the first time I saw them play; but John Pruett of The Huntsville Times says the first Alabama-Auburn game he ever saw was in 1953, and Alabama wore crimson jerseys, Auburn wore orange jerseys. Alabama won, 10-7.

"I was 12 years old at the time and my father took me to the game at Legion Field. We sat together in the old south end zone, which was horseshoe shaped at that time," Pruett remembers. "I think that was the only time the two teams wore crimson and orange in that game, at least after the series was resumed."

Ben Barnes, who has degrees from both universities and attended many of the games, has researched The Tuscaloosa News and Google Archives and has come up with a list of jersey colors worn by Alabama and Auburn in every game from 1948 to the present.

In old photos of the 1948 game, the year the series was resumed, it appears Alabama was wearing crimson and Auburn was wearing white. Alabama won that game, 55-0.

The next year, 1949, when Auburn won what may have been its biggest upset in the series (14-13), the teams wore those same colors – Alabama crimson, Auburn white.

In 1950 Alabama donned crimson and Auburn wore Navy blue; but in 1951, Ralph Jordan's first year as head coach, he had Auburn wear white and Alabama stayed in crimson.

Barnes says Alabama wore crimson and Auburn blue in the 1952 game; and returned to those colors for the three games in 1954 through 1956.

In 1957, when Auburn won the AP national championship, Auburn wore Navy blue, its home jersey; and Alabama wore white. Auburn won, 40-0. That was J.B. "Ears" Whitworth's last game; being replaced by Paul "Bear" Bryant.

In 1958 and 1959, Bryant's first two years at Alabama, the Crimson Tide wore crimson and Auburn wore Navy blue.

In 1960 Alabama wore crimson, Auburn white. From 1961 through 1963 Alabama wore crimson. Auburn wore blue in 1961 and 1963 and white in 1962.

Television, which was primarily black and white at the time, was coming into play and it was hard to distinguish which team was which if both were wearing colored jerseys. So the NCAA mandated that all home teams had to wear dark and visiting teams white, with few exceptions, such as LSU, whose home jerseys were white.

In 1964, the first year THE GAME was televised nationally, Alabama wore crimson and Auburn white. Beginning with that year, the teams have alternated wearing dark (home) and white (visitor), including the games that were played at Legion Field.

Auburn has worn orange jerseys a few times, but only that one time (1953) against Alabama.

M.L. Brackett says when he played (1953-1955) the team wore orange jerseys two times. "In 1953 in the 10-7 loss to Alabama, a game we should have won, and in 1955 against Tulane in New Orleans. We lost that game, too, 27-13," he said. "After that loss Coach Jordan burned them and we never wore them again."

When Doug Barfield was head coach (1976-1980) he put the Tigers in orange four times. That was in the 1978 game against Georgia, a 22-22 tie; in 1979 a 14-3 win over Mississippi State; and in 1980 a 31-0 win over Southern Mississippi and a 21-31 loss to Georgia.

Although Auburn has not worn orange jerseys in over 30 years, many fans still wear that color to a lot of games. This began during the tenure of Coach Tommy Tuberville, who encouraged Auburn fans to wear orange, even though he never put the Auburn team in orange.

-30-

A Favorite Story About a Favorite Coach

For many years in the past century newspapers in Alabama would print a special football section before the annual game between Alabama and Auburn. It would usually run on the Sunday before the annual game. Each paper had its own name and content, but it was all about the Crimson Tide and Tigers.

At The Times, our special was called THE GAME and the sports staff started working on it weeks before the game. Because of the Sunday publication date, we had to have it to the press for pre-printing on the previous Wednesday. That meant we had to build the pages the early part of that week; so everything had to be written well in advance.

Because of these deadline constraints, I would set up interviews with coaches at least two or three weeks in advance.

I remember one year I had phoned both Auburn and Alabama and set up interviews with the head coaches.

I went to Auburn first, on a Wednesday I believe, to talk with Pat Dye. He was gracious and gave me plenty of time, answering all my questions and adding

Coach Ray Perkins, left, and the author

* * * * *

comments about the upcoming game. I never had to worry about getting a good story from Coach Dye.

    The next day I drove over to Tuscaloosa to meet with Ray Perkins. I had covered Ray when he played for Alabama and we had renewed our friendship when he returned as head coach. It was always a pleasure to visit with him.

    That day I walked into his office grinning, and was a little shocked that he was stoned-faced and cast a steely-glare my way. The greeting was pleasant enough; but when I pulled out my notebook and pen, and opened the interview with, "So what about the Auburn game?" Perkins exploded.

    I don't remember his exact words, but it was something about, "I'm not talking about them this week. We play one game at a time and we've got another game to play Saturday and that's all I'm thinking about. You know I never talk about any opponent except the next one."

He had several more choice words, and there was no mistake about his feelings on the subject. But I knew Perkins, had always liked him and still do, so his charade didn't bother me. I politely rose, folded my notebook, stuck it in my pocket and started for the door. After a few steps I stopped and looked back.

"Ray, you knew in advance why I was coming down here today; but if you don't want to talk about THE GAME, then I'll just write what Coach Dye said, and say that you refused to comment," I told him, and continued toward the door.

Perkins said, "Hey, wait a minute. Did you talk to Pat yesterday?"

"I sure did."

"Did he talk about THE GAME?"

"He did."

"What did he say?"

"I'm not going to tell you."

"OK, then come on back, sit down and let's talk," said Coach Perkins, now grinning as he walked around his desk and gave me a bear hug. He added, "You know I don't want to comment until next week, but since you're here let's do it."

That was just Coach Perkins. He had intended to do the interview all along, but wanted to have a little fun first; just wanted to see what kind of reaction he could get out of me.

-30-

Covering THE GAME via TV

By Jimmy Smothers, written in 2011

Auburn football fans remember THE GAME of 2007 as the "Other Hand" game. It was the year that Auburn defeated Alabama for the sixth time in a row; it was the year that head coach Tommy Tuberville held up the index finger of the "other hand" signifying the sixth straight win over Alabama, 17-10.

The year before, in Bryant-Denny Stadium, Auburn had beaten Alabama for the fifth time, giving Tuberville the opportunity to show Tide Fans his thumb, holding up one hand with all four fingers plus a thumb extended.

Alabama fans hated the thumb; Auburn fans loved it.

Then came 2007 and the "Other Hand". Those six years added a new twist to the series, and gave fans something different to talk about during the year. Will Auburn give Alabama the thumb? Will Tuberville hold up his other hand?

It was a new craze and fun for a while. Alabama broke the string the next year, 2008, and Tuberville is no longer the Auburn coach. Although it's fun to read about, and recall the past, I haven't heard anyone talking about any of that in recent years.

The thing I remember most about the game of 2007 is more personal; actually, there are two things about that game that remain vivid.

One, it was the first time in 45 straight years that I had not been in the press box covering that game first hand for The Gadsden Times. I had also been to three previous games, two as a photographer, one to write a sidebar.

Secondly, in 2007 I was able to fulfill a lifetime goal. During most of those 45 years I traveled with John Pruett, sports editor of The Huntsville Times. Several times each season we would be watching a movie on television in our motel room when it came time to leave for the stadium. Every time that happened we would vow that before we retired, that we would remain in the room, watch the remainder of whatever movie we were watching, and then cover the game on television.

I wasn't in a motel room at Auburn in 2007, where the game was played, but I did cover it on television – sort of.

I had retired at the end of the 2006 season, but continued writing for the Times. I went to bowl games with both Alabama (Independence Bowl) and Auburn (Cotton Bowl). Then I went to most of their games that fall. But when it came to THE GAME, I stayed home and for the first time, I watched that game on television and wrote a post-game column.

It was fun not having to buck the crowd at the stadium or get caught up in traffic after the game. During the first few years after retiring, I wrote several post-game columns, some from the press boxes at various sites, some from home after watching a game on television. It had taken more than 50 years, but finally I was able to keep that promise to cover a game on television before I stopped writing.

-30-

END OF HALFTIME

Van Tiffen kicked a 52-yard field goal as the game ended to give Alabama a 25-23 win over Auburn in 1985.

THE GAME - 1985

By Jimmy Smothers, written in 2011

The game was played on the last day of November at Legion Field in Birmingham. As with many of the other games in this series between these two teams, it has been given a title. Tide and Tiger fans now simply refer to that game as "THE KICK". A big part of the Alabama football tradition is Van Tiffin's 52-yard field goal on the final play to win the game.

I had already left the press box and gone down on the sideline with other writers so we'd be on hand for post-game interviews. Normally, we left with 5 minutes remaining in a game and there would be a couple of minutes remaining when we found a spot on the sideline to watch the final stages of the game.

I remember standing there on the opposite side from the press box as Van Tiffin lined up to try the field goal. I was thinking that he couldn't kick it that far and Auburn would win, 23-22. As the ball was snapped I moved into the area with the players and coaches near midfield to get a better look. I had a clear view of the snap, the placement and Tiffin's kick. It was perfect – high and long and right down the middle.

As the ball rose in a long arc toward the goal post, time seemed to stand still. I can still see the ball in flight, and everything still seems like it was in slow motion. It was like those kicks you see in the movies where it takes forever for the ball to reach its destination. Every eye was focused on the ball – every person was standing, watching, hoping – half wishing it would make it, half wishing it wouldn't. The players on both teams all stood, turned and watched.

Even before the ball got to the crossbar, Alabama fans started celebrating. There was no doubt that Tiffin had nailed it. Auburn people were stunned, the players frozen in motion, unable to move. A game they felt they had won was suddenly kicked from their grasp.

I don't know how I felt. Reporters don't pull for either team, there is no cheering in the press box (or on the sidelines, either). There is a job to do, and I had a story to write. But what a story. I had never seen anything like that before, nor since.

This was the second straight win for Coach Ray Perkins over Auburn. He'd lost his first one, and would lose his last, winding up 2-2 in his career at the Capstone.

Earlier that week Auburn's offensive coordinator, Jack Crowe, spoke to the Gadsden Quarterback Club. That is something you won't see today. Coaches rarely, if ever, speak to any club the week of a game; and certainly not before this game.

-30-

Pre-game column

Crowe won't make a prediction

(Original version published in The Gadsden Times, Tuesday, November 26, 1985)

Who's going to win Saturday's football game between the Auburn Tigers and Alabama's Crimson Tide?

That was the No. 1 question among football fans in this state this week.

So, naturally, Jack Crowe wasn't surprised when he was asked, "Who's going to win?"

Crowe is the offensive coordinator and quarterback coach for the Tigers. If he ever decides to change professions, he should consider politics. He already knows how to answer a question without really answering it. And he can stand the heat.

Lend an ear: "The team that can be emotionally stable will be the team that comes out in the end," Crowe said. "I think in a close football game, that composure is what gives you a win."

True. But will that team be the one from Auburn or Alabama?

"Up to now, Florida has been the best team we've played. Alabama will be the best we've played against Saturday," he said.

"Alabama is a team with no weaknesses, a team with an outstanding quarterback, a solid passing game, a sound running game and good kicking game."

The Auburn coach also said Alabama plays outstanding defense.

"We think we're as good right now as we've been at any time this year," he said, referring to the Auburn Tigers.

Will that be good enough to beat the Tide?

The redhead who calls all offensive plays for the Tigers called a defensive one for members of the Gadsden Quarterback Club – "Don't pick this one."

"If you've got any sense at all," he said, "you won't bet on this game because there is no telling what will happen."

The fact that Crowe was in Gadsden, speaking to its Quarterback Club the week of the Auburn-Alabama game, is an example of what he meant.

"I just can't believe I'm here instead of in Auburn working on fourth-and-one calls," he said. Reference was to last year's game when Auburn failed to score from the one on a fourth-down play and lost to Alabama.

Crowe has been able to accept the Alabama jokes about that play, which have haunted Auburn people for a year. Like the other Auburn coaches and players, he has felt the heat and withstood the pressure.

"I'm bringing it up before you do," he said. "It was a logical call – not something that was done in the excitement of emotion."

Here is the way he explained the most talked about play in Alabama during the past 12 months.

"On the fourth-and-one deal we knew we'd get the ball back. We knew we'd be in better position to kick a field goal than from the angle at the one-yard line. From there, the space between the uprights isn't very much.

"Some people have said we should have taken a penalty and backed up for a better angle. But Alabama could have declined a penalty. The only way we'd been allowed a penalty would have been if they were crazy. And they were certainly not crazy.

"Besides, we thought we were going to make a touchdown. And if we didn't, Alabama had the ball on the one. And with the lead, they were not going to come slam, blam, thank you ma'am out of there. They were going to be conservative like they had been since taking the lead.

"We would get a punt back at the 45 or 50 and have time to drive down and be in better field goal position. We did and we were. But we missed the kick.

"On the fourth-and-one Coach Dye wanted to send Bo over the top. But I reminded him we hadn't practiced it since Bo's shoulder injury early in the season against Texas. There would be a good chance we'd never get it handed off.

"Another thing was to go with the sweep. But we'd had three consecutive third-and-short in the fourth quarter that we'd run. We just gave the ball to Bo on the sweep and we hadn't made it.

"The coaches got together and said we didn't want to be running into Emanuel King (Alabama's star defensive end). Bo's on the right side and they knew what to expect. If we'd run the sweep then we'd have been running right into Emanuel. And he wasn't there by accident, either. They know.

"We had Brent (Fullwood) and we don't have to apologize for him. We didn't feel like we were playing left-handed by giving him the ball. We felt equal about our tight end. So we decided to run away from Emanuel King.

"It was a personnel decision – and one that didn't work for us. It was a logical decision, but it wasn't made the next day after sleeping on it."

Crowe said it could happen again Saturday, but that it won't.

He was certain about that, and about a lot of other things. But, you know, he never did get around to saying which team is going to win THE GAME come Saturday.

-30-

Game

Tide turns back clock to fourth-quarter wins

(Original version published in The Gadsden Times, Sunday, December 1, 1985)

BIRMINGHAM – Turn back the clock to yesteryear, to an era of Alabama football when the Crimson Tide did the impossible. Take a trip through the portals of time, back to when Alabama won in the fourth quarter, when the Crimson Tide made a habit of coming from behind with unbelievable finishes.

There was once such a time. And that time is now, again.

Alabama, here Saturday at capacity-filled Legion Field, thrilled its fans with the kind of performance on which the Crimson Tide tradition was built.

The Crimson Tide refused to be beaten, coming from behind twice in the fourth quarter to edge rival Auburn 25-23.

Ray Perkins was a part of that tradition as a player. Saturday, he said the team has regained that same kind of oneness – that same kind of desire – that he knew when he played for Alabama.

Perkins, humble in a victory which he said thrilled him more than any other, said he doesn't deserve to be associated with such a team – but he is.

When Van Tiffin kicked a 52-yard field goal on the final play of the game, it was as if time stood still.

His kick was dead center and even before it passed over the crossbar a shock went through the crowd.

Auburn players, who had taken a 17-16 lead with 7:03 to play, and a 23-22 lead with 0:57 left, were stunned. Some dropped to the turf, others were like stone figures. Motionless. They couldn't believe what was happening to them.

Auburn people throughout the stadium couldn't believe what they were witnessing.

Underdog and unranked Alabama, for the second year in a row, had defeated favored and nationally ranked Auburn.

For a moment Alabama fans held their breath, then the old stadium shook as the shouts of victory erupted.

This Crimson Tide, which doesn't know the meaning of impossible, had pulled off another miracle victory. It was almost a repeat of the opening game of the year when Alabama came back in the final minute to beat Georgia.

Although Alabama needed a near-miracle to pull out the win, the early battling gave no indication it would come down to that.

Bama, after two days of feasting on Thanksgiving turkey, tried a menu of Tiger meat.

Playing from the beginning like it was a Top 10 team, the white-shirted Tide made hash of the highly regarded Tigers in the first quarter, rolling to a 10-0 lead. It was 16-10 at the half and stayed that way throughout the third quarter.

But then the real Tigers took charge, driving 80 yards to go on top, 17-16.

That score, 17-16 and Punt, Bama, Punt, was an omen to Auburn fans. And the fact that Auburn had been faced with a fourth-and-goal from the one also brought back a lot of memories from a year ago.
When Bo Jackson dived over for the touchdown, supporters of the Blue and Orange had justice of a sort from a year ago.

It was short-lived.

Freshman Gene Jelks saw to that, running 74 yards to put the Tide back out front, 22-17.

But Auburn did it all over, just for good measure. This time the Tigers drove 70 yards for a go-ahead touchdown, going on top 23-22 with less than a minute to play.

Surely, that would stand good.

Not so.

Cool-hand Mike Shula, Big Play Bell and Slippery Jelks refused to accept defeat. Each came up with big plays in moving the ball 45 yards, with no timeouts, to the Auburn 35. There was 0:06 remaining.

True-toed Tiffin took it from there, the littlest man on the field turned in the biggest play; and it was over. Time had expired on the Tigers.

Alabama players didn't want to leave, lingering to absorb the sweetest victory of them all.

Auburn players were too stunned to move. Finally, they started walking off the field in a daze.

Hundreds of fans stormed the field, in an orderly manner, with none attempting to go for the goal posts. They just wanted to stand there on Legion Field's turf with the players. They wanted to touch, to feel a part of this game.

Like other great games in this famous series, this one will live on in memory. Alabama fans will recall it with joy down through the years. For Auburn fans, it will eat at their insides.

That's the way of most Alabama and Auburn games – for the winners and the losers. That's what makes it so big in this state where football is king. And for another year, Alabama will be wearing the crown.

-30-

Post-game column

Bama blazing new image

(Original version published in The Gadsden Times, Monday, December 2. 1985)

Alabama's win over Auburn has passed the test of time. It's for real. Alabama 25, Auburn 23, it was, and is, and shall remain.

Fans in this football-crazy state were not sure for a while. It was so unbelievable, the 50th game between Tide and Tigers. Especially so, the fourth quarter, that it left the 75,808 fans at Legion Field Saturday last, in a state of shock.

First Alabama, then Auburn, appeared to have the game won. Then Alabama regained the lead. But again Auburn fought back out front, this time 23-22 with 57 seconds remaining.

Auburn had won. No doubt about that. But no, wait, what's that happening?

Mike Shula and his white-shirted teammates refuse to accept defeat. Even when it's third and 18 from the 12 and seconds remain, the Crimson Tide of 1985 isn't giving up.

Gene Jelks catches a pass from Shula for 14 yards. Al Bell picks up 20 on a reverse, and Greg Richardson catches a pass from Shula for 19.

Every snap, every play, gives Alabama another hero in this 50-year old rivalry that is packed with legendary games, plays and players.

Then with 0:06 remaining, Van Tiffin gets the call. The littlest Tider of them all, probably no more than 5-8, 150 pounds, kicked a giant 52-yard field goal as the game ended.

It is a fitting climax to a most unbelievable Alabama vs. Auburn game.

It left both winners and losers in a state of shock; they were numb, speechless, dazed.

Surely it was a dream. Football games with this kind of ending are made in Hollywood not played out on Legion Field.

Sunday the fans of this state's football world were still shaking their heads in disbelief. It was a "Pinch me, I must be dreaming" kind of reality. But today, with the Thanksgiving holiday over, the wild weekend is a thing of the past.

Football fans are back working at their jobs; life is back to normal.

Yet, the game has not gone away. It was no dream. It was for real – Alabama 25, Auburn 23, in a storybook fairy-tale finish.

With this game, that Tide win of a year ago takes on a different meaning. It may not have been so much a miracle win as some like to believe.

This Alabama team and this Alabama coach have suddenly come out of the shadows of the past and are blazing a new image.

Ray Perkins has finally thrown off the Bear Bryant yoke with which he's been burdened since succeeding the legendary Alabama coach.

Perkins may have turned in the best coaching job in the nation as he brought Alabama back from a 5-6 season in 1984 to 8-2-1 this year.

That record is even more remarkable when realizing that each loss was by two points – and in both games the Tide was still on its feet at the end, fighting for a game-winning field goal just as it did Saturday.

It is time that Alabama fans realize what they have in this coach and this team.

Don't forget Bryant, what he did and stood for; don't forget the former players; don't forget the great wins. But don't try to live in the past.

Keep the memories, relive them from time to time, but don't dwell on them.

This Alabama team is worthy of the same kind of adulation. This Alabama team, Saturday last, played on a par with any of those that have gone before.

Although Alabama has been overlooked in the polls, is deserving of a bigger and better bowl that does not lessen the quality, the achievements, of this Tide.

Ray Perkins has Alabama on the way back to the top; soon it will again be recognized among the nation's elite.

Before the youngsters of this era are through, the names of Shula, Bell and Jelks; Bennett, Richardson and Tiffin, will be as familiar with this generation as are those of Stabler, Perkins and Musso or Jordan, Homan and Davis to previous generations of Tide followers.

A dream ending? Sure. But these kinds of players make dreams come true.

-30-

Alabama head coach (1987-1989) Bill Curry and Auburn head coach (1981-1992) Pat Dye, surrounded by photographers during their pre-game conversation on the field in 1989 at Auburn's Jordan-Hare Stadium.

THE GAME - 1989

By Jimmy Smothers, written in 2011

This game had all the hallmarks to make it a legendary game in the colorful series between Alabama and Auburn, with the No. 2-ranked and undefeated Crimson Tide being upset by the Tigers, who already had two losses and were ranked No. 11 in the Associated Press poll. Alabama was looking at another national championship, with only Auburn and then Miami in the Sugar Bowl standing in the way.

Everything pointed to this being another of THE GAMES between Tide and Tigers that would have fans remembering for years to come, especially after the underdog Tigers pulled off a 30-20 win. But this isn't exactly the way it turned out.

Oh, people remember the game of '89, but primarily for another reason. That was the "First Ever" game; the first time that Alabama played Auburn in Jordan-Hare Stadium. It broke the long-standing tradition of that game's history at Legion Field.

Bill Curry was in his third year as Alabama's head coach. The Tide's record had improved each year under him, going from 7-5 to 9-3 his first two years, yet only tying for fourth place in the Southeastern Conference each year with 4-2 and 4-3 records. But in 1989 he seemed to have turned things around and the Tide went into Auburn on December 2 with a 10-0 record, leading the SEC and in second place nationally.

Despite his winning record, which got better each year, Curry had not been a popular hire. He was a nice guy, but he was a Georgia Tech guy – having both played for the Yellow Jackets and had been coaching there before being hired to replace Ray Perkins who had succeeded Paul Bryant.

A brick had been thrown through his office window the previous year after Alabama lost to Ole Miss on homecoming. And the week before the game with Auburn, despite the unbeaten record and needing only two more wins to be National Champions, it was reported that Curry had received death threats and had reported it to the FBI.

The week before the game things seemed tense in Tuscaloosa and Curry was uptight. In Auburn there was a lot of anxiety, this being the first time this game was to be played there, but Tiger coach Pat Dye was cool and relaxed. When I visited him with a couple of other sports writers that week to get information for pre-game articles, he spent more time reading to us from a book about children than he did talking about this important game against rival Alabama.

Dye was experienced with this game, having been an assistant coach at Alabama for nine years; and this was his ninth (of 12) years as head coach at Auburn.

Dye had also taken the game out of Legion Field, so bringing the Tide to Auburn was his deal. Because of that, and the fact that it was greatly opposed by Alabama fans, he was having a ball.

Auburn went into the game with an 8-2 record and ranked No. 11; but it came out with a 30-20 win and moved up to No. 9 in the Associated Press poll. The win also gave Auburn a tie (with Alabama) for first place in the SEC, each with 6-1 conference records.

Auburn defeated Ohio State in the Hall of Fame Bowl game in Tampa, Fla., ending the season with a 10-2 record and No. 6 national ranking. It was an identical record as Alabama, which wound up 10-2 after also losing to Miami in the Sugar Bowl. But the Tide dropped to No. 9 in the final AP poll.

Curry was on the way out, resigning before leaving New Orleans and taking the head job at Kentucky, where former Alabama basketball coach C.M. Newton was then the athletic director.

Although the season ended on a high note for Dye and Auburn, it didn't last. The following year the team dropped to 8-3-1, then won only five games each of the next two years. Gene Stallings had replaced Curry and Alabama won all three of those games. Dye resigned before the Alabama game at Legion Field in 1992. Alabama went on to win the 1992 National Championship.

-30-

Pre-game column

Auburn coach reveals different side

(Original version published in The Gadsden Times, Thursday, November 30, 1989)

AUBURN – It was a busy time on the Plain. An atmosphere of intensity seemed to be everywhere.

In the hallways of the athletic complex, doors, normally open, were shut; assistants, usually cordial, were uptight; some players were skipping the noon meal at Sewell Hall to avoid running into reporters.

An appointment had been made with head coach Pat Dye to talk about the Alabama vs. Auburn football game.

"Better start off with some light and friendly conversation before you start asking questions about Alabama," the sports information director told me.

But Dye wasn't like the others. He was relaxed, joked a little, managed a chuckle or two, even pulled a book from his briefcase and read a page aloud.

Here are a few of the lines:
"Most of what I really need to know about how to live and what to do and how to be, I learned in kindergarten. Wisdom was not at the top of the graduate-school mountain, but there is the sand pile at Sunday school.
"These are the things I learned:
"Share everything.
"Play fair.
"Don't hit people.
"Put things back where you found them.
"Clean up your own mess.
"Don't take things that aren't yours.
"Say you're sorry when you hurt somebody."

There were others.

When he got near the bottom of the page Dye looked up, peering over the top of his reading glasses and across his desk to make a point.

"This is what is strong with me," he said, *"When you go out into the world, watch out for traffic, hold hands, and stick together."*

He closed the book, which is currently a No. 1 bestseller by Robert Fulghum.

"It's so true," Dye said. "There's just something there."

Remember, this is the week of the biggest football game of the year in Alabama. Yet, the Auburn football coach took time out to talk about his philosophy of life.

"Life is so simple, but we make such a mountain out of it," he said, "because of jealousy and envy and greed and all the things that people pull and tug away at."

This was a side of the Auburn football coach that fans seldom, if ever, see. It's a side of the man that is private, just as are his charity projects for handicapped children.

On the surface Dye is tough, strong-willed and, perhaps, even hardheaded at times. He runs a tight ship, with the regimentation of the military. His players, his assistants, are afraid to cross him.

Because of his success, because he has built the Auburn athletic department into one of the richest and most powerful in the nation, Dye is able to speak his piece on any subject without fear of reprisal, even if it happens to be opposite the view taken by the university and conference leaders.

But there is a different man inside. And that person can take common things; simple rules, such as author Fulghum expressed in his book, and put the wisdom of a child in kindergarten to use in the big-business world of major college athletics.

That speaks loudly of the man Auburn has running its athletic department; of the man who some have criticized for the exploitation of student athletes regarding academics.

A man who finds it worthwhile to read to others such things as: "Wash your hands before you eat" and "Live a balanced life, think some, play some, work some every day" and "Warm Cookies and cold milk are good for you."

He is a man who cares, and it stood out loud and clear on this day.

Oh, Coach Dye also had a lot to say about the Alabama football team.

Some of the things were:

"They have had a great season. It is obvious they are playing together and playing the game the way it's supposed to be played.

"Saturday's game will be interesting from both a strategy standpoint as well as for intense, hard hitting play on the field.

"Alabama has an awful lot of talent on offense, a star-studded defense and for Auburn to win it will have to have a total team effort in all three phases of the game."

But regardless of the score of Saturday's game, Pat Dye is a winner in life. And so are the young men who follow his teachings.

-30-

Game

Jordan-Hare, Bama's Waterloo

(Original version published in The Gadsden Times, Sunday, December 3, 1989)

AUBURN –It was defense; it was big play offense; it was Auburn 30, Alabama 20.

It was the historic first game between the two teams here that has been grossly overplayed the past two weeks.

THE GAME has been made to seem bigger than life.

It wasn't.

It was big, but it didn't begin to live up to the pre-game hype.

Like the Super Bowl, the game was almost anti-climatic after all the buildup.

It almost seemed as if there had been more excitement around the stadium Friday night than in it Saturday afternoon.

And this is not to take anything away from the game.

Auburn coach Pat Dye said the past two days had been the most overwhelming experience he'd ever been through.

"What happened on this campus today was tremendous," he said.

Alabama's Bill Curry said this was the biggest game he'd ever been in, that he'd never been more excited, more motivated, than he had been coming into this game.

Dye suggested that because of what happened here, Alabama ought to take the game to Bryant-Denny Stadium.

He said the game has a lot of tradition in Birmingham, but that there is something special about it being played on campus.

True.

For people who were part of this happening, no football game will be the same again. Perhaps that is good, because after Saturday, no game can stack up when compared to what happened here the past two days as fans flocked into town.

The Alabama team came to play a football game in Jordan-Hare Stadium and it ended up as its Waterloo.

Auburn, so high its feet seldom touched the turf, showed up as the team people expected it to be all fall.

The Tigers, picked to repeat as SEC champions, wound up sharing the title with Alabama and Tennessee.

It's the first time in 50 years there have been SEC tri-champions. It is the first time Auburn has ever won three titles in a row.

The win was also the fourth straight over Alabama. But don't take anything away from the Tide.

This was a game between two great football teams. Auburn took the lead and led except for part of the second and third quarters. But the Tide never gave up and was battling to catch up until Win Lyle eliminated that possibility with a late field goal.

Auburn receiver Alexander Wright was sensational catching the football and was the difference in Auburn winning or losing.

Quarterback Reggie Slack was tremendous, so was tailback Stacy Danley. The offensive line, which struggled early, did not allow Slack to be sacked for the third straight game.

Alabama quarterback Gary Hollingsworth brought the Tide back with a big drive in the fourth quarter. And Keith McCants played his heart out on defense.

Alabama missed its chance for a perfect season, for a shot at the national championship. And that takes some luster off the Sugar Bowl.

And Curry must spend another season, at least, of hearing about never having beaten Auburn.

But the thing he said he hated most about it was that after losing to an in-state rival, the players never get the recognition they deserve. They hear about it every day of the year.

He said these Alabama players deserve better for the kind of season they have had (10-0 before that game). As for Saturday, Curry said, "We just got whipped by a better football team. Thank goodness, we still have another game to play."

Dye said he wished Alabama well in the Sugar Bowl, that the Tide deserved to be in that bowl and if it plays well, can win. He wished Tennessee well in the Cotton Bowl.

He said he is tickled to death to be going to the Hall of Fame Bowl to play Ohio State.

After Saturday's game, Dye has a lot to be tickled about.

-30-

Post-game column

Different kind of postgame comments

(Original version published in The Gadsden Times, Monday, December 4, 1989)

THE GAME had been over less than an hour, but coaches Bill Curry and Pat Dye were already preparing their players and fans on the importance of winning and losing.

Sounds of victory celebrating could be heard in the interview trailer beneath the south end of Jordan-Hare Stadium; the sights were still fresh in the minds of those inside.

The colorful crowd that packed the arena was mostly a sea of orange tinted with blue. More than half of the north end zone and part of the east side were red on a field of white.

The din was typical of any big sporting event. But this will not be a day remembered as one when fans tore the goal posts down. They didn't, and probably couldn't had they tried, since security people surrounded the field. Nor will this be a day that I will remember as the most emotional game I've ever covered.

The crowd reaction, the emotion of fans and players, did not compare to some other games involving these two teams.

The occasion was more of a happening, a spectacle, something bigger than a college football game. There was just something different about the event.

Perhaps that was one reason the two head coaches took different approaches to their post-game comments.

Alabama's Bill Curry talked about what a man could learn from such an experience.

Two weeks ago, when it became clear what this game had become, he told his players it would be an experience they would remember the rest of their lives.

After the game he told them that when a team loses, especially after giving it everything they have, rather than be dejected or lose their self-esteem, they must learn from it.

He said a player can learn to deal with death, with tragedy that's real in life.

He said a player can learn how to come back, how to pick himself up after a setback, after a keen disappointment.

The Alabama players will hear about the 20-30 loss to Auburn every day. So he said the important thing now is how they deal with it.

Curry said they did it by respecting the opponent, loving people who are spiteful to you, treating people the way you want to be treated, and honoring God in everything you do.

He said he would approach the bowl game by telling the players their greatest achievement may be getting back up after being knocked down. And they will have that opportunity later this month.

Auburn coach Pat Dye, naturally, took a different approach. He joked with the writers who had picked Alabama to win, kidding them about criticizing him when he had been wrong. And when the few writers who had picked Auburn to win spoke up, Dye said that they just didn't know any better.

He jokingly said some Auburn fans were dumb and he'd have to talk to them.

He said when the quarterback holds his arms out, it means for the fans to be quiet so he can audible at the line; that when he holds up his hands, they are to pick it up.

At times Saturday, Auburn fans were so noisy that their players couldn't hear the signals.

Dye pointed out that once he had studied Alabama on film, he felt Auburn would have a chance to win – would be able to pass on them.

Alabama just did not have the speed to cover the Auburn receivers, who would go deep if the defenders moved up and would be open short if they played back.

On a serious note, Dye talked about a letter from a 73-year-old veteran of World War II who had been a tank commander under General Patton.

The guy had written about a battle when his outfit of 300 men had been trapped by 3,500 Germans; but they elected to fight their way out. In the end, only 60 survived and were captured.

They were marched through the street of a German town, bloody, dirty, tired and beaten. But once the citizens turned out to see them, they dressed right and double-timed through town.

The SS and high-ranking German officers were so impressed they saluted them.

"The only way a man can take your pride and self-respect is if you give it away," the veteran wrote Dye. "We went in as boys and came out as men."

Dye compared that to the Auburn football team this fall.

The boys lost a couple of battles along the way, but in the end, the men won the war.

-30-

Quarterback Reggie Slack (1986-1989) is listed sixth, seventh and eighth among Auburn's career passing leaders in the categories of completion percentage, yardage and number of completions, respectively. During his four years on the Plain, Auburn won all four games against Alabama. Slack had a tremendous game in his senior season, leading Auburn to a 30-20 win over Alabama in the Tide's first game in Jordan-Hare Stadium.

Photo Courtesy of Todd Van Emst, Auburn Athletic Department

Alabama Coach Gene Stallings (1990-96) played for Coach Bryant at Texas A&M in the 1950s and later was his assistant at Alabama. As coach of Texas A&M in 1968, Stallings became the first of Coach Bryant's protégés to win a game against the master coach.

THE GAME - 1992

By Jimmy Smothers, written in 2011

This was the year that Alabama had been waiting for. It had taken 10 years and three head coaches since the death of Paul Bryant. But finally the Crimson Tide was on the verge of another National Championship – and Auburn's decade of football supremacy in the state was ending.

Bebes Stallings was in his third year as the Alabama coach and was taking the Tide into THE GAME with an unbeaten record, No. 2 national ranking, and a shot at both the SEC and National championships coming up.

For the first time since 1979 Alabama fans were preparing to get out those big plastic hands with the forefinger raised proclaiming "We're No. 1". For the second year in a row Auburn was looking at five-win seasons, and facing serious NCAA sanctions.

To say Alabama's football program was on the upswing; and Auburn's was in a downward spiral seemed at the time to be an understatement on both counts. Stallings was Bryant reincarnated, Dye's reign was ending.

The year before, on Friday, Sept. 27, 1991, as John Pruett and I were driving to Knoxville to cover the Auburn at Tennessee football game the next day we heard on the radio that former Auburn player Eric Ramsey had accused an Auburn booster of giving him money, tires and steaks during his Auburn career that had ended the year before. He said that Dye knew all about it and he had it on tape.

"I sure hope that booster isn't from Gadsden," I told Pruett. Turns out he was.

When we checked into the motel we tried to get comments from Auburn people, but no one was talking – on the record. But we got a few comments "off the record" and were able to write the first of many articles on the topic that would go on for more than two years, even after the NCAA sanctions were handed down on Aug. 18, 1993.

Auburn lost to Tennessee (21-30) that Saturday; and finished the year 5-6, after a 6-13 loss to Alabama in its final game of the year.

Throughout 1992 the Ramsey story still dominated the sports news from the Plain, and Auburn went into its final game against Alabama with a 5-4-1 record. Dye had resigned as athletic director in the spring, and word had leaked out that he was going to announce his resignation as the university's football coach at the Auburn-Alabama game.

Ramsey and the NCAA was the buzz all week, despite the fact that Alabama had improved week-to-week and gradually moved up in the polls. The Tide had closed out October with wins over Tennessee and Ole Miss and moved to No. 3 before the Nov. 7 win over LSU. It had moved up to No. 2 the next week and remained in that position for the games against Mississippi State, Auburn and Florida, in the first SEC Championship Game. That put Alabama facing No. 1 Miami for the National title in the Sugar Bowl.

By then Dye and Auburn had been forgotten, and the focus was on Alabama winning another National Championship. Stallings was the head coach, but in the bowl game Brother Bill Oliver got much of the attention with his defensive plan against the Hurricanes. At times it appeared all 11 defenders were on the line of scrimmage and the Miami quarterback Gino Terretta and his receivers were all confused. When they came to the line of scrimmage, there was no secondary to read.

It was said that before THE GAME that Dye was going to tell his players it would be his final game, hoping they would go out inspired and upset the Tide, thus winning a final time for their old coach; and burst Alabama's bubble. It didn't happen. Alabama won 17-0, and for the first time that I can remember, most of the writers went to the loser's interview room for their post-game stories.

That year, however, was not the turning point which had been expected. Stallings did not win another National Championship at Alabama; and Auburn's program did not falter – at least not for six years, when it went 3-8 in 1998 and 5-6 in 1999. In fact, after 1992 Auburn hired Terry Bowden and the team won 20 straight games, and was tied by Georgia, before it again lost to Alabama.

-30-

Pre-game column

Auburn, Bama always produce unexpected

(Original version published in The Gadsden Times, Wednesday, November 25, 1992)

Coaches like to talk about each team having its own personality.

Even when a lot of the players are returning from the previous year, the teams are not the same. Each season, each team is different.

Even when coaches talk about the breaks having a way to even themselves out, when the process carries over from one year to the next, from one team to the next, somehow it isn't the same.

That will be the case this year when Auburn faces Alabama Thanksgiving Day in Birmingham.

These are not the same two teams as last year, or as the year before that, even though many of the players are the same.

I am writing this two weeks before the game is to be played, before the teams hold their pre-game press conferences. So it is likely a lot of things will be said, a lot will have happened, between the time this is written and when it is published. But regardless of what may have transpired during that interval, and what effect it may have on the people involved, some things will never change.

One of them is that when Auburn and Alabama play, you can always expect the unexpected.

I'm not referring to an upset victory. The history of the series reveals that most of the time the favorite wins. I'm talking about how the games are won.

In big games, normally, a few plays make the difference; a few plays will go down in history and be talked about each year when the game comes back around.

Sometimes it's the average player who makes such a play, who becomes legendary to Auburn and Alabama fans. Sometimes it's a superstar who exceeds expectations, or falls on his face. But whichever, he will be remembered.

For most of the guys, just playing in THE GAME is special. It's an experience no player ever forgets, something they live with every day of the year, from one of these big games to the next. And if they are seniors, their final Auburn-Alabama game stays with them for a lifetime.

It seems like everything that could possibly happen has happened in this series, the good and the bad; the close games and the upsets, the runaways and the last-second victories. It's all been well documented.

Tucker Frederickson's performance one year, despite an Auburn loss, overshadowed all the Tide runners; Bo Jackson turned in a super performance one year, but then there was the "Wrong way, Bo" game.

Of course, it wasn't Bo's fault that Auburn lost that year. But Alabama fans had a lot of fun with the label, just as Auburn fans did with the "Punt, Bama, Punt" game a few year earlier.

There was Van Tiffin's last-play, 52-yard field goal in 1985 that gave Alabama a victory over Auburn; Auburn's reverse with the wrong player (Lawyer Tillman) getting the ball and scoring a late winning touchdown.

Remember Bill Newton and David Langner of Auburn who caused lightning to strike twice; and Snake Stabler's "Run in the Mud" for a winning touchdown. And there was the sensational performance of Gene Jelks his freshman year, but I don't know if Alabama fans will want to be reminded of that right now.

For the past two weeks fans have been remembering Dec. 2, 1989. That was the day that Ray Perkins said would never come. He said Alabama would never play a football game in Auburn. But it happened.

Bill Curry took his 10-0 and No. 2-ranked Crimson Tide into Jordan-Hare Stadium. The team was one win away from a National Championship showdown with top-ranked Miami in the Sugar Bowl.

It didn't happen. Auburn won that game, 30-20, then Miami won 33-25 in the bowl and Curry resigned and accepted a job with Kentucky before leaving New Orleans.

This year Alabama is again unbeaten; and with a win will face Miami in the Sugar Bowl for the National Championship. Again Auburn stands in the way and fans are asking, "Will the Tigers be the stumbling block?"

They could be. Auburn played well enough against Georgia to be on the verge of pulling a stunning victory. Such a win would erase a lot of the disappointment so far during the season.

Alabama will go into the game favored to win against the 5-4-1 Tigers. And through the years, the favorite has won most of the time. Since the series was renewed in 1948 I can't remember the underdog winning more than seven or eight times.

So tradition, in addition to the odds, favors Alabama.

Alabama has also won the only other game that was played on Thanksgiving Day. It was on November 26, 1964. That year also, Alabama was unbeaten and ranked No. 2.

Auburn's Frederickson was the game's most valuable player, but Alabama won, 21-14.

At that time, the national champion was named at the end of the regular season. Alabama, 10-0 with the win over Auburn, moved into the No. 1 spot, replacing Notre Dame, which had lost to Southern Cal.

It was Alabama's second national title under the late Paul Bryant.

That Thanksgiving win was also the beginning of a five-year winning streak over Auburn, before Pat Sullivan arrived to direct the Tigers on a two-game streak of their own.

This Thanksgiving Auburn goes into the game having lost its last two games to the Tide. Not since 1989 have the Tigers defeated their cross state rival.

Of the 49 games played in Birmingham, Auburn has won 18, Alabama 30 and there has been one tie, 6-6 in 1907.

This year is also the beginning of the new home-and-home agreement.

Last year Auburn ended its contract to play its "home game" against Alabama in Legion Field. Alabama is the "home team" this year and elected to play at Legion Field rather than on its campus. In 1993, the game will return to Auburn, where it will be played in Jordan-Hare Stadium in odd years from then on.

This year is also the first time when the game does not end the season for Alabama. Next week the Tide will play in the SEC's first Championship Game. So this is, really, not THE GAME anymore.

At least not to some of the players who told me the other day that "This is just another football game to us. Our BIG GAME now is the Championship Game."

However, if Alabama doesn't beat Auburn, it will no longer be in the running for a National Championship. So that makes this game pretty important, it seems to me.

-30-

Game

Tide defense too much for the Tigers
(Source, The Gadsden Times, Friday, November 27, 1992)

BIRMINGHAM – Second-ranked Alabama defeated Auburn 17-0 before 83,091 fans at Legion Field, taking the first of three final steps in its bid for another National Championship.

Alabama (11-0 overall, 8-0 in the Southeastern Conference) will take the second of those three steps here on Dec. 5 in a game against Florida in the inaugural SEC Championship Game. A win in that game will put the Tide in the Sugar Bowl against top-ranked Miami.

Auburn (5-5-1 overall, 2-5-1 in the SEC) will not go bowling for the second year in a row. The players will spend the holidays at home while school officials begin a search for a new coach.

Pat Dye had worked out details of his resignation Wednesday afternoon, and told his staff and players that night. Later the Auburn president announced that he had accepted Dye's resignation.

Fourteen hours later, Dye was pacing the sidelines at Legion Field. He was wearing his familiar blue baseball cap, an orange and blue Auburn tie, his white coaching shoes and a collegiate blazer.

From a distance, everything seemed normal as the Auburn coach paced back and forth in front of the bench like a tiger pacing inside his lair, stalking his prey. But this was a final time for Dye. This was the end of an era on the "Loveliest (sic) village on the plain…"

For half the game plus a few plays the men of Auburn were on course to give their old coach a farewell victory.

The Tigers had battled favored Alabama to a scoreless first half; and their defense even held Alabama 124 yards below its season average in rushing and passing for the game.

Auburn took the second half kick and had picked up 36 yards on five plays. One more first down and they would be within field goal range; two more first downs and they would be knocking at the end zone.

Then it happened. Then the magic spell burst.

Alabama's defensive back Antonio Langham intercepted a pass and returned it 61 yards for a touchdown. Before the quarter ended Michael Proctor had kicked a 47-yard field goal.

Emotion can carry a team just so far; then talent takes over. Langham's interception and return for the touchdown was just the break Alabama needed. After that, talent took over and the best team won, just as everyone had expected.

Although Auburn moved the ball at times against Alabama's No. 1-ranked defense, it could never sustain a scoring threat.

Auburn gained 139 yards (20 rushing, 119 passing). Quarterback Stan White was sacked five times and left the game in the fourth quarter with a shoulder injury. Before leaving the game, he had completed 14 of 23 passes and had two intercepted. James Bostic was the leading rusher with 55 yards on 15 carries.

Martin Houston was Alabama's top rusher with 68 yards on 14 carries. Jay Barker completed five of 13 passes for 63 yards. He had two passes intercepted.

Dye did not get his 100th coaching victory at Auburn; he did not go out on a high note. But neither did those who went before him. Shug Jordan also lost his final game against Alabama; and so did Doug Barfield.

And the last time Paul Bryant coached against Auburn, he didn't win. Dye did.

Alabama's coach, Gene Stallings, said, "Give Auburn credit. They played extremely tough and I thought they were playing hard in the latter part of the game. Obviously, it was another outstanding performance for us, especially the second half.

"We struggled a little big offensively, and Jay had two passes intercepted. Yet he came back and made a key third down throw that helped his confidence. We moved the ball and came away with points. Defensively, we did an outstanding job of keeping them in tow. Our line put a lot of pressure on them and we did a good job on coverage."

(Gadsden Times sports writer Greg Bailey contributed to this article)

-30-

Sidebar

Game takes back seat as Dye says goodbye

(Original version published in The Gadsden Times, Friday, November 27, 1992)

BIRMINGHAM – Alabama had just beaten Auburn in this state's biggest football game of the year; had just won bragging rights for a year.

Wearers of the Crimson and White were celebrating.

Roll Tides still echoed throughout Legion Field. But in the interview rooms, the game took second place.

Hundreds of writers jammed their way into the Auburn room and overflowed out into the hallway. A smaller group was in the Alabama room.

It had been announced that Coach Pat Dye and his players would spend 30 minutes together before talking to the press, but no one complained. The silence was like a funeral wake, so quiet it was almost deafening.

To one side sat Dye's wife and children, standing by their man during his final press conference. One of the girls wore an "I love Auburn" button.

Dye said his resignation was old news and started talking about THE GAME. But the game wasn't the story on Thanksgiving Day in 1992. The BIG STORY was Dye, who had just coached his final game.

He said that was not the way he would have preferred to go out, but under the circumstances, it was the best thing to do.

"I'm a builder, not a tear-er down-er," he said, explaining that by staying and fighting for the opportunity to continue coaching at Auburn it might tear down more than he had built.

"I don't want to tear down Auburn, to break up a family," he said. "Auburn is my family, my family's family. And we plan to live in the area."

Three of his children graduated from Auburn and a fourth is a senior there now.

Dye said he was not forced to resign, that it had been his decision.

He said there were a lot of uncertainties surrounding his health – he had a tumor removed from his liver last summer – but that had not kept him from working.

"I'm going back to the doctor on Dec. 10 and hope he tells me I'll have another three months to live," he said. "I live every day like it was my last day and I live every day like I'll live forever."

The straw that broke the camel's back, he said, was the letter of inquiry from the NCAA that was made public on Nov. 5. Dye was mentioned in two of the nine allegations.

He said Auburn had been fair about his settlement, allowing him to remain on the payroll and receive health benefits.

"I need the benefits, with my health problems," he said.

Dye said, "I hadn't planned to coach forever, anyway. When I came to Auburn 12 years ago I wanted to coach 14 years, but it didn't work out that way."

He said he hoped the NCAA would have some compassion for the innocent young men on the Auburn team, and would take into consideration that Auburn had suffered through two years already.

"The timing of my resignation, the night before the Alabama game, was not the best," he said, explaining it might have been better last week, or next week. But that as soon as the negotiations were finalized and approved, he wanted to tell his players and staff before word leaked out.

The agreement was completed late Wednesday afternoon.

Dye said there were some people he'd like to see hired as his replacement, but would not name them.

"I'm not going to have anything to do with who they hire. But I will be for the guy they hire and I will support him every way I can," he said, adding that he would never coach again – unless something should happen at Auburn and they needed him.

"I have a big old house in Auburn that will be for sale soon. We won't need a house that big now. But we'll live somewhere in that area."

He has a farm nearby and some young birddogs he wants to work with.

In addition to his family, Dye was joined by his players and coaches. He paid tribute to them, and to his former players.

"I'm pleased to have coached some great players, some great people, and to enjoy the special relationship between players and coach," he said.

"This may sound corny to you, but I'm more concerned about what kind of people they are than what kind of players they are. And they know that."

Dye said he didn't go out on the field early because it was very emotional going out for his final game and seeing a lot of old friends.

"I'm kinda sentimental anyway, and it needed to be a business deal. I didn't want to get emotional," he said. But when he called his wife and children to join him at the speaker's platform, he did.

"Come on up here and stop crying," Dye told the girls. "We ought to be celebrating."

When his family joined him, he said, "This is one of the reasons a man has to do what he has to do."

Mrs. Dye and their daughters hugged him and his eyes became moistened.

He said a few more things, then suddenly words could no longer come. He stepped away from the speaker's platform, walked out of the room with his family and never looked back.

"Thank you gentlemen," Sports Information Director David Housel said. And it was over. The Pat Dye era on the Plain had ended.

-30-

Post-game column

Did Auburn really do right by Dye?

(Original version published in The Gadsden Times, Sunday, November 29, 1992)

You've read the phrase: *"The King is dead. Long live the King."*

At first I didn't know what that meant. America has no kings. Not really.

Oh, they called Elvis the king. But Elvis is now dead and no one has taken his place.

Recently, King Richard retired. And no one will ever do for stock car racing what Petty did.

Even the Bear died.

Bebes Stallings has the Tide back competing for No. 1 and Alabama people are again talking about a National Championship, which Bama hasn't won since 1979.

Stallings is the coach Alabama needed from the day Bryant retired. But it took a while before they brought him in.

Now Auburn faces a similar situation.

The King Tiger is gone. And it may take a while before the shout goes up: *"Long live the King."*

All of this happened too quickly for me.

At halftime of Thursday's Auburn-Alabama football game, before Pat Dye even had an opportunity to say his final farewell, Mike Lude was talking to writers in the press box at Legion Field about finding a new Auburn coach.

I understood, just as I understood Lyndon Johnson being sworn in as president with Jackie Kennedy standing there with the blood of her husband still wet on her dress.

Kennedy is dead, long live Johnson!

I didn't like it. I felt there should have been a grace period, a time of mourning.

Nor did I like to hear the new man at Auburn University talking about replacing Dye, when Dye was still down on the sideline coaching.

To me, Pat Dye is Auburn football now, just as Shug Jordan used to be.

I believe Dye should still be the Auburn football coach.

William Muse is the new Auburn president, but he is not really an Auburn man. Not yet, anyway. Neither is Mike Lude.

They have been in the Loveliest Village of the Plain less than a year; they don't know anything about the tradition – the Southern heritage – the way people here think about college football.

They are smart men, both evidently know their business or they wouldn't be the president and athletic director at Auburn. Yet somehow it seems strange that "outsiders" can come in and suddenly have so much authority.

When Pat Dye was hired in 1982 and put in charge of the athletic program he led Auburn to its greatest decade. Just look at the stadium, the new athletic fields, the new complex. Look at plans on the drawing broad.

And look at the records of his football teams.

Pat Dye was a doer; a man with drive and foresight.

He was a tough man, testy at times, and could rub a man the wrong way.

However, he cared for his players. Too much, perhaps, and that was his weakness.

Dye wasn't a politician; he didn't cultivate friends the way he might have, and that may have hurt him.

Dye was, basically, a football coach; he was a man who wasn't afraid to take a stand. He spoke out for what he believed, even if it went against the grain of many college presidents today.

There is nothing wrong in that, except it isn't "politically correct" these days to speak out for discipline and hard work; for God, country and motherhood.

I don't understand why Muse did not stand behind Dye until the NCAA case was completed. He could have stood and said Dye is the Auburn coach and I support him.

Isn't that the American way? Isn't a man innocent until proven guilty? And right now Auburn has only received a letter of inquiry, not the final verdict of wrongdoings.

When the NCAA finishes its investigation; when all the findings are in, if it becomes evident at that time that Auburn needs a new coach, than the Auburn president would be correct in announcing that the circumstances had changed and there would be changes made in the athletic department. There is a time and place for everything; and I don't believe that the day Auburn played Alabama at Legion Field was that time and place to treat Dye like that.

* * * * *

When the above was written the facts were not all in, and much had yet to be made public. However, it was a matter of record that Shug Jordan wasn't fired because of probation; neither was Doug Barfield or Tommy Joe Eagles. So some people were wondering why Auburn officials were doing a rush job on getting rid of Dye. -- JS

The author, right, stands next to Auburn coach Pat Dye as the foursome poses during one of Dye's annual Media Golf Tournaments. At far left is Auburn assistant coach James Daniel. (Fourth party unidentified.)

Auburn quarterback (1992-1995) Patrick Nix.

THE GAME - 1993

By Jimmy Smothers, written in 2011

Gene Stallings had rebuilt the Alabama program in the image of the late Paul Bryant and was coming off a national championship season when he took the Crimson Tide to Jordan-Hare Stadium for the second time.

Pat Dye's Auburn program, which had been dominant in the 1980s, had fallen on hard times. Auburn had won only five games each of the two previous seasons; and had not beaten Alabama since its first visit to Jordan-Hare in 1989. Now Dye was gone, and Terry Bowden, in his first year as head coach, was on the verge of an unbeaten season.

Auburn was 10-0 and ranked No. 6 in The Associated Press poll; Alabama was 8-1-1 and ranked No. 11. Because of NCAA probations, the game was not on television, but because of the keen interest in this rivalry, and the records of each team, fans flocked to the Plain. Many didn't have tickets, and had no prospects of getting any, but they just wanted to be a part of the happening.

Some fans, both Alabama and Auburn, went to Tuscaloosa. An arrangement had been made to broadcast the game via closed-circuit TV in Bryant-Denny Stadium. A huge screen was set up in the south end of the stadium; and a small admission may have been charged. But the venture did not go over as expected, with 15,000 - 20,000 fans turning out.

Auburn came from behind to win the game, 22-14, with quarterback Pat Nix throwing the winning touchdown pass on the first play he was in the game. It was a huge story for me since he was from Attalla and The Gadsden Times was his hometown paper.

The win gave Auburn an 11-0 record overall, 8-0 in the SEC. The National Championship Foundation named Auburn its National Champions for that season; although The Associated Press poll only voted the Tigers No. 4. The UPI coaches' poll did not recognize Auburn because of the NCAA probation. I wrote at the time that if a team was allowed to play games, that team should be recognized. After all, Auburn went 8-0 in the powerful SEC and should have played in the SEC Championship Game and gone to a bowl game.

Alabama was 8-1-1 and ranked No. 11 going into that game. It was named Western Division champions, and then lost to Florida in the SEC Championship Game. Alabama defeated North Carolina in the Gator Bowl and wound up the year 9-3-1 overall and 5-2-1 in the SEC.

The year was a fantastic start for Bowden, who went on to become the first coach to start a Division 1-A career with 20-consecutive wins. In the following year, 1994, Auburn won its first nine games before closing out that season with a 23-23 tie with Georgia and a 14-21 loss to Alabama. The 1993 team gave Auburn its first 11-win season.

-30-

Pre-game column

A whole lot of talking going on

(Original version published in The Gadsden Times, Thursday, November 18, 1993)

Fact or fiction - and what people are saying about THE GAME:

* Auburn is a good team playing over its head. Alabama is a great team that has failed to reach its potential.

* Auburn cannot match up with Alabama in individual talent.

* Six times this fall, one of Auburn's players has been named SEC Player of the Week. Alabama players have received that honor but three times. From Auburn, Stan White and James Bostic have each been named twice, Chris Shelling and Brian Robinson once. Alabama's David Palmer twice has been player of the week, Lemanski Hall once.

* "We're going to go at them all kinds of ways. They will probably double David (Palmer), but he's going to get open regardless because he's a great player." - TODERICK MALONE, Tide receiver.

* The demographics of football fans at Alabama and Auburn reveal that Auburn alumni are in the higher income bracket, are conservative, and own businesses. Alabama alumni make less money, are liberal and belong to labor unions. This is a flip-flop from the pre-Bear Bryant years when the Alabama family was largely a country-club group, and Auburn fans wore blue jeans and drove pickup trucks. - from Dr. WAYNE FLYNT, data for his book on the Deep South.

* "We're going to pass the ball and run the ball, so they will have to stop one of them." - REID McMILION, Tiger fullback.

* "It doesn't matter whether they play zone or man. When they're in the zone, we're going to tear the middle up until they come out of it. And when they go to man, we're gonna beat 'em deep." - TODERICK MALONE, Tide receiver.

* "I'm glad we don't have the week off in between. That extra week gives you too long to think about this game - too long to prepare. This way, we just keep going, don't have to wait a week or worry about our intensity level." - ANTONIO LANGHAM, Tide cornerback.

* An Alabama win Saturday would give the Tide four in a row over Auburn, its longest winning streak in the series since Alabama won nine in a row from 1973-81. Auburn won four in a row under Pat Dye, 1986-1989.

* The last time Auburn went into the Alabama game undefeated was in 1971, the year Pat Sullivan won the Heisman Trophy. Alabama won that year, 31-7, due largely to the defensive schemes of Bill Oliver.

* "I don't know much about the folk who make us underdogs. Most of them don't play. Very few of them ever coached. Now if Coach Bryant told me we were the underdog, I'd run the antenna up." - GENE STALLINGS, Alabama coach.

*"If there is any one person who can change the outcome of this game, it's David Palmer." - TERRY BOWDEN, Auburn coach.

* "This will be Gene Stallings' final year. He will resign after the bowl game and be replaced by Bill Oliver." - RADIO TALK SHOW HOST.

* "This will be Clemson coach Ken Hatfield's final year. He will resign after the season and be replaced by Bill Oliver." - RADIO TALK SHOW HOST

* Saturday will be the earliest ending for an Auburn football season in 96 years. Not since 1897 has an Auburn football season ended so early in the year. That year the season ended as John Heisman's team, also undefeated going into its last game, played a scoreless tie at Sewanee on October 30.

* Although thousands of fans will be arriving in Auburn Friday, neither team will be there. Alabama will work out briefly at a high school stadium in Montgomery and spend the night in that city. Friday is an off day for Auburn. The players will go to a 3 p.m. movie, eat supper, then leave town for the night. Both teams will bus into Auburn before Saturday's game. I asked assistant coach Wayne Hall what movie the Auburn team will see. "I don't know the name of it, but it's going to have a lot of fighting in it," he replied.

-30-

Game

These Tigers make history

(Original version published in The Gadsden Times, Sunday, November 21, 1993)

AUBURN - "Miracles do happen", I heard someone say as I walked off the field toward the Auburn locker room. Auburn had just beaten Alabama 22-14, ending its season at 11-0. Auburn had never been 11-0 before.

The fans were ecstatic, waving their orange and blue shakers, screaming and shouting. They didn't want to leave their seats; the players didn't want to leave the field.

This win was something to savor as long as possible. It had been a long time coming; now they wanted it to last.

This was the second coming of the Tide, and the first time since '89 that Auburn had beaten Alabama.

It was worth celebrating until the wee hours of the morning; it was worth rolling Toomer's Corner.

This win was historic, and there was no limit to whatever enthusiasm the fans could muster.

But this Auburn crowd did not storm the field; they did not tear the goalposts down. They showed their support from the stands while the players celebrated on the field.

Wayne Gandy grabbed the huge Auburn flag and went around the field waving it; Derrick Dorn had a smaller one, doing the same thing. Stan White stood under the goalpost on crutches, taking it all in.

This was White's last game. He said it was his most enjoyable victory, although he'd sat out the fourth quarter with a knee injury.

Coach Terry Bowden and his players went to the student section, then to the opposite side of the field, thanking their fans.

The crowd went wild.

Former Auburn coach Pat Dye, who witnessed the final minutes of the game from the sideline, went to the locker room with the players. He said, "This has been one of the most rewarding years of my life."

White said Dye was as much a part of this Auburn team as anyone.

Old players, school personnel, students and fans will long remember the season of '93. They will never forget this team. And that's what it was, a team. No individual standouts, no one-man efforts.

This was a team that played with heart and head; this was a team that has done what no other Auburn team has ever done - gone 11-0.

This Auburn team is the best in the SEC - and has proven it on the field. As one of the banners read, "No Bowl, No TV, No Problem."

Another said, "If this is probation, let's do it more often."

But it wasn't easy, and it wasn't a sure thing. At least not until the fourth quarter. Then there was no stopping the Tigers.

Auburn went on top 3-0, but trailed 5-14 at the half and 12-14 going into the fourth quarter, with its senior quarterback on the sideline.

Sophomore Patrick Nix, who threw a 35-yard touchdown pass on the first play he was in the game, led the Tigers to the comeback win. And in doing so, he gave Auburn fans a preview of the future.

This was a game of big plays. And mistakes. Alabama was penalized 12 times for 112 yards, Auburn four times for 37.

Alabama made a mistake and drew a 15-yard penalty when Auburn missed a 52-yard field goal. So instead of the Tide getting the ball at the 35, Auburn got a first down at the 20. A few plays later a 23-yard field goal was good.

In the second quarter Alabama got a big play from Kevin Lee, who scored on a 63-yard reverse. And two more big plays, as Jay Barker passed 34 yards to Lee and handed off to Chris Anderson on a 19-yard touchdown run.

Alabama had a 14-5 lead and the momentum at the half. But a 15-yard penalty following a pass interception in the third quarter prevented the Tide from cashing it in. And the Tide began to turn.

Nix helped it along when he went in on fourth-and-15 at the 35, and completed a touchdown pass to Frank Sanders.

After that, there was no stopping the Tigers.

James Bostic, who had been limited to 20 yards in the first half, gained 24 and 13, 14 and 70, and wound up with 147, more than the entire Alabama team.

Although Alabama seemed to have overcome its mistakes in the first half, they hurt in the second. Auburn made an interception; Alabama failed to convert on fourth and six inches.

Later, when Auburn botched a field goal attempt, it got the ball back by a second interception on a fourth-and-10 play.

Auburn was leading by one, 15-14, with just over two minutes to play. And the fans sensed a victory. Bostic made it certain, with his 70-yard burst for a touchdown on the next play. Auburn 22, Alabama 14.

Barker went out with a knee injury. Brian Burgdorf and the Tide fought back, trying to tie the game in the final two minutes. It didn't happen.

Two hours after the game Bostic, Nix, and other players were still talking to reporters and signing autographs at one end of the field.

The fans had moved uptown to continue their celebrating.

It won't end for a year.

-30-

Post-game column

Special moment makes Nix hometown hero

(Original version published in The Gadsden Times, Monday, November 22, 1993)

AUBURN - It looked like the aftermath of a snowstorm. And late Saturday night, with the Christmas lights on, it was a sight to behold.

The trees were white, so were the streets and sidewalks. But at mid-morning Sunday, where the street sweepers had passed, there were huge piles of the stuff that resembled snow which had been pushed into heaps.

A lot of people were taking pictures.

Toomer's Corner had been hit with a tissue storm, leaving the town beyond description. This was something one had to see. Even then, it was hard to believe.

The celebration by Auburn fans here Saturday night was not unlike that of Alabama fans after the Sugar Bowl last January.

Remarkable, the success of Alabama one year, Auburn the next. And people outside the South wonder why football is a religion in this state.

It's a shame that such non-believers could not have been here over the weekend to see first-hand what happened at the second coming of the Tide.

It rates right alongside the Georgia-Florida game in Jacksonville, the infield crowd at a stock car race in Darlington, Mardi Gras in New Orleans.

I attempted to walk the two blocks from my hotel to the stadium before the game, but the crowd was so thick I had to circle the masses and wound up walking more than a mile. But the sights were worth it.

So was the game.

Alabama-Auburn games always are. It seems that each year something unusual crops up that sets that game apart. A play, a player, the unexpected.

And when those involved in these unforgettable, history-making moments are from my town, it is extra special.

Such was the case in THE GAME of '93.

Patrick Nix, backup quarterback to Stan White, came off the bench to lead Auburn to a come-from-behind victory.

The nation saw the highlight film on TV dozens of times Saturday night and Sunday. No. 10, Auburn, dropping back and lofting a 35-yard touchdown pass to Frank Sanders, who out-fought Tony Johnson for the ball. He dived into the end zone as he was hammered by Chris Donnelly.

No. 10 was Nix, a sophomore who played at Etowah High in Attalla.

He quarterbacked the rest of the game for the injured White, leading the Tigers to an additional 10 points in the fourth quarter to nail down the 22-14 win.

Afterwards, Nix conducted himself like an old pro before a jam-packed room of media. He said his role was the smallest - crediting the offensive line and the receiver as the real heroes.

He said the things a quarterback is supposed to say.

But when White hobbled into the room, he told a different story.

"Patrick has been poised - he's been there all year ready to play," White said. "The hardest job you can have is being a backup quarterback."

As a backup quarterback, Nix had to be ready to play every down, yet he was aware that he might not play at all.

It takes a special kind of man to prepare to quarterback a game, not knowing if he will play.

"You don't know if, or when, the starter is gonna get hurt or when something is gonna happen," said White. "Also, you've got to be able to call plays, suggest plays. So he has a hard job as far as mental preparation for a game goes. He's got to be ready to go in every minute, but he never knows when it is."

Auburn coach Terry Bowden said Nix represents all this Auburn team is about, although he hasn't played that much. He said Nix is a team guy who uses all his ability.

"There are certain things he can do; he has great presence and is comfortable out there," Bowden continued. "I'm so proud of him, how he sat back and cheered Stan on and helped him while never getting a chance.

"Then he finally got in there in the biggest game of the year. He threw a touchdown pass and led the team to a come-from-behind win.
"It gives him a good position for the future with the other quarterbacks and made this a special day for him, too."

For Auburn fans, it may have been a preview of the next two years.

Nix has paid his dues; he has learned the trade behind White. Now, it's time to step up. People in Gadsden and Etowah County should be proud for Patrick, whether they are for Auburn or Alabama.

An important thing here is to be hometown proud. That translates into being Patrick Nix fans.

-30-

THE GAME - 1995

By Jimmy Smothers, written in 2011

Going into THE GAME this year neither Alabama nor Auburn was looking at championships. The Tide was 8-2, ranked No. 17 in the polls, and banned from bowl competition; Auburn was 7-3, ranked No. 21 and needed a win to get a nice bowl invitation.

Biggest story line for The Gadsden Times focused on the starting quarterbacks, Alabama's Freddie Kitchens and Auburn's Patrick Nix, who had once been teammates at Etowah High School in nearby Attalla. This was the first time quarterbacks from the same high school had started for opposing teams in THE GAME.

This was Kitchens' sophomore year at Alabama; Nix was a senior, going into his final game in Jordan-Hare Stadium.

Kitchens had not played earlier that year, but was substituted into the game against LSU, played well in a 10-3 win, and started the following game against Mississippi State. Again he led Alabama to victory, 14-9, and got the nod going into the game at Auburn.

"Suddenly it hit me, that Patrick was going to be the starter on the other side," recalls Kitchens. "I thought it was a big deal locally – around home in Attalla, in Tuscaloosa and Auburn. It turned out to be a big deal nationally."

Kitchens says that it was something special, not only to him and Patrick, but to all their high school teammates – those in Nix's class, those in his class, and the ones in between.

"Everyone we had played with all realized that it was going to be a big deal under those circumstances," Kitchens says. "I never expected the game to turn out like it did, but I think both of us did fairly well in the game. I might have outplayed him a little bit, but they won the game, so, you know …"

Kitchens, who is now coaching in the NFL and has been to the Super Bowl, says that game was one of his best memories from his collegiate career.

The week of that game the two did not phone each other nor talk; but they met on the field after the game in what Kitchens recalls as "a hit-and-miss" kind of thing.

"Patrick was more in a consoling mode and I'd rather have been the consoler," Kitchens said. "I also had a chance to talk with Coach Conrad Nix after the game. Seeing in his eyes how much that special moment was to him is a … "

Conrad is Patrick's father and coached both boys at Etowah.

"One thing you realize, as you go through life, sometimes the things that happen are not always about you. I think just being there at the moment and seeing how it affected other people is what made it so special," Kitchens added.

Since then the two old friends and high school teammates talk two or three times a year, but that game has never been brought up.

"I'm glad," said Kitchens. "I certainly don't want to talk about it because we lost that game; and because of the bad calls in the back of the end zone there at the end. I'm thinking about that right now, but only because you brought it up. Patrick and I have never talked about that game, not once."

Toderick Malone, another former Etowah High Player, also played in that game.

"When Patrick was quarterbacking at Etowah High School, Freddie and I were his receivers," Malone recalled. "I was the wideout, Freddie the tight end. After Patrick went to Auburn, Freddie became our quarterback and threw to me at both Etowah and Alabama."

Malone said it was a great feeling when he learned that Kitchens and Nix would be the starters that year in THE GAME at Auburn.

"It was a competitive game and came down to the wire," he said. "It came down to the fourth down and we were trailing by four and driving. But unfortunately, Curtis Brown didn't get his foot in on what was a big controversial play over whether he was in bounds or not. We would have won, but we didn't get the call. Patrick was all excited and happy over them winning."

Malone remembers Nix coming up to him and Kitchens after the game and telling them, "You all played a heck of a game and it was unfortunate that one of our teams had to lose; but keep your heads up and move on."

Malone says he sees Nix occasionally; and sees Kitchens more often. "We grew up together and our parents were friends," he said. "When we get together we talk about high school and college, we talk about the good and the bad, but mostly about the good ol' days."

They don't talk about Alabama and Auburn games unless some fans ask questions. Then Malone might mention that his best game against Auburn was in 1995 – a game in which he lost to the Tigers.

"I had a pretty good game, gained close to 200 total yards and scored two touchdowns. I caught one long touchdown pass when Freddie threw me a bomb for about 60 yards. The other came on a reverse when I ran about 60 yards."

I remember talking with Nix after the game long after most of the other writers had left the interview room   Auburn's sports information director David Housel mentioned later that it appeared to him that Nix and I had a special relationship. Nix was always available when I went to Auburn. "I can't talk to all my friends and fans back home, so talking to my hometown newspaper is a means of sharing my thoughts and communicating with them," Nix told me.

-30-

Pre-game column

Nix-Kitchens typifies Tide-Tiger rivalry

(Original version published in The Gadsden Times, Friday, November 17, 1995)

The football world knows by now that for the first time quarterbacks from the same high school will be opposing each other in THE GAME.

Senior Patrick Nix will be starting for the Auburn Tigers; sophomore Freddie Kitchens will be starting for the Alabama Crimson Tide. And forevermore, these two Etowah High graduates will be a part of Alabama-Auburn history, regardless of how the game ends Saturday.

Auburn coach Terry Bowden says he thinks it is neat that the two quarterbacks come from the same school, one growing up loving Auburn, the other growing up loving Alabama.

It typifies the rivalry in this state, where families are often split over their loyalties to one school or the other.

For fans who say that players on one team differ from those of the other, they need look no further.

While visiting Alabama and Auburn earlier this week, I talked with the quarterbacks, asking questions about themselves and about each other.

Kitchens said that Nix's strength is his weakness, now more so than ever.

"His mental part of the game is so sharp. He's studied the game a lot and he learned a lot growing up from his father," Kitchens said, mentioning Conrad Nix, one of their high school coaches.

"Patrick's strength is definitely something I need the most work on."

"Off the field, it is basically the same. Patrick's a real good guy and he always tries to do the right thing. Obviously, I've made some mistakes along the way. Hopefully, I'll learn from the way he handles himself," Kitchens continued.

"I guess in a nutshell you could say that he's more mental and I'm more physical. But you know Patrick's got a ton of talent, too."

Nix returned the compliment, saying that Freddie could be great, and with his ability, he could become one of the better quarterbacks in the nation.

"Freddie will tell you, obviously, that he has the stronger arm," Nix said. "And he'll tell you that he is taller than I am, and faster. He always told me that in high school. But he wasn't. He just believed it."

Nix said he is the more experienced quarterback, knows the game a little better, but that Freddie has enough experience, and knowledge of the game, to get the job done, "with his strong arm."

"The bottom line is that we both get the job done, we are both winners and both highly competitive," said Nix.

"Basically, my dad taught us both everything we know about being a quarterback."

Jokingly, Nix said Freddie has about 50 pounds more muscle and gut, and he has about 50 pounds more brains.

"I'm a lot better looking than he is, too," the redhead kidded.

In a nutshell, Nix said, "Freddie is tough, hard-headed, and competitive."

Tide receiver Toderick Malone, who caught passes from both quarterbacks at Etowah, says Kitchens throws the ball harder and farther, Nix has more of a soft touch.

Where Nix would just lay the ball in there, Kitchens would put it up and Malone would go get it.

"Patrick knows the game well, is an inspirational leader, and does what it takes to help his team win," said Malone.

"Freddie is a competitor who will do whatever it takes to win, whether it is running or passing. He wants to make the big play."

Gene Stallings says the more Kitchens plays, the better he gets. "There is no doubt that he has a strong arm. And against Mississippi State, he ran the ball extremely well."

Although both quarterbacks are Etowah graduates, Nix's parents don't live here anymore. But he has seen Ernie Payne, Etowah principal, and some of the teachers at some games. And he keeps up with old friends through mutual friends.

Kitchens' parents still live in Attalla and he is home often. Freddie's and Toderick's mothers often attend games together -- and will Saturday.

"Regardless of who wins, we'll always think of Patrick as Freddie's big brother," said Mrs. Brenda Kitchens. "That's the way it was when they were playing together. Coach Nix and Patrick always looked out for him. They are good people."

-30-

Game

THE GAME was AUsome for Auburn

(Original version published in The Gadsden Times, Sunday, November 19, 1995)

AUBURN -- AUsome! That's what it was to Auburn. The word, coined by Coach Terry Bowden before his first win over Alabama here two years ago, was flashed over and over on the big scoreboard in the south end zone.

AUsome! AUsome!

That's what the Auburn fans felt about the 31-27 win over Alabama here Saturday night.

It did not necessarily refer to the way the game was played, but the fact that Auburn had defeated Alabama.

That's the way it is when Tide and Tigers meet; when every single person in this state seems to live or die with this game.

Fans of the winning team earn a year of bragging rights. Last year it was the Crimson Tide; this year it was the Tigers. And school officials wanted everyone to know.

Long after the celebrating had ended, after the players had left the field, the fans had left the stadium, and only a few workers and members of the media remained, the big scoreboard told the story.

AUthentic. Tigers State Champs, it read. And there was the score, lest any could forget, 31-27.

The words are good ones for Auburn people; and who can question the winner; for the next 365 days the Tigers will have the right to say whatever they want, whenever they want.

But as the game wound down another word came to mind.

Suspense.

Alabama had the ball the final 3:14, time for 13 plays. Freddie Kitchens threw 10 passes, ran three times, and on any of those plays he had the capability of scoring a winning touchdown.

Alabama had moved from its 31 to a first-and-10 on the Auburn 22. Thirty-four seconds remained.

Curtis Brown caught a pass out of the end zone; Marcel Weldon missed one at the one; Kitchens threw twice more into the end zone.

Two seconds remained. Patrick Nix ended it, sealing Auburn's win.

"It is never over until it's over," Auburn coach Terry Bowden said after the game.

He was right. But despite the game coming down to Alabama throwing for a win as time ran out, touchdown-favored Auburn met the challenge earlier and turned back upset-minded Alabama by taking advantage of its mistakes.

Alabama had more first downs, more yards rushing, more yards passing, and more total yards. But the Tide also made more mistakes, which turned out to be the difference in the game.

Alabama lost a fumble at the Auburn 27; then drew two penalties as Auburn drove 73 yards to a go-ahead touchdown.

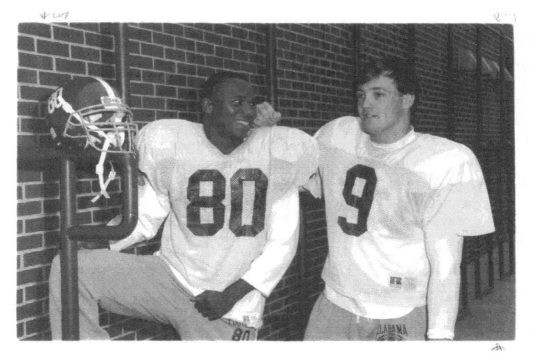

Alabama receiver Toderick Malone (80) and quarterback Freddie Kitchens

* * * * *

Kitchens threw to Toderick Malone for a tying touchdown.

Patrick Nix made some good plays, especially by avoiding Alabama's rush, letting the Tide defenders go by him as he stepped up to make play after play as Auburn went back up 14-7. But on first down after the kickoff Malone ran 59 yards on a reverse for another touchdown.

The first quarter, which had taken an hour to play, ended tied, 14-14.

The highly publicized battle between Auburn's offense and Alabama's defense did not materialize and Auburn scored 10 points in the second quarter to go up 24-14. Then in the third quarter Alabama matched it and the game was tied again, 24-24 going into the fourth quarter.

Suspense.

Michael Proctor, who had missed a field goal in the first half, kicked one in the fourth quarter after Alabama had gotten a first down at the 16 but couldn't score.

Auburn went back up in five plays, with Patrick Nix always coming up with a big play when it was needed; then its defense came up with the play that turned the Tide.

Alabama made but one yard on a third-and-four, and had an incomplete pass on fourth-and-three, turning the ball over to Auburn at the Auburn 37 with 6:27 left.

The Tide defense limited Auburn to three downs and a punt, giving the offense one more chance.

The highly publicized battle between the quarterbacks was about what was expected, with the strong-armed Kitchens throwing more times for more yards and longer passes; and the more-experienced Nix just plugging away, doing whatever it took to win the game.

Kitchens threw for one touchdown, Nix for two; Kitchens was sacked five times, Nix four; Kitchens completed 19 of 43 passes, Nix 18 of 36.

Nix converted six of 17 third down plays, Kitchens five of 17.

The first half belonged to Auburn, the last half to Alabama.

But Auburn won. And the celebrating went on and on, with the players staying on the field to celebrate. Jon Cooley, Harold Morrow, Terry Solomon and others ran around the field waving the big Auburn flag, Eric Reebals went around taking snapshots of cheerleaders; the Christian athletes of both teams met at midfield for prayer; Nix looked up Kitchens, and those two old friends had a long talk.

Bowden said it's a shame the fans don't get along like the athletes.

It certainly is.

-30-

Sidebar

Nix satisfied with accomplishments

(Original version published in The Gadsden Times, Sunday, November 19, 1995)

AUBURN -- Auburn quarterback Patrick Nix, who played his final game in Jordan-Hare Stadium here Saturday night, said he is leaving with no regrets.

"I'm happy with what I've accomplished and what I've been able to do," he said after the 31-27 win over Alabama in which he threw two touchdown passes.

"This was a game of big plays. It was a game where people stepped up and made the big play," Nix added.

"I don't think I was the difference at all. I could have been the difference in us losing in the second half. I'm just thankful my teammates and I were able to make the plays we had to make."

Nix's two touchdown passes gave him 15 this season, which moved him past Stan White (1990) and Loran Carter (1968) into fourth place on the single-season Auburn touchdown pass chart.

Establish the run

Tigers' coach Terry Bowden said that he wanted to start the game by establishing the run.

"We tried to do it, but that is their forte. They stuffed us," Bowden said of Alabama's defense. "Then we got back out to the full receiver set. They really made all of the adjustments you could make and we couldn't get anything open.

"Finally, we went right back to the I (formation) and rammed it right down there, and were able to do what we had to do.

"I never thought we would have scored 31 points on that defense."

Seniors happy

Auburn linebacker Jason Miska, who received the biggest applause when the seniors were introduced at Friday's pep rally, said it feels great to win the last home game, especially beating Alabama.

On Alabama's last drive, Miska said, "We all had butterflies, but we just had to win it. That is what playing college football is all about."

Tight end Andy Fuller said it is the best feeling he's ever had, coming into his last home game in front of all the fans.

Tiger records

With its 31 points Saturday, Auburn has now scored 424 points this season, averaging 38.5 per game, a school record.

Stephen Davis' touchdown reception in the first quarter gave him 17 touchdowns this season, which ties Bo Jackson's single-season school record. Davis also tied Jackson's record of 102 points scored in a season, and topped the 1,000-yard rushing mark for the year with 1,068.

No. 200

The win was Auburn's 200th victory in Jordan-Hare Stadium.

Auburn's 31 points were the most scored by either team in this series since 1980, when Alabama scored 34. The combined 58 points were the most scored by both teams since 1977, when they scored 69 points.

First sacks

Charley Dorsey made two sacks (minus four yards) against Alabama, the first sacks in his Auburn career.

Auburn's leading tackler was Larry Melton with eight.

-30-

Post-game column

Fans will remember this game

(Original version published in The Gadsden Times, Monday, November 30, 1995)

AUBURN -- Sunday morning coming down College Street everything was all white. The street, the trees, the bushes. If the sun had not been shining and the weather shirt-sleeve, one would have thought a blizzard had hit overnight.

What it was, though, was the aftermath of another victory celebration at Toomer's Corner.

Auburn 31, Alabama 27.

AUsome, the Auburn crowd called it.

Even in defeat, Alabama people cannot deny it was a fantastic football game.

There were big plays on both sides; key plays that decided the outcome; everyone who played was a hero.

The lead changed hands; so did the momentum. Both teams could have won, and both deserved to. The outcome wasn't decided until the last two seconds, which had everyone on edge to the end.

I've seen the last 35 games between Alabama and Auburn, and a couple of others before that; and each game had moments to remember.

There have been plays and players that stand out through the years. And this one may top any of those in the past. Nix and Baker; Davis and Beasley; Kitchens and Malone; Riddle and Blackburn.

It was an unusual game from the beginning; a game when nothing much was riding on the outcome; yet a game that drew tremendous attention.

And it lived up to its pre-game hype.

Auburn coach Terry Bowden said last week that he would take 31 points.

Ironically, that's what Auburn scored.

Alabama receiver Toderick Malone said the Tide would have to score more than 26 points.

Alabama scored 27.

Malone also said he'd like to get a couple of celebration penalties. He could have, scoring on a 52-yard pass and a 59-yard run.

The game was billed as Auburn's offense vs. Alabama's defense, strengths of each team. Yet at the end it came down to Auburn's defense vs. Alabama's offense.

Alabama's defense had given up an average of 15.7 points per game, and had scored 40 points, an average of five points per game.

But Saturday night, the Tide defense did not get a turnover or score. Those five points would have made the difference.

In the first half, Nix seemed to turn Alabama's speed on defense, to his advantage. On numerous occasions, the aggressive Tide defense would whiz past, and then Nix would step up and make the play.

Credit it to his experience, to his ability to see what is happening on the field and to take advantage of whatever the defense gave him.

Alabama adjusted at the half, shut the Tigers down in the third quarter, while scoring 10 points to tie the game at 24-24.

Early in the fourth quarter Proctor kicked a field goal to put the Tide in front, 27-24.

Now was the time for Alabama's defense to take charge, to ice down a win.

But it was Nix who came up with the big play.

On third and nine at his 40, he called a play that had been put in for this game — 178 Baker.

The wideouts gave Alabama's defense the same look as earlier, but instead of cutting to the outside, Robert Baker faked it, cut to the inside, and was wide open. He gained 34 yards to the Alabama 26.

Two plays later, Fred Beasley took a handoff and shot off the left side, going 22 yards untouched, for what proved to be the winning touchdown.

Alabama couldn't match it. Late in the game, after getting a first down at the Auburn 22, victory was a play away. But the Tide couldn't make that play. Kitchens threw four incomplete passes.

For Nix, it was a fitting climax to a brilliant career at Auburn. He made the plays; he led his team to a win over Alabama.

For Kitchens, it was a preview of great things to come. He played well enough to win most games. At the end, he could not make the play; but the fact that he was in there, gaining experience, will pay off. He'll get that touchdown next time.

-30-

Coach Gene 'Bebes' Stallings and the author.

THE GAME - 1999

By Jimmy Smothers, written in 2011

This was a turnaround game of sorts for both Alabama and Auburn; it was also the beginning and the end for the opposing coaches. So the story lines were many. Even after more than a decade, fans, especially Alabama's, still wonder what might have happened if the aftermath of that season had been different.

Alabama had never won a game in Jordan-Hare Stadium; having lost the four previous games played there after Pat Dye pulled the Tigers out of Birmingham and scheduled their home game with Alabama in Auburn. Auburn had won in 1989, 1993, 1995 and 1997 – the first three against Gene Stallings, the last against Mike DuBose, who had stepped up to the head coaching position that year.

DuBose's first team (1997) had won only four games, but showed promise in a 17-18 loss to Auburn. The next year (1998) Alabama went 7-5, winding up the regular season with a 31-17 win over Auburn in Birmingham. The team earned a bid to the Music City Bowl, and lost to Virginia Tech in a cold, miserable late night game. Hardly anyone noticed.

As 1999 began DuBose appeared to have the Tide back among the elite of college football's national powers. Other than an upset loss to Louisiana Tech early in the season, Alabama had won every game except against Tennessee, and was ranked No. 7 nationally when it went into Auburn for a night game. It won 28-17, then beat Florida 34-7 in the SEC Championship Game.

Alabama fans were riding high and a 34-35 loss to Michigan in the Orange Bowl did little to dampen their spirits. They were digging out those old "We're No. 1" signs and talking about winning a national championship in 2000. After opening the 2000 season ranked No. 3, the team fell apart, winning only three games. It was the end of the DuBose era; it was the last of what only a year before had been expected to be the beginning of another power program.

The 1999 game had been the benchmark for DuBose; it might also be said it was a beginning to the end. But for the opposing coach, Tommy Tuberville, in his first year on the Plain, it was just the opposite. The Tigers wound up 5-6 and stayed home over the holidays. But that was the only losing season for Tuberville at Auburn until 2008, when the Tigers went 5-7 and he resigned.

In between those two losing seasons Auburn rose to great heights, including a 13-0 season, 11-2 season, and four nine-win seasons.

I walked uptown Sunday morning after the '99 game to get breakfast, but there had not been a "snow blizzard" after the Auburn loss the night before. Toomer's

Corner looked drab, cluttered with leftovers from the previous week's win over Georgia. Alabama had closed out the 20th century the way it had played in most of the games – winning. As I think back at that mess of dirty paper hanging from the trees and lying on the ground, it might have been an omen, marking the end of one reign and the beginning of another.

-30-

Pre-game column

Tide vs. Tigers: The talk now ends

(Original version published in The Gadsden Times, Saturday, November 20, 1999)

AUBURN -- Alabama and Auburn will meet for the 64th time in a night game with far-reaching implications for both teams.

Kickoff will be before a standing-room only crowd in Jordan-Hare Stadium; a national television audience will be looking on.

Bragging rights may be the most important of the spoils that go to the winner of the state's biggest rivalry. But other things are also at stake, such as a first win for Alabama in Jordan-Hare Stadium.

No. 8 Alabama (8-2) could clinch a spot in the SEC Championship Game in Atlanta. However, a loss would not necessarily eliminate the Tide from winning the Western Division title and playing Florida for the conference championship.

Even if Auburn won, the Crimson Tide could still win the Western Division title if Mississippi State lost to either Arkansas that day or to Ole Miss on Thanksgiving. Florida has already won the Eastern Division, so the Dec. 4 Championship Game would be a rematch between Bama and the Gators. Alabama won 40-39 in overtime during the regular season,

If unranked Auburn (5-5) won, it would give the Tigers a winning season and make them eligible for post-season play. However, Coach Tommy Tuberville had said that a win would not assure Auburn a bowl berth.

"There are a lot of teams in the Southeastern Conference eligible for bowls this year," he said. "We would only be one of many hoping to be selected."

This is also the final game in Jordan-Hare for the Auburn seniors, the final game played there in this century, and this team did not want to be remembered as the first to lose to Alabama in Auburn.

Alabama is a four-and-one-half point favorite and has not lost a road game this season.

The game could be a defensive struggle with the teams almost equal in scoring defense. Alabama has given up an average of 20.6 points per game, Auburn 20.8. Alabama's defense has held foes to less than 100 yards rushing in the last three games and five during the year. That may not figure in this game since Auburn averages only 68 yards a game.

Auburn relies on its passing game, featuring quarterback Ben Leard and the receiving of Ronney Daniels, who is especially talented running with the ball after catching a pass.

Auburn's best runner is Heath Evans, who has rushed for 214 yards the last three games.

Alabama's offensive formation is similar to Auburn's, but the Tide makes it work with a strong running game featuring Shaun Alexander. He leads the SEC in rushing (129 ypg) and touchdowns (20).

Alexander is also a big-play receiver but the go-to guy for quarterback Andrew Zow is Freddie Milons.

Daniels and Milons each caught nine passes in big wins for their respective teams last Saturday.

Alabama may be without tight end Terry Jones and his backup Shawn Draper. In practice this week, fullback Justin McClintock has played the position.

"About half our offense last week was two tight ends or two backs," said Alabama coach Mike DuBose. "If we don't have them, it takes away a lot of runs and play action."

Alabama is also without three players who started most of the season on defense.

Auburn appears to be at full strength, although the flu went through the team this week faster than Daniels went through the Georgia secondary the previous week. But Tuberville said the team is about as healthy as it's been all year.

"Anyone who can walk and breathe will play," he said.

Although this is Tuberville's first time to coach in the Alabama-Auburn game, he was aware of the rivalry.

"Fortunately, I have been to this game before as a coach. In 1989 I was Miami's defensive coordinator and we were going to play Alabama in the Sugar Bowl," Tuberville said. "I scouted the game. I was a little bit in awe. It was the first time Alabama played in Auburn."

He said he didn't go through Tiger Walk or a week of preparations, but it was still overwhelming.

"You can't let it overwhelm you. You have to tell your players to stay totally focused. If they don't, then walking out of that stadium is not going to be very much fun," Tuberville said.

DuBose has been there before, as a player and coach. He knows about playing in a hostile environment, and said that just "stirs competitive juices and makes you play a little bit better."

"In a game of this magnitude, there will be a few plays that decide the outcome. And the team that makes those five or six plays will be the team that wins," DuBose said. "You never know when they are going to occur. But they are going to occur.

"If you are playing hard on every snap, and you have prepared the way you should, then you will have an opportunity to make those plays."

-30-

Game

Half Tigers, Half Tide

(Original version published in The Gadsden Times, Sunday, November 21, 1999)

AUBURN -- The last Alabama-Auburn game of the millennium was one worthy of the ages, a game fitting the tradition of great games between the men in Crimson and White and those in Orange and Blue.

The tale on this chilly, damp night before an overflow crowd in Jordan-Hare Stadium was one of two halves.

The first half of this tale was of Auburn, playing its best of the season, beating Alabama with the passing game, stopping Alabama's running game.

Auburn led 14-6 at the half, but the game had not been that close.

This was the kind of football Auburn fans had not seen in Tiger country in a long time.

A popular sign around town and on T-shirts and banners said, "No Bama, not in this millennium."

In the first half, that saying appeared to be coming true.

The all-night tailgate parties, sitting in hour-long traffic jams, walking long distances in the rain, waiting all day for this game, THE GAME, was about to be worth the sacrifice for Auburn fans. And for Alabama, it would be just another version of "wait 'til next year."

The setting for this tale began 10 years ago, when Alabama first played in Auburn. Auburn upset the Tide that day, had won the three games here since. But this was to be the year of the Tide. Finally, Alabama would win in Jordan-Hare. And by doing so, sew up the Western Division title and a berth in the SEC Championship Game.

At first, it didn't seem it would happen. But in the end the Tide won, 28-17.

For a half, Auburn played like the King of the West. Although having to come from six points down, the Tigers were pretty much in charge from the beginning.

They had the momentum.

Ben Leard was picking the Tide secondary apart with his passing. Heath Evans had more yards rushing than Shaun Alexander. And the Auburn defense had twice stopped Tide drives after turnovers, giving up two field goals rather than two touchdowns.

The first quarter ended 6-0, Alabama. But it was a shaky lead.

Twice in the second quarter Leard commanded 80-yard scoring drives, converting five third downs. In each drive he completed six passes without an incompletion.

In the second half, the Tide turned. Auburn had a first and goal at the seven, then missed a field goal attempt on fourth and four.

Alabama drove to a first and goal at the six, and Auburn stopped Alexander four times and took over on downs.

Then on first down, Kindal Moorehead sacked Leard for a safety.

Thus begins the tale of the second half.

The Tide took the kick and scored, held Auburn to three and out, then drove for another touchdown and a 22-14 lead.

Only 3:45 remained and it was over, except for the shouting. Although Auburn got a final field goal, and Alabama another touchdown, the battle had been won.

This time it didn't come down to the final minute, with a field goal deciding the outcome. This time there was no suspense to the end with fans hanging on their seats.

In the end it was a sound Alabama victory, with Alexander making the difference. He rushed 33 times for 182 yards and three touchdowns. He set the SEC record for touchdowns scored, and the Tide career record for yards rushing.

Coach Mike DuBose told Alexander before the fourth quarter that God had given him the talent, that he had the ability to take over the quarter. And he did.

His performance was a fitting climax for this tale. It was a fitting way for Alexander to wind up regular season play with Alabama.

After failing to score on four plays from the six, he felt he had let the team down. But rather than stepping aside for his backup, it inspired him to play harder.

When it was over, DuBose said Alexander was the best player in America, and that Chris Samuels, his lead blocker, was the best lineman.

The tale of two halves was also one of two quarterbacks. Tide starter Andrew Zow couldn't get anything going in the first half. Tyler Watts led the Tide to victory in the second.

An ugly incident as the players left the field killed enthusiasm for extended celebrating. Someone from the Auburn student section threw a bottle at the Alabama players as they left the field. It struck a TV cameraman in the head, dropping him instantly. Suddenly the mood turned sober. There is no place for this type behavior on any college campus.

-30-

Post-game column

DuBose speechless after big victory

(Original version published in The Gadsden Times, Monday, November 22, 1999)

AUBURN -- Beating Auburn for the first time in Jordan-Hare Stadium was so special that it left Coach Mike DuBose at a loss for words.

"It was a tremendous win. This football team has come so far," he said. "I am so unbelievably happy for them (the players). I really don't know how to express it in words."

Auburn controlled the line of scrimmage, both on offense and defense, in the first half. And Alabama controlled the line of scrimmage, both on offense and defense, in the second half.

Auburn coach Tommy Tuberville said it was obvious the Tigers didn't play very well in the second half. But the difference in the game was one guy -- Shaun Alexander.

"He was a one-man show. We couldn't tackle him, we couldn't make any plays and we couldn't get the ball back," Tuberville said.

The Auburn coach said he was proud that his players did not quit. He did not mention that many of the players had been sick with the flu leading up to the game.

"Both teams came to play, but we came up short," he said.

DuBose said Tuberville had as good a game plan as Alabama has seen all year.

"They really gave us some problems with some of the things they did offensively," he said.

"I didn't think we were flat in the first half. I felt like Auburn did such a good job with their game plan, both offensively and defensively, that they had us scratching our heads at times."

DuBose said Alabama was lucky it wasn't down more than 14-6 at the half.

Tuberville said the difference in the second half was that Alabama came out and started running the ball instead of trying to throw it.

"They began to get the ball to No. 37 (Alexander)," he said.

"We gave our guys an opportunity to win the game, it just didn't work out. We were making plays, but their defense kept coming and our offensive line got tired in the fourth quarter. When we got behind, we had to try to get the ball down the field further."

Regarding his first Alabama-Auburn game, Tuberville said, "It is fun for the players, fun for the fans and fun for the coaches. We just got beat by No. 37."

DuBose said offensive coordinator Charlie Stubbs had suggested just before the half to put Tyler Watts in the game. The decision was made to start him in the second half.

"It was a good decision," DuBose said. "He was effective when he first went in and we stayed with him for the rest of the half. He played as good as a player could play in that situation, coming off the bench."

He said Zow was disappointed that he didn't get to finish the game, but that he was excited that Tyler played well.

Tuberville said it looked like Alabama played better with Watts, and that it is good for a team to have two quarterbacks.

On winning the SEC Western Division, DuBose said, "We accomplished some of our goals, but we haven't accomplished all of them. We put ourselves in a position to go to Atlanta and now we have the challenge of a great Florida team."

-30-

THE GAME - 2000

By Jimmy Smothers, written in 2011

The year was 2000, the beginning of the 21st century. That doesn't seem like so long ago to me. Earlier when I was writing about THE GAME of 1989, I mentioned that it was a recent game in this bitter series. The pretty woman I live with, reading proof, called my hand; she said that was more than 20 years ago and crossed out the word "recent."

So I dare not say this year's game was played recently, although it was hardly more than a decade ago. I'm fearful the use of that word (recently) might again bring out her blue editing pencil. So I'll just say that year's game is yet vivid among my memories.

Actually, so are most of the games in this series. But there was something special about this one – both on the field and in the stands. There was also a lot of talk about "firsts" and some mention about it fitting into a category of "last".

All this may sound confusing, so I'll try to explain.

This game was the "first" time that Auburn had played a game in Tuscaloosa in 99 years; and the first time the Tigers would play in Bryant-Denny Stadium. Alabama had played its first game at Auburn 11 years previously.

This was also going to be the "last" game for Mike DuBose as the Alabama head coach. There wasn't too much concern over that, since the Tide had only won three games that season. The Alabama family was ready for a change. Tommy Tuberville was in his second year on the Plain and had already turned the Tigers' program upward.

Auburn entered the game with an 8-2 record; Alabama was 3-7. But surprisingly, the Tigers were not a big favorite. Alabama's faithful expected the Tide would win, that the gods of the gridiron would not let the Tigers actually win on Bear Bryant turf.

Dawn broke on game day to miserable weather conditions. It had already turned cold, and during the night it had started to rain. By game time the rain had turned to sleet. Surprisingly, the fans were going to stick it out. After all, this was Auburn and Alabama, and THE GAME was only played once a year. Who cared about a little ice? The "Ice Bowl" seemed to fit the occasion better than "Iron Bowl" anyway.

Amazingly, the playing conditions were not all that bad, and Alabama played well. But neither team was able to score a touchdown. Auburn kicked three field goals to win, 9-0.

Normally, when a game begins, I am focused on the action. But that day, for the first time in my career, I turned some attention to the stands. That was the first time my grandchildren had asked me for tickets to a football game. Earlier in the week I had been proud that they were finally taking an interest in the game, but when the weather turned bad, I was wishing they were back home safe and warm. Thank goodness for cell phones, because I was able to keep check on them until they stopped answering my calls. They were having fun, and not paying any attention to the weather. They didn't want to be bothered by their old grandfather, especially one who was high and dry up in an enclosed press box.

-30-

Pre-game column

Fans getting into spirit as game nears

(Original version published in The Gadsden Times, Friday, November 17, 2000)

TUSCALOOSA – Thirty-two hours and counting until kickoff of THE GAME – Auburn playing Alabama in Bryant-Denny Stadium for the first time.

Tension is beginning to build, fans are getting excited.

Now that kickoff is nigh, things are a little different than earlier in the week when the game was ho-hum and people were talking about a new coach (for Alabama) and going to a bowl game (for Auburn).

Suddenly, THE GAME has become important, there is a little spark out there and the glow is bound to become full-blown by Saturday.

People are making predictions and the most asked question is, "Who do you think is going to win?"

Most people are sticking to the party line – Auburn people are picking the Tigers; Alabama fans are taking the Crimson Tide, perhaps a little gingerly.

Both sides can make a point.

Auburn is a one-to-two point favorite, which is about the same as a toss-up

Sports editors and beat writers from papers around the state have made their predictions in the annual Associated Press poll. The majority favors Auburn.

The home team usually wins this game, so that's in the Tide's favor.

Still, Alabama would probably like to recall its invitation to Auburn to visit the Capstone, or postpone the game to a later date.

Perhaps 2002 would be better. By then the Crimson Tide should have a new coach in place and he will have had a couple of years to get the program back to its traditional winning ways.

It took Alabama 10 years to win its first game in Jordan-Hare Stadium, which is a lengthy waiting time.

Auburn seems certain to break the Southern decorum of not kissing on the first date and will smack the Tide right in the mouth with its version of smash-mouth football. That's more than a little peck on the cheek, but look for it to happen Saturday.

The game will be hard-nosed.

Auburn has returned to winning with a running game and a running game is physical football.

Rudi Johnson has given the Tigers the added punch. He will be the difference Saturday.

Former Auburn coach Pat Dye said this week that the difference will be the confidence Auburn has because it has been winning.

Former Alabama coach Gene Stallings says Alabama will have the emotional edge because the game is being played in Tuscaloosa and it will be Mike DuBose's last game.

Still, Stallings is aware that to win, Alabama must slow Johnson while establishing its own running game.

Look for the game to be close and to be decided in the fourth quarter, which has become a tradition when Tigers and Tiders meet.

Last year Alabama outscored Auburn 20-3 in the fourth quarter to win 28-17; the year before Auburn went up 17-0; but Alabama won, 31-17.

Through the years there was Van Tiffin's last-second field goal for an Alabama win; and Bo over the top for a late touchdown to give Auburn the win.

Even in 1992, when Alabama won its last national championship, the score was 0-0 in the third quarter. Bama wound up winning 17-0 in Dye's last game at Auburn.

Coaches' say when these teams meet you can throw the record book out the window. But during the past 20 years only twice has the team with the best record failed to win.

In 1984 Alabama won 17-15 and wound up 5-6. Auburn was 8-3 going into the game and wound up 9-4, counting its bowl win over Arkansas. The other time was in 1990 when Alabama went into the game 6-5 and won 16-7 against Auburn, which was 7-2-1 and ended the season 8-3-1.

The only time a team with a losing record has won during the last 20 years was in 1984.

Another misconception about this game is that the winning team will gain the upper hand in recruiting.

That isn't necessarily the case. Few recruits ever have a choice between Alabama and Auburn, and the ones who do don't normally base their decision on the outcome of any one football game.

Alabama will have recruits at this game, something the Tide could not do when it was played in Birmingham. But that will be no more of an advantage than Auburn has when the game is played in Jordan-Hare Stadium.

A difference this year will be that Athletic Director Mal Moore will speak to the prospects, not out-going Coach Mike DuBose.

Now, to answer your question, I'm picking Auburn, 21-10.

-30-

Game

Tigers win 9-0 on first trip to Bryant-Denny

(Source, The Gadsden Times, November 2000)

TUSCALOOSA – It wasn't typical football weather in the Deep South, where fans enjoy sitting in the stands soaking in the mild autumn temperature, while watching a good football game. Instead when Auburn came into Bryant-Denny

Stadium for the first time it was cold, raining and sleeting. Describing it as miserable would be a compliment.

Despite all that, the stands were full and the game was played. Neither team managed to score a touchdown, but Auburn kicked three field goals to win, 9-0.

Game hero was Auburn kicker Damon Duval, a senior, who kicked three field goals from 22-, 42- and 27-yards out. The win gave the Tigers a 9-2 record, the Western Division title and a spot in the SEC Championship Game against Florida.

In only his second season as the Auburn head coach Tommy Tuberville had brought a team with back-to-back losing seasons to one of the top in the Southeastern Conference.

This was Tuberville's first win over Alabama, but nobody wanted to beat Bama more than Auburn fullback Heath Evans.

"I've thought about it every day since last year," Evans said after the game. "I can still hear those Alabama fans singing, 'Hey, Auburn! We just beat the (heck) out of you!' I thought about it every day. I had never known a pain like that before."

The previous year Alabama had beaten Auburn for the first time at Jordan-Hare Stadium. After that game Evans said as long as he was on the team, Alabama would not beat Auburn again.

Auburn had won its last four games; Alabama was on a four-game losing streak and at "Low Tide" having won only three games all year. Head coach Mike DuBose had already been told that he would not be retained after this game.

Still, the Alabama seniors wanted to win, after all this was Auburn; and they wanted to win a final time for their coach.

Despite a wet field, it was a hard-fought and physical game. Both teams played well, especially on defense. Auburn held the Tide to 23 yards rushing and only 135 yards of total offense.

"Anytime a team comes in and shuts you out in your own stadium in miserable conditions like this, it is hard to swallow. We have to live with it for a whole year and that's just hard to take," said Tide tackle Jarret Johnson.

Alabama quarterback Tyler Watts said the Tide was at the bottom, emotionally. That it was the worst feeling he'd ever been a part of.

Tuberville said, "What a night. It was one of those we'll always remember. It was bad weather but we had a great crowd. I thought we played great on defense; and Alabama played great on defense, but they couldn't stop Rudi (Johnson). Our offensive line blocked as well as it has blocked all season. I thought Cole Cubelic had a heck of a game at center. It was one of those times we were bound and determined to run the football no matter what they did on defense.

"They put seven or eight guys up there to stop the run, and Rudi was still gaining yards. If it had been a nice night where we could have thrown the football more, I think we could have moved it a little better through the air. But we'll take what we got."

Tuberville pointed out that nine wins was kind of a dream come true especially for the seniors, as well as for the entire football team. The two previous seasons Auburn had gone 3-8 and 5-6. .

(Gadsden Times Sports Correspondent Lori Johnson contributed to this article)

-30-

Sidebar

Auburn making an Amazin' run

(Original version published in The Gadsden Times, Sunday, November 19, 2000)

TUSCALOOSA – It's not anything new, the term was used once when Shug Jordan was coaching the Auburn Tigers and Terry Henley was shocking people by the way he was running the football.

That year the team was called the Amazin's because it did things no one expected.

This year's team is doing the same thing.

Auburn keeps getting better and continues to win. Rudi Johnson is amazing, the way he runs with the football.

He gained 130 yards against Alabama, the 10th time this year he's had 100 or more yards. His 37 carries were a career high.

And the end doesn't seem to be in sight – for Johnson or the Tigers.

It's amazing that this team, which was expected to be in the middle of the pack in the Western Division, will be playing for the SEC Championship in two weeks.

Even with a win over Alabama, the Tigers needed Arkansas to upset Mississippi State in order to win the tie-breaker for the Western Division title. Fat chance of that happening.

Amazingly, it did.

The Razorbacks won 17-10 in overtime.

The Tigers have a 9-2 record; will be headed to a big bowl and a high national ranking.

It's amazing the way the season turned around for Alabama and Auburn, each doing an about-face from preseason predictions.

Three months ago, even three weeks ago, hardly anyone expected Auburn to beat Alabama on its first visit to Bryant-Denny Stadium.

After back-to-back losses to Mississippi State and Florida, breaking even in its last four games seemed logical. But the Tigers won out. And Alabama lost out, ending the year with five straight losses.

Amazing.

Even with Alabama's losing record, Auburn was only a shaky one-point favorite. But the Tigers shut down the Tide, allowing only 47 yards rushing, 112 passing. The closest Alabama came to scoring was a missed 48-yard field goal in the closing minutes of the game.

All the reminders of Alabama's winning tradition – the replays of great plays and pictures of Coach Bryant on the video screen, had no effect on this game. Neither did the return of some of the Tide's greatest players who took part in the halftime show.

This was the Tigers' day to growl. And growl they did.

After a week of hype about "firsts" going into the game, it is only fitting that the "unusual" will be most remembered about Auburn's first game in Bryant-Denny Stadium.

The weather was unusual, with rain and sleet off and on throughout the game.

It was unusual that it didn't seem to affect the crowd or the play on the field. But then, no one seems to notice a little rain and cold when Auburn and Alabama play.

There was a capacity crowd, many arriving on campus two or three days early, and at the stadium two or three hours before game time. It created an enthusiastic atmosphere, although the game drew little attention outside the state.

That was unusual, too, because now it's Auburn, not Mississippi State, paired against Florida in the SEC Championship Game.

Auburn won 9-0, scoring all of its points on field goals by Damon Duval, who has become an incredible player.

This is somewhat of a credit to the Tide defense, keeping Auburn's offense out of the end zone. Kenny Smith, for example, played a super game.

Going into the game neither coach expected to win without scoring a touchdown, nor expected to win by scoring only nine points. But it happened.

Unusual, perhaps, but when Auburn and Alabama play, anything may happen. Mike DuBose said the difference in the game was Auburn's defensive front.

"They just lined up and beat our offense at the line of scrimmage," he said. "They whipped us at the point of attack."

It had been a difficult week for the Crimson Tide and at times DuBose said he had trouble staying focused on the game because he would start thinking about it being his last time to be doing this or that.

The game was the last for DuBose as the Alabama coach and at times during his post-game press conference he became emotional.

It's sad to see a man lose his job, especially one he loves. It was difficult for him to go out losing, especially this game. But he predicted that a good coach will be hired, that the team will quickly be restored.

What happened this season, what happened against Auburn, was not a lack of effort. He said for whatever reason, there was no chemistry and the team continued to miss.

"We'd have a breakdown here and a breakdown there," DuBose pointed out.

That was what happened Saturday.

Alabama failed to make the plays, Auburn made them.

What was a sad ending to a season for Alabama; to a career for DuBose, was just the opposite for Auburn; and for its coach, Tommy Tuberville, completing his second year with the Tigers.

It's that way in sports – joy in winning, sadness in losing. And when it's Auburn and Alabama both last for a year.

Coach Tuberville said it was a fun day; that it has been a fun year. And by winning, the Tigers earned themselves another game. Auburn fans earned the bragging rights for the coming year.

-30-

Post-game column

Tide's giddy feelings supplanted by misery

(Source, The Gadsden Times, Monday, November 20, 2000)

TUSCALOOSA – The fairy tale has the clock striking 12, ending Cinderella's dream world. For Alabama, its football coach and its throng of followers, that doomsday number was three.

After winning last year's SEC championship coaching the Crimson Tide to its first 10-win season since the Gene Stallings era, Coach Mike DuBose had been talking all summer about taking the next step in the fall of 2000. And Alabama fans, who hadn't enjoyed a national championship in eight years, jumped on the band wagon.

Going into the season Alabama was ranked No. 3 nationally; but when it was over, the only number three was the Crimson Tide's win total.

Multiply those two 3s and you get 9, which was the number of points the Auburn football team scored in a 9-0 win over the Crimson Tide in its first game at Bryant-Denny Stadium. It also proved to be the end of the dream job for DuBose, who had once played for Alabama, had been an assistant coach there, was familiar with the school's tradition and championships.

When he was named head coach, when the team went 10-3 and won the SEC his third year, earning him "Conference Coach of the Year" honors, he surely felt like Cinderella. He was living out his dream.

Then it all came tumbling down. But on this November day, when Auburn came calling for the first time at the stadium that Bryant built, his team played well. But Auburn played better.

Auburn was unable to score a touchdown, but managed to kick three field goals for a 9-0 win. It was the first win over Alabama for Coach Tommy Tuberville, in his second year as head coach on the Plain. The previous year Alabama had won for the first time in Auburn, Tuberville's first year there. But on this cold and rainy day the Tigers got their revenge; and sent Alabama's coach packing.

Big as this loss was, at a site where Alabama fans felt that Auburn would never win, it wasn't the reason for DuBose's demise. In four seasons under him Alabama had gone 4-7, 7-5, 10-3 and 3-8. Those first and four years were a throwback to the mid-'50s, when J.B. (Ears) Whitworth was the coach during the era of the Low Tide.

DuBose had offered to resign after a 0-21 loss; and after a homecoming loss the last Saturday in October had been told he would not be back.

Alabama senior tackle Kenny Smith said after the game: "We really wanted to come in here and give Coach DuBose a win for his final game. We did everything we could, we just couldn't do it."

-30-

Running back Rudi Johnson (2000) is second (behind Bo Jackson) in Auburn's single season rushing records with 1,567 yards and in average yards per game at 130.6. He is first in total carries in a single season with 324. In his only game against Alabama, he was the leading rusher in the "Ice Bowl" game of 2000 at Tuscaloosa, which Auburn won 9-0 with three field goals. Johnson signed with the Cincinnati Bengals in 2001 and wound up his pro career in 2009 with the Detroit Lions.

Photo Courtesy of Todd Van Emst, Auburn Athletic Department

THE GAME - 2002

By Jimmy Smothers, written in 2011

This game isn't on a "Notable Games" list that can be found on the Internet, but it has all the makings necessary for a game to remember. The only thing missing is a down-to-the wire, fantastic finish that sets many of the games in this series apart.

This was a game that no one expected Auburn to win, but it did, upsetting No. 9 Alabama (9-2 going in) 17-7. Auburn (7-4) was unranked; but that's not why no one was giving the Tigers a chance to win. Here are some of the reasons why: (1) the game was being played in Bryant-Denny Stadium and Auburn had not scored a touchdown in Tuscaloosa since 1903, although it did defeat Alabama 9-0 on three field goals two years earlier; (2) Auburn's team was riddled with injuries and was starting some third stringers in key running positions; and (3) Alabama had the nation's No. 1 defense.

Auburn's star running backs Carnell Williams and Ronnie Brown had a broken leg and injured ankle, respectively; Chris Butler was also injured as was fullback Brandon Johnson. Tre Smith, who had opened the season at fourth string, started at tailback; third string tight end Cooper Wallace played fullback.

Smith stole the show, rushing for 126 yards, 15 more yards than the entire Alabama team. But he refused to take credit, telling the media after the game that Auburn's running game all year had been founded on the offensive line, not the running backs. And that was the way it was that day against Alabama.

After the game coach Tommy Tuberville said the line blocked well the first half; then the defense took over in the second half. He also praised the game plan of offensive coordinator Bobby Petrino.

After the game Alabama's Brodie Croyle, who replaced Tyler Watts in the second half, said Auburn did a lot of blitzing and Alabama's blockers could not pick it up.

Alabama, which had a big win over Tennessee earlier, was hoping to move up in the polls with big wins against Auburn and in a big bowl game. But what had been a special season suddenly turned sour, dropping to No. 14 in the polls. The Tide wound up playing Hawaii. It ended the season at 10-3 and ranked No. 11. Auburn defeated Penn State in the bowl at Orlando, Fla., winding up 9-4 and ranked No. 14 in the final AP poll.

In the first quarter quarterback Jason Campbell passed seven yards to tight end Robert Johnson for a touchdown, the first for Auburn in T-Town in 103 years. Alabama never caught up, scoring its only touchdown with 1:38 left in the third quarter on a one-yard run by Santonio Beard.

The win was Auburn's fourth against Alabama in Tuscaloosa; by a combined score of 91-7. The three previous wins were 48-0 in 1895, 17-0 in 2001 and 9-0 in 2000; then in 2002, Auburn won again, 17-7, starting the string of six wins. Tuberville kept Auburn fans updated by holding up the correct number of fingers, plus one thumb, after each of the wins.

Rumors had been circulating all week that Tide coach Dennis Franchione would announce his resignation after the game and take the head job at Texas A&M. After the upset defeat, it was rumored that Alabama had not been prepared for the game because he'd been focusing on the job with the Aggies.

Naturally, Franchione denied all this, saying he wasn't leaving and that the team had been prepared for the game. Alabama had an NCAA bowl ban at the time so Athletic Director Mal Moore scheduled a regular-season game in Honolulu to be played after the Auburn game.

There was speculation over Franchione leaving for Texas A&M, even as the team was winging its way back across the Pacific. After the team returned to Tuscaloosa, maybe a day or two, A&M sent a school plane to pick him up.

When he got on the plane and flew out to College Station, it began to sink in that he was probably going to take the job. All heck broke loose among the Alabama fans. I don't think he ever came back to Tuscaloosa after that. Never even met personally with the team to tell them he was leaving.

Mike Shula, a former Alabama quarterback who had beaten Auburn two of his three games against the Tigers, was named head coach.

For Auburn, this was the beginning of a six-game win streak against Alabama, the longest string in the series for the Tigers. Alabama had once won nine in a row during the Paul Bryant era. Tiger coach Tommy Tuberville held up his index finger as he greeted them from the field after the game.

-30-

Pre-game column

Tuscaloosa buzzing, Auburn must be in town

(Original version published in The Gadsden Times, Saturday, November 23, 2002)

TUSCALOOSA – There is a caravan atmosphere around the University of Alabama campus and spreading across town. RVs have been coming in since mid-week, fans have filled the motels and hotels and the highways are jammed with traffic coming into town for the football game with Auburn.

People are having tailgate parties galore; flying their colors, playing their loudspeakers and having a ball.

The festivities are almost like New Orleans during Sugar Bowl week.

This could be Alabama's bowl game, since the Tide is on NCAA probation this year. But Coach Dennis Franchione says no. Nor is he treating next week's game in Hawaii as Alabama's version of a bowl.

He said this is a special day and a meaningful game, but that he doesn't look at it any other way. He said he doesn't think the Alabama players do, either.

Some may not, but most of the players grew up surrounded by the rivalry between Auburn and Alabama. They know what this game means.

Tide quarterback Tyler Watts said, "It isn't just a game people talk about one week, then it's over and they move on. It's something that's carried over and talked about 365 days every year. It's amazing how much people look forward to this game and how it affects their lives."

Auburn's players have had a daily reminder of last year's loss, staring at an Alabama jersey, with 31-7 on it, hanging on the wall of their weight room.

"It lingered for 365 days and now it's coming up again," said Auburn guard Monreko Crittenden.

Still, it is just another game to Franchione, who approaches every game with the same attitude.

"Preparation, practice, focus is how I handle my team," Franchione said. "It doesn't change from week to week."

Tide cornerback Waine Bacon agreed.

"We're going to be staying the same. There's not a lot of change in Coach's way of doing things. It's a game, it's a business. Every time we go on the field he approaches everything the same," he added.

Watts said the time to be emotional about a game is after it is over. "You have to approach every game the same way. If you don't, the North Texases of the world will beat you."

Despite his "sameness attitude" Franchione is aware that this is a big game with people in Alabama; and says he doesn't know any way to make it any bigger. So he just wants to be a part of it. Before the game, he will take 5 minutes to reflect on it and let it all soak in, and then it will be back to business as usual.

Despite all of Auburn's injuries that have weakened the team, Coach Tommy Tuberville said, "Somehow, someway we've just got to find a way to put a game plan together on offense to score some points."

Most of the talk all week among Auburn fans has been about how banged up their players are. They seem shocked that Alabama is only favored by a touchdown and field goal. But the Auburn players don't see it that way.

"It's going to be a knock-down, drag-out fight," said cornerback Junior Rosegreen. "Whoever wants it most is going to win. I know for a fact, that if we come in and handle our business and win this game, everybody's going to forget about the loss to Georgia."

If Auburn beats Alabama this year, Auburn fans will be talking about a double-dip in T-town all next year.

-30-

Game

Running game carries Auburn past Alabama

(Original version published in The Gadsden Times, Sunday, November 24, 2002)

TUSCALOOSA - There was no dancing in the end zone and around the goal posts after this win in 2002, such as there had been at Legion Field in 1982 when Auburn defeated Alabama 23-22. But the lack of an Auburn celebration on Bryant-Denny turf after a 17-7 win this year was only because fans were not allowed on the field.

Alabama went into the game an 11-point favorite. Most thought it should have been by more.

"No one in the country gave us a chance," said Tre Smith, who gained 126 yards, more than the entire Crimson Tide, which had 111.

Smith was a fourth-team tailback when the season started at Auburn; that was before Carnell Williams suffered a broken leg, Ronnie Brown had an ankle injury and Chris Butler was also injured.

No one expected Auburn to be able to run the football without them or fullback Brandon Johnson, who is the team's leading blocker. He was replaced by Cooper Wallace, a third-team tight end.

"People said with me and Cooper, Auburn didn't have a running game," Smith said, pointing out the Auburn running game wasn't Williams or Brown during the season; nor was it he and Wallace Saturday night.

"We have been able to run the football because of our offensive line," he said.

Alabama's defense was ranked No. 1 nationally, but Smith said the way the Auburn line blocked, it didn't seem like it; that Alabama's defense wasn't as good as Auburn had expected; and that this wasn't the first time this season Auburn had gone against a defense ranked No. 1 nationally.

"Both sides of the line of scrimmage made the difference in this ball game." said Auburn Coach Tommy Tuberville. "We blocked well the first half. They turned up the heat the second half on blitzing, but we still tried to run the football. Our defense was what made it."

Tuberville said this game was a classic case of guys not being denied. And he mentioned the history of Auburn-Alabama games played in Tuscaloosa. Auburn had won the three previous games by a combined score of 74-0.

"It took them 103 years to score here, but they did get some points today." said Tuberville. "When it was all said and done, the key tonight was our special teams.

"We set up field position good. Roderick Hood had a great night returning kicks. It was fun to watch us have fun," he said. "We haven't had a lot of things go our way the last few weeks.

"We played with emotion most of the year, and I think that was the reason we've played so well since the fourth quarter of the Florida game. This group believes in what they're doing.

"It's just unfortunate that some bad things happened to us down the stretch. But it doesn't get any better than winning the Iron Bowl on the road. Last year people said we quit. But we didn't quit then, and we didn't quit tonight."

Tuberville said Alabama has a good football team and played hard. But that Auburn's defense took away the option, took away the sprint draw and forced them to throw the ball.

Shaud Williams gained 49 yards, Santonio Beard 41 for Alabama. Quarterbacks Tyler Watts (126) and Brodie Croyle (83) combined for 209 passing, 40 yards more than Auburn's Jason Campbell.

But Auburn's defensive plan worked. So did the offense.

"Our offensive line - tremendous," Tuberville said. "Their defensive line is very athletic, and we were very concerned. We didn't know whether to keep an extra tight end in to block, or a back in to block. But our front five offensive linemen did a super job.

"We slowed their initial rush down. We did miss some blocks, and Jason paid for it in some situations, but our offensive line has gotten better all year."

Tuberville praised his offensive coordinator, Bobby Petrino, for coming up with his best game plan.

"We saw some things in their secondary we wanted to take advantage of. We were a little concerned with our protection, but our protection looked great," Tuberville said. "Campbell had a great night, but we pulled the plug in the fourth quarter. I wouldn't let him throw the ball."

With Auburn's win, the Tigers are still in the running for the SEC's Western Division title. But the players or coaches were not thinking about that, amid all the celebrating.

"We aren't concerned about national championships. We got the championship we want. We got an Iron Bowl. When you win an Iron Bowl, you've done a day's work," Tuberville said.

-30-

Post-game column

Auburn win over Bama a scene to behold

(Original version published in The Gadsden Times, Monday, November 25, 2002)

It's been 36 hours since Auburn defeated Alabama 17-7 in one of the biggest upsets in this series. Fans are still celebrating and will be for a long, long time.

Actually, don't look for it to stop until the teams play again next year in Jordan-Hare Stadium. Even then, this game won't be forgotten.

Fans talk about every Auburn-Alabama game for a year. This one will have a much longer life span. It was a storybook performance by the Tigers those Hollywood script writers would have trouble duplicating.

From the way fans rally around this rivalry, there is no denying the hype may be justified. This game, more than any other, grabs the attention of people throughout the state; even many who pay no attention to football the rest of the season.

Fans roll into the game site days in advance, flying their colors and showing support for their school. That's all great for people who enjoy that kind of stuff.

My favorite games are Alabama and Tennessee, Auburn and Georgia, and whichever team, Tide or Tigers, is playing at Arkansas, Baton Rouge, or Oxford.

People are always asking writers which team they are for. The usual answer is both, or neither, although there are a few newsmen who are more fans than reporters.

Naturally, it's more fun to cover a winning team. And since I usually alternate between Alabama and Auburn I like to see them both win.

When they play each other, I have no favorite. I simply cover the event and write about the game. There have been times when the biggest story was about the losing team; but usually it's about the winner, as was the case last Saturday.

Auburn won a game no one expected the Tigers could, or would, win. Being on the sideline at the end of the game and seeing up close the joy and exuberance in the faces of the Auburn players, coaches and fans as they erupted in excitement is something I will remember. The celebration, long and loud, was something to behold.

Before the game, Auburn Athletic Director David Housel kidded me about "being for that other team" because I was wearing a red and white press credential issued by Alabama. He failed to mention that his credential also had Alabama printed on it in big red letters. But he knew that I played it straight down the middle and had been with him at as many Auburn games as I have been with Alabama.

This was my 45th Auburn-Alabama game. Since no one knows what the future may hold, there is no guarantee there will be a next year for me, although players and fans from the losing team did a lot of talking about it.

"Wait 'till next year", quickly became the Alabama motto. The Crimson Tide may even hang an Auburn jersey with 17-7 on it in their locker room as a reminder of what happened, and that they will have another shot in 12 months.

Auburn did that last year and it seemed to have played a role in motivating the Tigers last week.

I just sat back, watched and enjoyed. Then I wrote about whatever happened, about one of the most surprising upsets I've ever covered. Now I'm going to take a few days off, and then go see the SEC Championship Game and travel with Auburn to some bowl game.

While many fans will talk about this game until next year rolls around, I'm anxious for the SEC basketball season to begin. The tournament will be in New Orleans. I can hardly wait.

-30-

Photo courtesy Craig Scott, Gadsden Public Library

Legion Field, Birmingham, was once known as "The Football Capital of the South" and was the scene of many of Alabama's and Auburn's most exciting games. At one time sports writers who covered games there would "dateline" their copy with LEGION FIELD rather than BIRMINGHAM.

THE GAME - 2004

By Jimmy Smothers, written in 2011

This year was to Auburn what the 1966 year was to Alabama. Auburn was denied a shot at the BCS championship in 2004; Alabama calls 1966 the year of the Lost Ring.

In 1966 Alabama beat Auburn, wound up the season at 11-0, but was ranked No. 3 by both AP and UPI, and got no cigar.

In 2004 Auburn beat Alabama, then won the SEC Championship Game and the Sugar Bowl; winding up with a 13-0 record, 8-0 in the SEC, and ranked No. 2 in both wire service polls. There were three unbeaten teams that year, and Auburn was the third-man out when it came to getting a berth in the BCS Game and a shot at that national championship.

However, the Tigers were named national champions by some other organizations, including People's Choice. But it was little consolation, considering 13-0 was the best record in Auburn history. The 21-13 win over rival Alabama, third straight over the Tide, had been huge at the time, but did little to calm the uproar of the Auburn faithful.

Auburn had gone into Tuscaloosa tied for No. 2. Fans expected an impressive win over the Tide would move the Tigers up at least a half game and into a solid position to get a berth in the BCS Game. But the game wasn't that impressive, with Alabama leading 6-0 during the first half on field goals by Brian Bostick.

Auburn rallied behind the passing of Jason Campbell and running of Carnell Williams in the second half, going out front 21-6. That performance might have been enough to impress the voters in the wire service polls. But in the closing minutes of the game Alabama rose up, scoring on a pass from Spencer Pennington to D.J. Hall, and was scrapping into the final seconds.

Auburn dropped from a tie for second to third in the polls, and stayed there even after a 38-28 win over Tennessee in the SEC Championship Game. The 2004 BCS Championship Game was won by No. 1 Southern Cal over No. 2 Oklahoma.

Here in 2011, because of NCAA violations by Southern California, the 2004 National Championship has been "vacated". Of course, it is impossible for 2004 Oklahoma and 2004 Auburn to play now for the championship game they should have played back then.

But one does wonder why the powers-that-be, instead of vacating the 2004 championship, didn't retroactively declare Auburn and Oklahoma co-champions for 2004.

-30-

Pre-game column

Upset would give Shula higher fan stature

(Original version published in The Gadsden Times, Wednesday, November 17, 2004)

TUSCALOOSA – Mike Shula said during a conversation Sunday night that he realizes there are definitely some things he needs to build on as a football coach, and one of those things is the Auburn-Alabama game.

As a player and coach, Shula is 2-2 against the Tigers. If Alabama can beat Auburn Saturday, it will be one of the biggest upsets in the colorful series and his image will shoot up in the eyes of Crimson Tide fans.

It isn't likely to happen, but it could. That's what makes this game special.

Pat Dye, who has coached at both schools, has seen what this game is about from both sides. He says it is a different kind of deal every year.

"Don't ever think that it isn't," he said.

When these two teams play each year, records, rankings, odds and predictions are meaningless and tossed aside.

Remember two years ago? There was no way Auburn could win without Carnell Williams, Ronnie Brown and Brandon Johnson. But it did, 17-7. It was the first time in 20 years that an unranked Auburn team defeated a ranked Alabama team.

This year, the situation is somewhat reversed in that Alabama has three starting backs out – Brodie Croyle, Ray Hudson and Tim Castille. Auburn is ranked (No. 2 tie), Alabama isn't.

This year Auburn has rolled through the season undefeated – its had luck of schedule and luck of injuries, two of a few things the late Bear Bryant used to say a team needed to win championships. LSU has been the only close game; there have been no major injuries.

This year Alabama is the team that is beat-up and short on depth. Still the Tide has won six games and played well much of the time in the four losses.

The fact that Auburn is only a nine-point favorite, when its average margin of victory is 24.9 points, makes a strong statement. With the exception of the one-point win over LSU (10-9), only Arkansas and Georgia stayed within 18 points.

On paper, it should be a Tiger romp, but that hasn't happened since a 49-26 win (23-point margin) in 1969. Alabama won by 24 points, 31-7, in 2001. But that was the first one-sided victory since the '70s.

It has been 20 years since there has been a huge upset. That was in 1984 when Alabama went into the game 4-6; Auburn (8-3) had won eight of its last nine games.

That was the game people remember as "Wrong Way, Bo" after Bo Jackson went the wrong way on a goal line play. Auburn got the ball back, but missed on a last-second field goal attempt.

That was said to be the biggest upset in the series since Auburn's 14-13 win in 1949.

That was Mike Shula's first time to play against Auburn and he recalled it being a tough game that ended on a good note.

"It showed me one more thing about this game – that it really didn't matter about the records or who had the momentum coming in," he said. "I remember Paul Ott Carruth's touchdown. I remember getting the wind knocked out of me. I remember as a player feeling good about the off-season. I remember we got some good recruits, such as Bobby Humphrey."

Alabama won again, 25-23, in 1985 on Van Tiffin's last-second field goal. Shula's last year. Auburn won 21-17 on Lawyer Tillman's reverse in 1986. So he was 2-1 against Auburn as a quarterback. He is 0-1 as a coach.

Someone asked Shula how many of today's players have asked him about what happened at the finish of the '85 game. "Zero," he replied. "Brodie (Croyle) is probably the only one who knows anything about it."

They are being told about the '84 game, hoping they can do a Crimson repeat.

Today's players were babies, if they had even been born, when Shula quarterbacked the Tide. Many of them are from out of state, so they grew up without any knowledge of the rivalry that is so intense within this state.

Shula was living in Miami when Ray Perkins signed him to play for the Crimson Tide.

"I remember my first year, hearing about it as soon as I got here. Then all of a sudden that week came and the upper classmen started talking about it," he said. "It started with them, and then everyone was talking about the game between meetings, on the practice field, in the dorm. The scout team players even get fired up because they want to give a good look to the first team."

The game may mean more to players from the State of Alabama, who grow up hearing about the game, whose families are for either one team or the other.

Shula said another thing that makes it neat is the way high school football is covered in Alabama; the players all know each other. Even if they didn't play on the same team, or against each other, they have read about one another.

Brodie Croyle and Carnell Williams, both from Gadsden, are an example. And there are others from other towns who are friends, and who will be phoning back and forth this week, then squaring off in Bryant-Denny Stadium Saturday.

-30-

Game

Auburn's victory might not be enough
(Original version published in The Gadsden Times, Sunday, November 21, 2004)

TUSCALOOSA -- Auburn won the battle, but may have lost the war in its campaign for a spot in the BCS national championship game. The Tigers went into Saturday's game against Alabama tied with Oklahoma for No. 2 in one poll and a close third to the Sooners in the BCS rankings.

The big question all week has been, "Who is No. 2?"

Oklahoma defeated Baylor 35-0 earlier in the day. Auburn needed an impressive win, also. Each team has a conference championship game remaining.

Auburn came from behind in the second half to beat Alabama 21-13 in a game that Auburn coach Tommy Tuberville said wasn't very pretty, but it was a win.

He talked about the rivalry, how it's usually even on the field despite the odds and how both Alabama and Auburn have won games when they were the underdog.

"It was a hard ball game," he said. "We knew we were going to be in for a battle. All week long we kept telling our players. Sometimes it soaks in, sometimes it doesn't."

Tuberville also said a lot of people who vote in the polls don't understand the rivalry in this game and they will look at the score and say Auburn struggled.

"Those people have never been to this game, they don't understand it's an even playing field," he said.

This is a game that Tuberville had rather people who vote not watch, at least not unless they understand what it's all about.

When Auburn and Alabama play, it's the win that counts, not the score, not even how the game was played.

The first thing a new coach is told when he is hired, and the first thing the players are told when they sign, is to win this game.

Beat Auburn.

Beat Alabama.

Whichever phrase applies.

That's what football is about in this state. How, or by how much, isn't important. But a lot of the voters, and none of the computers, who will decide the BCS rankings don't understand that.

Alabama played its best game of the season, especially in the first half.

"Our whole football team laid it on the line," said Tide coach Mike Shula after the game.

The remarkable thing is how well Alabama played with a patched up team - with some players on offense, defense and special teams who would never have thought at the beginning of the year that they would be playing against Auburn at the end of the season.

Some of the Tiders played with bad ankles and other injuries. All of the players gave it their all, leaving everything on the field.

Even Tuberville praised the Alabama team for playing hard, noting they had a lot of injuries.

"They came to play and played well," he said of the Tide. "We just didn't have any rhythm in the first half and Alabama did something about that."

Auburn just couldn't seem to find the right combination in the first half, not until that final drive. Then they came out in the third quarter playing like champions -- scoring on long drives the first two times they had the ball.

Tuberville said when Jason Campbell was able to start throwing the ball downfield; it got Alabama out of the eight- and nine-man fronts.

"They just took a chance doing that in the first half and it worked," Tuberville said. "In the second half, it didn't."

It wouldn't have made any difference if Auburn's defense hadn't stepped up in the first half and shut down Alabama's powerful running attack. Ken Darby, the SEC's second leading rusher, averaging more than 100 yards per game, was limited to 19 yards on 14 carries.

Overall, Alabama had 50 net yards rushing, Auburn had 74. Alabama 226 yards passing, Auburn 224.

The first half was Alabama, and Tuberville said the Tiger defense saved the day.

"This thing could have been over at halftime if our defense hadn't shown up, as many mistakes as we made," Tuberville said.

It was only the second time Auburn had been behind all season, but the players didn't lose their poise, and never lost confidence.

Auburn came out in the second half and started making plays and found a way to win.

Tuberville said Mike Shula and his staff did a tremendous job, in spite of all the injuries.

"We knew coming over here that it would be a battle to the end and obviously, it was," the Auburn coach said.

The players on both teams will get a few days off. Then Auburn will begin preparing for the SEC Championship Game against Tennessee.

After that, both teams will go to a bowl somewhere. There were representatives at the game from bowls at Orlando and Shreveport. But that probably doesn't mean a lot at this point in time. Auburn will probably wind up at the Sugar Bowl and Alabama may go to the Music City Bowl.

Sidebar

A Ballgame of Opposites

(Original version published in The Gadsden Times, Sunday, November 21, 2004)

TUSCALOOSA -- Auburn has been a first-half football team this fall, running up a big score on the opposition then coasting through the second half. Saturday, it was just the opposite. Alabama led 6-0 at the half, and had rushed for only 51 yards. Thirty-five of those came on a 78-yard drive just before the half that ended with a missed field goal.

The second half was just the reverse, Auburn still didn't do a lot of running, but it scored three touchdowns and won the game, 21-13.

Offensive coordinator Al Borges said that is what championship teams are all about.

"It's not all about leading 30-6 at the half, and we've had some like that when we jumped on our opponent," Borges said after the game -- his first against Alabama. "Champions are about when you are down by six and haven't done a thing; the crowd is in the game on the opponent's side; everything is looking pretty dim on being able to recover, but you find a way to win the game."

Borges talked to the Auburn players about this, telling them that is what being a champion is all about.

"When you go 11-0 and blow your opponents out, that's talent, but not many teams do that. You've got to have a few games, and we've had two (LSU and Alabama) when we were not hitting on all cylinders. But we found a way in a crucial situation to get it down. That's what champions are all about."

Alabama jumped on Auburn in the first quarter, shutting down its running game to three yards on three carries; and limiting Jason Campbell to minus one yard on three of six completed passes.

Auburn finally drove 78 yards just before the half -- 43 on three passes, 35 on six rushes.

During previous games this fall Borges had given Auburn some new plays, some finesse plays to run in the first half. But he said Alabama did an outstanding job of changing its defensive look and taking away those plays.

"I had a few left on the sheet because I didn't think they would work," he said.

At the half, he took what had worked in the final drive and expounded on it and Auburn scored on two long drives the first time it had the ball in the third quarter.

"What I did was go back to the basic plan of run and pass out of a simple formation. I tried not to confuse our kids and it paid off," Borges explained. "But I'll say this; I don't think you can win every game doing that. I don't think you can line up in the I formation and play like that and win every game. You have to be able to do some other things."

However, it worked this time. Borges said the changes at halftime made it easier for Auburn to execute, made it easier for the linemen to see who they were supposed to block and how they were supposed to block.

In the first half Alabama's defense was packing the box to stop Auburn's running attack. At the half Ronnie Brown had 26 yards, Carnell Williams 23. They gained about the same number of yards in the second half, but they came at more opportune moments and each scored a touchdown.

The difference was that Jason Campbell started completing some passes and forced Alabama's defenders to move back. With fewer men to block, the offensive line was able to give Campbell better protection.

Although he started slow, Campbell wound up completing 18 of 24 passes for 224 yards and one touchdown. He completed two or more passes to seven different players. One was for 51 yards to Devin Aromshodu to set up Auburn's first touchdown, scored on a five-yard run by Williams. Another was a 32-yard touchdown pass to Courtney Taylor. The final touchdown came on a two-yard run by Brown.

Alabama scored its only touchdown on an 18-yard pass from Spencer Pennington to D.J. Hall with 1:26 remaining in the game.

-30-

Post-game column

Auburn doesn't impress voters in win

(Original version published in The Gadsden Times, Monday, November 22, 2004)

Consistency: that's the key word for winning championships. A team must also be talented and have a lot of luck.

The Auburn Tigers have a lot of talent and they have had a lot of luck. They have had luck of schedule and luck of injuries, to name a couple. But they have not been consistent, at least not when it would really have counted.

Except for the game against LSU, Auburn has jumped on opponents at the beginning and rolled up a big first half score. Even against Tennessee and Georgia, Auburn all but had the game won at halftime.

It has been an impressive season.

The way the Tigers played against Georgia, one of the top teams in the country, they could have probably beaten any college team.

That day, on Nov. 13, Auburn was the best football team in the country. Few people could have argued against a No. 1 rating then.

A week later, on Nov. 20, Auburn wasn't the same football team. The Tigers were sluggish in the first half against Alabama; the offense was out of sync. Alabama's defense was shutting down the running game and timing was off in the passing game.

Auburn was going three-and-out, three-and-out; inconsistent with the way it has played all year. If Alabama had had a good offense, it might have put the game away by the half.

Even Auburn coach Tommy Tuberville said as much.

But the Tide could manage only a field goal in each of the first two quarters for a 6-0 lead.

Just before the half ended, Auburn finally mounted a long drive and the offense got moving, although it did not score.

Jason Campbell told offensive coordinator Al Borges during the break that he had picked up the rhythm and to give him an opportunity to throw the ball downfield and get the Alabama defenders to back out of the box.

He did, and Campbell led the Tigers on long scoring drives the first two times they had the ball. That was the difference in the game -- Auburn finally playing like the team it has been all year.

But in the fourth quarter, this consistency did not continue as each team scored a touchdown and the game ended 21-13. The eight-point margin of victory did not impress the voters.

Auburn remained third in the coaches' poll, dropped from a second-place tie to third in the writers' poll, and will probably still be third when the BCS rankings are announced later today.

Auburn had gotten a lot of attention with its dominating win over Georgia and picked up some votes. It needed another impressive win against Alabama, a team struggling to stay above .500, especially after Oklahoma defeated Baylor 35-0.

Tuberville tried to make a case about the rivalry -- how big it is in Alabama. But it doesn't get a lot of attention in other parts of the country.

He talked about the tradition of this game, and how hard it is to win, regardless of the score. He reminded writers, and anyone else who would listen over the television broadcasts, of the times the games would go down to the wire, and how often the underdog would win.

During the 57 games of this series, there have been upsets and last-second wins; there have also been one-sided victories.

Fifteen times one team has been a decisive favorite, but the other team would go into the game convinced it could pull an upset. Just as the Crimson Tide did Saturday, the underdog would compete at an amazingly high level, demonstrating great courage, playing above its perceived capabilities.

*   *   *   *   *

Auburn coach Tommy Tuberville, left, and the author.

That was what happened Saturday. Spencer Pennington, for example, had his best game. The Alabama defense held the famous duo of Carnell and Ronnie to a combined 96 yards (although each scored a touchdown).

The underdog even led for a half, but the stronger team finally came back to win. Alabama never gave up, competing hard to the end and gained much praise and admiration, not only from the Crimson Tide supporters, but from Auburn fans.

Such games, such gallant performances, have happened before -- at least eight times by Auburn teams; seven times by Alabama, including this year's game.

A few such examples are Auburn in 1964 and 1973, 1981 and 1992. Some gallant efforts but no wins by the Crimson Tide were in 1958, 1970, 1983 and 1997.

This is what Tuberville was talking about. This is the kind of rivalry that doesn't fit into the scheme of things. Those who vote in the polls should take these things into consideration. But they don't. They primarily look at the results, and the record of the opponent.

Tiger quarterback Campbell took another approach. He said that if a team is undefeated, especially if it goes undefeated in the SEC, it should be No. 1.

He said he can't imagine a team going undefeated and winning the SEC championship, not playing for a national title. That has pretty much been the tradition. Remember Alabama, Florida, Tennessee and LSU in recent years?

Georgia was expected to do that this year, and when Auburn beat the Bulldogs badly, the Tigers were expected to jump up in the polls and rankings.

It didn't happen and now it probably won't.

Campbell says he thinks Auburn deserves more credit than it's getting, but that the Tigers can't worry about that.

The SEC Championship Game against Tennessee is coming up. And if Auburn doesn't win that game, it won't matter anyway. However, Auburn can go 12-0, then 13-0 in the Sugar Bowl, which would be something special, regardless of what happens for the Tigers with the BCS bowl committee.

-30-

THE GAME - 2006

By Jimmy Smothers, written in 2011

Auburn gave Alabama the thumb that Saturday night, back in the year of 2006. Yes sir, head coach Tommy Tuberville walked right out on the field in Bryant-Denny Stadium and held up one hand, extending his thumb, along with four fingers.

That thumb was something fans of both teams had been talking about the past year. It signified a fifth straight Auburn win over Alabama; and since Tuberville had held up four fingers the previous year following Auburn's win in Jordan-Hare Stadium, War Eagle fans had been telling their Roll Tide buddies to "Fear the Thumb".

Now the damage had been done, right there in Tuscaloosa. It happened on November 18 in the stadium that Bryant built. Kickoff had been at 2:37, but it was dark when the game ended and Auburn had won, 22-15.

It had not been an easy win, although Auburn had a much better record. In fact, earlier in the year the Tigers had been ranked No. 2 nationally for three weeks, then Arkansas upset the Tigers, 27-10. Auburn dropped out of the Top 10, but had worked its way back to No. 5 before a second loss – this time 15-37 to Georgia.

The Tigers (9-2) had dropped to No. 15 when they rolled into T-town. Alabama (6-5) was struggling to break .500 and earn a bowl bid. It should have been a cakewalk for Auburn, but it wasn't. Alabama gave Auburn a struggle, with the lead switching back and forth. Auburn won in the end, then went to the Cotton Bowl and won again, winding up 11-2, but ranked only No. 9 in the Associated Press poll.

Joe Kines was named interim coach after Mike Shula was dismissed; he made a pitch for the job permanently at the Independence Bowl, where the Tide again played well, but was beaten 34-31, winding up 6-7.

Losing that bowl game didn't compare to what had happened the previous month in Tuscaloosa – a fifth straight loss to Auburn was something that had not happened in half a century. It was something that Alabama's fans had said would never happen again.

After that Saturday's win, Tuberville jogged before the Auburn cheering section and band, waving his orange cap with his right hand and pumping his left arm up and down with four fingers and a thumb extended.

It mattered not that the game could just as easily have gone the other way. This was a game that neither team actually lost, but Auburn just wound up with a few more points. However, it was a win; which gave Auburn fans bragging rights for another year.

-30-

Pre-game column

Despite 1 vs. 2, Tigers-Tide still The Game

(Original version published in The Gadsden Times, Thursday, November 16, 2006)

There is a big football game Saturday that has everyone talking and it isn't Auburn at Alabama. Actually, the huge in-state rivalry between the Tide and Tigers rarely gets much notice outside the state. And this year it is getting even less attention on the national level.

The spotlight game this week is No. 1 Ohio State against No. 2 Michigan. That game is so big this year that I have heard some Auburn and Alabama fans say they were going to install a second television so they could watch both games.

I have considered staying home and doing the same thing. And if the weather is bad Saturday, I just might do that. But this will be my 45th consecutive Auburn-Alabama game to cover for this newspaper and that has a special ring. It will be my 48th game overall, having shot pictures at the game on three occasions for other newspapers before coming to work at The Times.

It would have been nice if I'd kept a scrapbook of my stories and pictures from all those games, but over the years, it was just another day on the job. Now as my career is winding down, every time I go to a game I wonder if it will be the final time to sit in that press box or walk across the field, looking up at the fans in the stands and being up close to the players and coaches.

I remember the first time I covered this game as a young sports writer. I was on cloud nine as I walked up through the stands to the old press box at Legion Field. It wasn't much, but it seemed like paradise to me. I'd grown up reading newspaper articles with that dateline: LEGION FIELD, Birmingham. Back then writers always used the name of the stadium as their dateline, since they were writing from the site. Finally the dream of putting my byline on that dateline was coming true.

That was in 1961 and Alabama won the game, 34-0 en route to a perfect season climaxed by Paul Bryant's first national championship.

There were a lot of great players on the field that day -- Pat Trammell, Billy Neighbors, Lee Roy Jordan, Mike Fracchia and others for Alabama: John McGeever, George Gross, Dave Woodward and others for Auburn. But my heroes that day were the writers covering the game more than the athletes playing it.

The game wasn't as big back then. At that time the big game for Alabama was against Tennessee and for Auburn, it was Georgia Tech. The Georgia game for both teams was about as big.

Games against Georgia and Tennessee are still important, especially to the older generation. But THE GAME of the year is now Auburn and Alabama. This is the game that fans talk about all year long.

It has been said that a team has a successful season if it wins this game, regardless of what happens in the previous games. This is the last game, the bragging rights game, the one that people remember from year to year.

I asked Mike Shula the other day if beating Auburn Saturday would mean this has been a successful season for Alabama, in wake of all the criticism the team has received this fall. He asked me to repeat the question, pondered it a moment, kind of smiled and fielded the next question.

He didn't need to answer. It is obvious that a win Saturday will be huge – not only to Alabama but to Auburn. An Alabama win could be the foundation for stepping up his rebuilding program. It will put the Tide in a bowl game, make the off-season program much easier and enable the team to open next season on a positive note.

Auburn needs the win for a different perspective; it needs to win to keep alive its dominance over Alabama, to stop a downward spiral that seemed to start in last week's loss to Georgia, to go into a bowl game and the off season on a positive note.

Except for the 13-0 season, Tuberville is being labeled as a nine-win coach.

A win Saturday will get him past that.

-30-

Game

Auburn win gives fans a reason to cheer

(Original version published in The Gadsden Times Sunday, November 19, 2006)

TUSCALOOSA -- Auburn gave Alabama the thumb Saturday, but it wasn't easy. The thumb signifies a fifth straight win over the Crimson Tide, something that hasn't happened for the Tigers in half a century. It was something that Alabama fans have said would never happen, that Auburn University's head football coach Tommy

Tuberville would not walk around in Bryant-Denny Stadium with his arm raised, holding up four fingers plus his thumb.

When he held up four fingers before the Auburn students after last year's game in Jordan-Hare Stadium acknowledging a fourth straight win, Alabama people thought it was in poor taste. Auburn fans told their cross-state rivals to "fear the thumb". That has been the focus the past year – thumb or no thumb.

After Saturday's game, which ended 22-15, Tuberville jogged before the Auburn cheering section and band, waving his orange cap with his right hand and pumping his left arm up and down with four fingers and a thumb extended.

Junior defensive end Quentin Groves, who had set up two Auburn touchdowns when he twice sacked Alabama quarterback John Parker Wilson, forcing him to fumble, climbed the ladder in front of the band and directed the music.

This was a night for the Tigers, who have never lost a game in Bryant-Denny Stadium. The win gives the team a 10-2 record and puts the Tigers in line for a big bowl bid. The fifth straight win over Alabama ensures that Auburn dominance of power in this state will continue for at least another year.

Bragging rights, you know. Win this game and the victorious fans can brag for the next year.

It matters not that the game could just as easily have gone the other way. This was a game that neither team actually lost; Auburn just wound up with a few more points.

Each team has its moments; each had the momentum at various times and made the big plays. But each also came up short, turned the ball over, failed to execute and drew penalties.

Alabama once came from behind to take the lead; at times the Tide made big plays and moved the ball; at times it appeared the Tide would win and its fans could get off Mike Shula and his staff.

But in the end, Auburn won; and the Tide had to again endure the disappointment of what might have been.

The game started on an unusual note when the Tigers won the toss and elected to receive. But rather than get a quick go-ahead touchdown, the Tigers punted and Alabama drove downfield making four big plays along the way. But after getting a first and goal from the 3, Auburn's defense rose up and the Tide had to settle for a field goal.

The first quarter ended, 3-0. But on the third play of the second quarter Groves sacked Wilson, forcing the fumble that set up Auburn's first touchdown, which Brad Lester scored from the 12.

On second down after the kick, Groves repeated the play. This time Auburn got the ball at the 8 and Kenny Irons scored on the next play.

Auburn missed a scoring opportunity just before the half, and Alabama made a huge play, with Wilson completing a 52-yard touchdown pass to Nikita Stover. That gave the Tide the momentum going in at the half.

Alabama came out, took the second half kick and drove 80 yards for a go-ahead touchdown, 15-14. Auburn finally got its offense going again late in the third quarter, as Brandon Cox completed passes for 32 and 22 yards in a four-play, 54-yard drive. The last pass was to Prechae Rodriguez for 22 yards and a touchdown, winding up the scoring at 22-15.

At one point in the fourth quarter Auburn lost a fumble that could have cost the game; but on the next play Alabama fumbled it back following a completed pass.

Auburn also needed a defensive stand with five minutes remaining.

Alabama had moved down field and wound up with a first down at the 14. Auburn's defense held, making a big play defending a pass into the end zone on third down. And on fourth down it made an even bigger play on another pass, taking over on downs.

After that, Auburn held on for the win. It doesn't erase the bitter loss to Arkansas early in the season, or the recent loss to Georgia. Even with 10 wins, there have been disappointments for Auburn; and some will say the team did not live up to expectations.

Auburn had been expected to win the SEC, but didn't make the Championship Game. But a win in this game is always a big win. And it doesn't matter what happened before. On this night Auburn defeated Alabama, for a school record-tying fifth straight time. And today, that's all that matters to Auburn people.

The Alabama family must again wait 'till next year.

Although the Tide played well at times, and had a chance to win the game, as has been the case several times, again it didn't happen. So the Tide winds up 6-6, a couple of wins below expectations. Now even a bowl game doesn't appear likely, although the players would like to get one.

-30-

Sidebar

Auburn gets super win

(Original version published in The Gadsden Times, Sunday, November 19, 2006)

TUSCALOOSA – It was a super win, Auburn's 22-15 defeat of Alabama Saturday. That's what Auburn coach Tommy Tuberville said after the game.

It is a super win for the Auburn football program, which has now defeated Alabama five years in a row. The only other time that has happened was 50 years ago, 1954-58.

It was a super win for Auburn fans, who will now be bragging about it all next year.

"People talk about that," Tuberville said, referring to 'fear the thumb', when someone mentioned it to him after the game. "But I'm more excited about four straight wins on the road. That's huge."

He was referring to four straight wins for Auburn at Tuscaloosa, beginning with the 2000 game. If you go back to the 19th century, it's six. Auburn first beat Alabama here in 1895 and again in 1901.

"We knew coming over here it was going to be a dogfight, we knew we were going to have to do a lot of things," Tuberville said. "Our players stayed together and played as a team, we weren't fancy."

Auburn went into the game with star receiver Courtney Taylor and starting fullback Mike McLaughin sidelined. Both were hurt in practice last week.

Tuberville said it has become well known in recent weeks, that Auburn is not a great football team.

"We were put on a pedestal early in the year, we fought hard and kept our heads above water," the coach said.

Auburn came into the game wanting to establish the running game, which Tuberville said it did although it netted only 124 yards rushing. Kenny Irons gained 85 of those on 19 carries. The first two touchdowns were by runs, 12 yards by Brad Lester, eight yards by Irons.

"We didn't have a lot of style points, but when you play good defense and you cause turnovers, you have a chance. That is the way we have played all year."

Tuberville said Alabama played tough and played hard.

"They are well coached and they schemed us a little bit," he added. "They tricked us early on the first drive and had us a little bit confused. I made a stupid call on the blitz right before halftime. We just took a chance, but we probably shouldn't have."

Alabama scored on a long pass to pull within five points, 9-14, at intermission.

In the second half Alabama gained a 15-14 lead on the opening series and held it until just before the third quarter ended.

Tuberville said Alabama's defense came back in the second half and confused Auburn quarterback Brandon Cox, putting guys in his face on certain plays and forcing him to throw quickly.

"We figured they would blitz, and they did," he said.

On what proved to be the winning touchdown, a 22-yard pass to Prechae Rodriguez, Alabama pressured Cox, but Rodriguez is a big receiver who made the catch.

Tuberville said that was a good call by Al Borges, the offensive coordinator.

Alabama coach Mike Shula said this has not been the script that he wanted the Tide to follow this year. He talked about what might have been if Alabama had done things differently against Arkansas, Florida and Tennessee.

"There is a lot of accountability and it starts with the head coach," he said. "Then the assistants, then the players."

Auburn quarterback Brandon Cox said he believes that Auburn came out with too much emotion. "We just needed to slow down and relax," he said. "Sometimes games like this are more mental than physical. I think we were just too fired up."

Alabama quarterback John Parker Wilson said, "We had good chances, we had some good play calls. It gave us the chance to put the lead up and set the tone of the game. We just couldn't execute, we couldn't make the plays when we had to."

The thing that would have made a difference for Alabama, Wilson said, would have been not to turn the ball over.

"The turnovers were what hurt us. That was the big thing," he said.

Alabama lost three fumbles and had one pass intercepted. Auburn lost one fumble and did not have a pass intercepted.   -30-

Post-game column

Tide season not all bleak news

(Original version published in The Gadsden Times, Monday, November 20, 2006)

The aftermath of yet another Auburn win over Alabama isn't pretty for Crimson Tiders. Things turned ugly in Bryant-Denny Stadium after the game as Alabama fans cursed and threw things at the Auburn players as they left the field.

It was just a game, and the world keeps on turning. Despite the loss, dawn came Sunday; and a new week began today.

The Monday Morning quarterbacks are holding council, pondering what can be done to get the Tide back on top. The onslaught began on Internet chat rooms shortly after the game ended last Saturday afternoon. It will continue on talk radio later today.

It is understandable that Alabama fans are disappointed. They aren't used to going 6-6; they don't like losing to any team, especially to Auburn. They feel it's a disgrace being at the end of the line when bowl bids are handed out, and not even sure of getting one at that.

Alabama, once the bowlingest team in the country, may stay home this year while Kentucky is playing in a gala post-season event.

Alabama, once among the nation's elite and annually competing for championships, is now an also-ran.

Sure, it hurt losing to Auburn Saturday night; it hurts losing any game. But it isn't as bad as it may seem. With the exception of Mississippi State, Alabama won every game it was supposed to win this season. And it played well enough to win the other ones.

Going into the season, it appeared Alabama would be favored in six games, be the underdog in four, and that two games would be up for grabs.

An 8-4 season would be a plus, but 7-5 was more likely. The 24-16 loss to Mississippi State was the spoiler, not the 22-15 loss to Auburn.

Tide Coach Mike Shula said after the Auburn game that finishing 6-6 was not the script he had for this season, that it was not the script he had for the seniors.

"Who knows what our season could have been like if we had done some things different in the Arkansas game, if we had done a couple of things different with the lead against Florida, and against Tennessee in the fourth quarter? We played a lot of new starters this year, young starters who aren't quite there yet. We want to get this team where we are playing with a lot of redshirt seniors and redshirt juniors."

Shula spent a long time talking to his players after the game Saturday night before showing up in the interview room. It was a tough loss and there were things that needed to be said.

He told the underclassmen how the seniors had come to Alabama at a time when a lot of players didn't want to be there. They could have gone elsewhere, but they loved Alabama, and signed with the Tide although they knew there would be some tough times. Shula says they should be appreciated for what they have done; and now it is time for those who are returning to get things picked up.

He promised to evaluate everything -- the offense, defense and recruiting; the head coach, assistant coaches and the players.

"We want to get through this together, we've got to make sure we do everything we can possibly do coaching the players," he said.

Shula seemed to understand the situation; now he needs to come up with a solution. I don't think it should be based on any one game -- not the loss to Mississippi State and certainly not to Auburn. But the overall picture should be taken into accountability.

Alabama did not play well against the minor opponents, but it won.

Alabama played well for most of the time against the major opponents, but failed to win. Missed field goals were the difference at Arkansas, and that can't be blamed on the coach. The team seemed to wear down in the fourth quarter at Florida, and a lack of depth isn't the coach's fault, either.

There was a three-point loss to heavily favored Tennessee, a game the Tide could and probably should have won. Then the 14-28 loss to LSU, which may have been Bama's best game of the year, especially during the last three quarters.

That performance, plus the way Auburn had folded against Georgia, was what gave Tide fans hopes of winning this final game. But the game against Auburn turned out to be like the season has been -- one of close losses, near misses and bad breaks.

Another coaching staff may have done better; but who knows; this coaching staff may have done better with more players. After all, it won 10 games the previous year and the fans were elated.

I don't know what changes, if any, will be made at Alabama. But I think Shula should be given another year to see if things begin to come together. And I think it only fair that he should have a free hand in picking his supporting staff. After all, his future at Alabama is at stake, so he should have the assistants he believes can make it happen.

-30-

Photo courtesy of Brad Green, Bryant Museum

Alabama celebrates 36-0 win over Auburn in 2008, snapping Auburn's six-game winning streak.

THE GAMES - My Final Two

By Jimmy Smothers, written in 2011

At Auburn (2005)

The game had ended and post-game interviews were winding down. Auburn had just beaten Alabama for the fourth time in as many years. Noise of celebrating War Eagle fans filtering into the interview room under the south end zone stands was beginning to fade. But I lingered a little while longer, wanting to get a long look around the room, taking in the scene and the odor, making sure I would remember this setting.

Once back outside, as I started the long walk back across the field, I repeated the gesture. Before moving on to the sideline and climbing up through the stands to the elevator, which would take me to the press box, I stopped at about the 20-yard line, right in front of the goal post, and slowly surveyed the surroundings.

Jordan-Hare Stadium was empty now, the fans having moved uptown to Toomer's Corner to continue their celebrating. The game had started in daytime, but it was now dark. A few stadium lights were on, giving this huge sports facility a feeling of loneliness. The scoreboard was still lit, beaming the score -- Auburn 28, Alabama 18. There was also a glow of light from the press box high up in the stands where other writers were at work finishing their stories.

I stood there, taking it all in before moving on to the press box to write my column and sidebar for the next day's edition of my newspaper. Someone else was now writing the game story.

Although I didn't realize it then, it turned out to be the last time I would ever cover an Alabama-Auburn football game in this stadium. That night, for whatever reason, I just felt a desire to not only take a special look at the scene, but to have it become ingrained in my memory.

During my long career as a newspaper man I covered 48 of these games, most of them in storied Legion Field. The series went to home-and-home in 1989, with 2005 being the eighth time the Crimson Tide had played on the Plain. Alabama did not take its "home game" in the series to Tuscaloosa until 2000.

I remember all of THE GAMES I covered, beginning with my first as a photographer for The Anniston Star back in the mid-50s. But standing alone on the field in that empty stadium that night is vivid; and has proven to be one of the special memories of my career.

Cliff Hare Stadium (circa 1970) before the name change to Jordan-Hare Stadium and the expansion to 87,451 seating capacity.

At Alabama (2006)

Going into this game I knew it would be a final time for me to cover a football game at Bryant-Denny Stadium. I had informed my executive editor that I was retiring at the end of the year, but would continue working through the bowl season. Plans were made for me to cover Alabama in the Independence Bowl, then drive on out to Dallas and cover Auburn in the Cotton Bowl.

I was to also cover select games in the 2007 season, continuing to travel with Huntsville Times Sports Editor John Pruett, who would retire after that season. But the Alabama-at-Auburn game was not on my travel agenda. I planned to watch it on television at home and write a Sunday column and Monday follow-up article.

For the 2006 game I went to the stadium early, as usual. I wanted to take in everything, knowing this would be my final time to cover a game at Bryant-Denny Stadium. As it turned out, it was also the last game that Mike Shula would coach at Alabama; but at the time writers didn't know he would be dismissed within days. I'm glad it wasn't announced before the game, as had been the case with Pat Dye (Auburn) and Bebes Stallings (Alabama) during previous years.

Looking back, I wonder if he would have been fired if Alabama had beaten Auburn that night. Probably, although he was making progress in re-establishing the team following severe NCAA probations.

Working space in Alabama's press box is limited and writers are squeezed in elbow to elbow. But that night I hardly noticed. This was to be my finale and I wasn't about to leave with memories that included anything negative. I stocked up on bags of parched peanuts and settled in.

This was a typical Auburn-Alabama game, hard-fought with the lead switching back and forth. I was thinking at the time it was probably the best Alabama had played all fall, yet in the end Auburn won the game, 22-15, and afterwards coach Tommy Tuberville celebrated by giving Alabama the thumb. Actually, he held up one hand, with four fingers and a thumb extended, indicating five straight wins over Alabama.

Alabama fans retaliated by shouting derogatory remarks and throwing things. But I don't think about that. My memories are of all those exciting games, last-second wins and unusual victories; yet I never considered myself a fan -- I never pulled for either team. There is a rule: "No cheering in the press box".

That night, although the home team lost and the stadium emptied quickly, the small number of Auburn fans cheered loudly, but briefly, before leaving the grounds. As usual, at these games, I went to the interviews with the coaches and the winning team's players. The visiting team's locker room at Bryant-Denny was on the southwest corner, so there was no need to get on the field going back to the press box.

I just walked back to the elevator, rode up to the press box, wrote my final story from that location and left. I never looked back, but my mind was filled with memories – good memories. And today, as I recalled all the games I've covered at that locale, the words that most come to mind are from Bob Hope – "Thanks for the memories."

-30-

Photo courtesy Brad Green, Bryant Museum

Bryant-Denny Stadium circa 2006, seating 101,821 fans.

Epilogue

Early in my career I started to write a book, and then I got bogged down with my regular job and put it aside. Actually, I did that three times. I always figured that when I retired I'd have plenty of time on my hands and I'd be able to get out the old manuscripts and complete the task.

It didn't happen. I discovered that this adage is true -- if you have something that needs to be done, do it before you retire, because after you retire you won't have time.

Fortunately, modern technology has changed that way of thinking, and my friend Ben Barnes came along with the knowledge to put it to use. Bingo! I have my first book, with assists from an old engineer, web search engines and archives, a self-publishing web site, and the Gadsden Public Library.

This book is a combination of past and present. Most chapters include articles written during a particular year and about a particular game. There are 20 of those game chapters, four from each of the decades in my career. Each of those game chapters is led off with an article I wrote especially for this book, as I looked back over the years at that game. Some of this has not been written previously, while some of it is being presented here from a different perspective.

I had forgotten many of the incidents, the players and interviews, but as I read my stories again, for the first time in years, the things that came back to mind were interesting and exciting.

They took me back in time; put me back in the press boxes, on the sidelines, in the locker rooms, visiting with coaches and players. Suddenly, I remembered being at those games, hearing the crowds and the bands, smelling the aromas, seeing the cheerleaders, watching the action, and writing on deadline while munching parched peanuts.

I hope you, too, were carried back to the sights and sounds of those games as you read the articles, just as they were written those many years ago in the press boxes at Legion Field, Bryant-Denny, and Jordan-Hare stadiums.

Some of the things you may have remembered, some you may not. But they are all about Alabama and Auburn football, all about what I call THE GAME, what many fans today call the Iron Bowl. Whatever you might call it, thanks for being so interested in it.

Finis

By Rick Bragg

One of these days, probably a long, long time from now, Jimmy Smothers will tap the last period on the last sentence of the last story, column or chapter he writes, and an era will come to a close in Southern journalism. But I cannot picture it in my mind. My imagination is pretty good, but I cannot imagine that.

For as long as I have been able to read, Mr. Smothers has been covering the lives, deaths, hopes, dreams, heartaches, tragedies, victories, defeats and pride of my Alabama, usually in stories linked to sports but always about life.

"I guess we thought we were doing something important," he told me the other day.

I reckon so.

If you ask him his proudest moment, at his Gadsden Times or anywhere else in his writing life, he does not start waxing poetic on this great Alabama-Auburn game, this great race at Talladega or a big story about this or that legend. He does not tell you how the hundred thousand fans roared.

He tells you about the day he wrote five stories in one day, about youth tennis, golf, a boat racer, little league baseball, and a high school football game under the lights. Mr. Smother knew what was really important,

"If I didn't have a byline every day," he said, "I didn't think I was doing my job."

He did not believe in saving up words. He believed in spending them, one drop of ink at a time.

"I like to write," he said, "and sports was all I ever knew."

In more than 50 years of it, he earned a reputation as a professional and a gentleman, who served his readers first, and somehow still managed to hold the respect of the people he wrote about.

And he had a good time doing it. "I saw things and went places a kid from Sand Mountain might not have seen. You didn't do it for the money. My wife asked me once when I was going to get a real job. I said, `Let me do it for five years…'"

-30-

OVERTIME

A Couple of Other Things	232
A Few Facts and Figures	233
Scoring Values	233
History in Intervals	234
The Missing Forty Years	235
Rubber Matches	237
Series Results	238

A Couple of Other Things, etc.

There are some other things that I would have liked to mention but I have run out of both time and space. I will, however, touch on a couple of them briefly.

One was in 1968 when Auburn's senior quarterback Loran Carter and junior center Tom Banks were having trouble with the snap exchange. This was Banks' first year to start and he and Carter just couldn't seem to get their timing down.

The possibility of turnovers was of great concern to Auburn coach Ralph Jordan going into the Alabama game that year. I remember writing a little advice column, suggesting Auburn athletic officials should ask the NCAA to allow Carter to call for a "fair catch" on the snap from Banks, thus eliminating the possibility of losing the ball on a fumble. This would allow the game to continue in a timely fashion.

Another thing I wish I had written more about was the transitions sports information directors had to go through when schools changed head coaches. This is a major function that the general public knows little about because the public relations people work primarily behind the scene. Yet what they do has a tremendous impact on the image of athletic programs.

David Housel saw five head football coaching changes while employed as the sports information director or athletic director at Auburn. The most traumatic may have been when Pat Dye announced his resignation the night before the Auburn-Alabama game in 1992.

Larry White went through the same number of changes at Alabama. He, too, had a dramatic experience at the Auburn-Alabama game in 1996 when Gene Stallings announced his resignation.

White said he had been informed earlier that week that Stallings would announce his resignation after the game, but he was to keep it under wraps. Naturally, word leaked out and after the pre-game TV broadcast, one of the announcers asked White if it was so.

"I can't comment on that," he told them. But pretty soon, word had spread throughout the press box and all the writers were bombarding White with questions. This was a night game, the writers were on a tight deadline, and White knew there would be little time for them to write after the game. So at halftime, he told the Alabama writers and a few national writers, they could expect a "major announcement" from Stallings after the game.

I remember spending most of the second half of the game writing background on Stallings. I then topped it off with a few words from him after the game; following the same routine as most of the other writers. Ben Thomas, another member of the Times staff, wrote the game story.

White said, although it was a shocking story, especially coming after that game, that isn't what stands out most in his mind.

"I remember after the game, when all the interviews were over and the players and media had left the locker room that Coach Stallings stepped outside. There was his son, John Mark, waiting with the security people. Coach took the little guy in his arms and gave him a huge hug. That was the most poignant scene that I ever saw," White recalls.

A Few Facts and Figures

The series originated on February 22, 1893, Auburn won that game, 32-22; but Alabama now leads the series, 40-34-1.

The largest victory was on December 4, 1948, when Alabama won 55-0. That was the first time the teams had played in 41 years.

The most points scored were 55 by Alabama, in that 1948 game. The most points scored by Auburn were 53, in a 53-5 win on November 17, 1900.

The most points scored in a single game by both teams were 75, when Auburn defeated Alabama 49-26 on November 29, 1969.

The lowest scoring game was played on November 26, 1960, when Alabama won, 3-0.

The longest win streaks: Alabama 9 (1973-1981); Auburn 6 (2002-2007)

JS

Scoring Values

Seasons	Touchdown	Field Goal	Extra Pt(s)	Safety
1889 – 1897	4 points	5 points	2 points	2 points
1898 – 1903	5 points	5 points	1 point	2 points
1904 – 1908	5 points	4 points	1 point	2 points
1909 – 1911	5 points	3 points	1 point	2 points
1912 – 1957	6 points	3 points	1 point	2 points
1958 – 2011	6 points	3 points	1 pt or 2 pts	2 points

History of THE GAME
Divided into Arbitrary Intervals

INTERVAL	AUBURN WINS	BAMA WINS	TIES
Early Years, 1892-1907	7	4	1
Renewal, before Shug or Bear, 1948-1950	1	2	0
Shug before Bear, 1951-1957	4	3	0
Bear vs. Shug, 1958-1975	5	13	0
Bear after Shug, 1976-1982	1	6	0
Rest of 20th century, 1983-1999	8	9	0
Beginning of 21st, 2000-2010	8	3	0
TOTALS	34	40	1

Auburn's most successful intervals as they are defined above have been the earliest and the most recent - here in the 21st century and the period including the 19th-century games.

The most one-sided interval above (6-1, .857) was when Bryant faced Auburn coaches other than Jordan.

Coach Bryant's 25-year tenure at Alabama (19-6, .760) gave the Tide the series overall lead for the first time and is responsible for their current lead in the series.

Coach Jordan was the most successful against Coach Bryant of any coach who faced Bryant at least 10 times (5-13, .278). His five wins against the master coach kept the overall series reasonably close.

Coach Tuberville (7-3, .700) has been Auburn's most successful coach in the series over a sustained period. Coach Dye was once 6-3 but finished 6-6. Coach Jordan was once 5-3 but finished 9-16.

BBB

The Missing Forty Years

For forty seasons, 1908-1947, the Alabama-Auburn football series was interrupted.

One is led to wonder and speculate what might have happened had the two teams actually played THE GAME during that interval, and suggested here is a method of approximating what we missed (or more accurately, what our grandfathers and great-grandfathers missed).

Tabulated on the following page are the win-loss-tie records for each team during the hiatus years. There were only 38 installments of THE GAME missed during those forty years, for there were two years when one or both schools did not field teams, once during World War One, once during World War Two.

The method proposed here is comparison of the season records for each year. If one team's wins exceeded the other's by two or more in any year, then the first team is deemed to have been the favorite to win THE GAME that year, had it been played. That ignores possible upsets, but the assumption is that the upsets would even out.

If, on the other hand, the teams differ in total wins by only one, or if their wins are equal, the game is assumed to be even, a toss-up. The assumption is that the two teams would equally split these "even" games.

These formulas have been applied in the table on the following page, and of the 38 missing games, 14 are deemed even, Alabama is deemed the favorite 19 times, and Auburn five.

So the conclusion of this admittedly speculative exercise is that if those 38 games had been played, Alabama would have won 26 of them, and Auburn only 12.

This is not too surprising, for beginning in the 1920s and lasting until the 1940s, Alabama led the emergence of Southern college football into a competitive level nationally. During that interval, the Crimson Tide was invited to the Rose Bowl six times, following the seasons of 1925, 1926, 1930, 1934, 1937, and 1945.

BBB

Hiatus Year	Alabama Record	Auburn Record	Speculative Favorite
1908	6-1-1	6-1	Even
1909	5-1-2	5-2	Even
1910	4-4	6-1	Auburn
1911	5-2-2	4-2-1	Even
1912	5-3-1	6-1-1	Even
1913	6-3	8-0	Auburn
1914	5-4	8-0-1	Auburn
1915	6-2	6-2	Even
1916	6-3	6-2	Even
1917	5-2-1	6-2-1	Even
1918	WW I	2-5	No Game
1919	8-1	8-1	Even
1920	10-1	7-2	Alabama
1921	5-4-2	5-3	Even
1922	6-3-1	8-2	Auburn
1923	7-2-1	3-3-3	Alabama
1924	8-1	4-4-1	Alabama
1925	10-0	5-3-1	Alabama
1926	9-0-1	5-4	Alabama
1927	5-4-1	0-7-2	Alabama
1928	6-3	1-8	Alabama
1929	6-3	2-7	Alabama
1930	10-0	3-7	Alabama
1931	9-1	5-3-1	Alabama
1932	8-2	9-0-1	Even
1933	7-1-1	5-5	Alabama
1934	10-0	2-8	Alabama
1935	6-2-1	8-2	Auburn
1936	8-0-1	7-2-2	Even
1937	9-1	6-2-3	Alabama
1938	7-1-1	4-5-1	Alabama
1939	5-3-1	5-5-1	Even
1940	7-2	6-4-1	Even
1941	9-2	4-5-1	Alabama
1942	8-3	6-4-1	Alabama
1943	WW II	WW II	No Game
1944	5-2-2	4-4	Even
1945	10-0	5-5	Alabama
1946	7-4	4-6	Alabama
1947	8-3	2-7	Alabama

THE GAME, RUBBER MATCHES: 1893, 1953, 1955, 1963, 1965

AUBURN WON FEB 1893 "RUBBER" GAME TO GO AHEAD 1-0

AUBURN LED SERIES 1893-1951
LARGEST MARGINS WERE 5 GAMES
6-1 AFTER 1902 GAME
7-2 AFTER 1904 GAME

ALABAMA PULLED EVEN AT 8-8-1 BY WINNING IN 1952

ALABAMA WON 1953 RUBBER GAME TO GO AHEAD 9-8-1

AUBURN PULLED EVEN AT 9-9-1 BY WINNING IN 1954

AUBURN WON 1955 RUBBER GAME TO GO AHEAD 10-9-1

AUBURN LED SERIES 1955-1961
LARGEST MARGIN WAS 4 GAMES
13-9-1 AFTER 1958 GAME

ALABAMA PULLED EVEN AT 13-13-1 BY WINNING IN 1962

AUBURN WON 1963 RUBBER GAME TO GO AHEAD 14-13-1

ALABAMA PULLED EVEN AT 14-14-1 BY WINNING IN 1964

ALABAMA WON 1965 RUBBER GAME TO GO AHEAD 15-14-1

ALABAMA HAS LED SERIES 1965-2011
LARGEST MARGINS WERE 11 GAMES
28-17-1 AFTER 1981 GAME
30-19-1 AFTER 1985 GAME
37-26-1 AFTER 1999 GAME
38-27-1 AFTER 2001 GAME

TUBERVILLE MADE UP 5 GAMES, GOING 6-1 2002-2008

MARGIN IS SIX GAMES AFTER 2010 GAME, 40-34-1

SERIES HAS BEEN GOING ON INTERMITTENTLY FOR 118 YEARS;
DURING FIRST 70 YEARS, ALABAMA LED FOR ONLY ONE YEAR, AFTER 1953 GAME;
DURING LAST 48 YEARS, AUBURN HAS NOT LED AT ALL.

BBB

THE GAME - Dates, Winners, Scores, Locations

DATE	WINNER	SCORE	SITE
Feb. 22, 1893	Auburn	32-22	Birmingham
Nov. 30, 1893	Auburn	40-16	Montgomery
Nov. 29, 1894	Alabama	18-0	Montgomery
Nov. 23, 1895	Auburn	48-0	Tuscaloosa
Nov. 17, 1900	Auburn	53-5	Montgomery
Nov. 15, 1901	Auburn	17-0	Tuscaloosa
Oct. 18, 1902	Auburn	23-0	Birmingham
Oct. 23, 1903	Alabama	18-6	Montgomery
Nov. 12, 1904	Auburn	29-5	Birmingham
Nov. 18, 1905	Alabama	30-0	Birmingham
Nov. 17, 1906	Alabama	10-0	Birmingham
Nov. 16, 1907	Tie	6-6	Birmingham

BEGIN MODERN SERIES

DATE	WINNER	SCORE	SITE
Dec. 4, 1948	Alabama	55-0	Birmingham
Dec. 3, 1949	Auburn	14-13	Birmingham
Dec. 2, 1950	Alabama	34-0	Birmingham
Dec. 1, 1951	Alabama	25-7	Birmingham
Nov. 29, 1952	Alabama	21-0	Birmingham
Nov. 28, 1953	Alabama	10-7	Birmingham
Nov. 27, 1954	Auburn	28-0	Birmingham
Nov. 26, 1955	Auburn	26-0	Birmingham
Dec. 1, 1956	Auburn	34-7	Birmingham
Nov. 30, 1957	Auburn	40-0	Birmingham
Nov. 29, 1958	Auburn	14-8	Birmingham
Nov. 28, 1959	Alabama	10-0	Birmingham
Nov. 26, 1960	Alabama	3-0	Birmingham
Dec. 2, 1961	Alabama	34-0	Birmingham
Dec. 1, 1962	Alabama	38-0	Birmingham
Nov. 30, 1963	Auburn	10-8	Birmingham
Nov. 26, 1964	Alabama	21-14	Birmingham
Nov. 27, 1965	Alabama	30-3	Birmingham
Dec. 3, 1966	Alabama	31-0	Birmingham
Dec. 2, 1967	Alabama	7-3	Birmingham

Date	Winner	Score	Location
Dec. 3, 1968	Alabama	24-16	Birmingham
Nov. 29, 1969	Auburn	49-26	Birmingham
Nov. 28, 1970	Auburn	33-28	Birmingham
Nov. 27, 1971	Alabama	31-7	Birmingham
Dec. 2, 1972	Auburn	17-16	Birmingham
Dec. 1, 1973	Alabama	35-0	Birmingham
Nov. 29, 1974	Alabama	17-13	Birmingham
Nov. 29, 1975	Alabama	28-0	Birmingham
Nov. 27, 1976	Alabama	38-7	Birmingham
Nov. 26, 1977	Alabama	48-21	Birmingham
Dec. 2, 1978	Alabama	34-16	Birmingham
Dec. 1, 1979	Alabama	25-18	Birmingham
Nov. 29, 1980	Alabama	34-18	Birmingham
Nov. 28, 1981	Alabama	28-17	Birmingham
Nov. 27, 1982	Auburn	23-22	Birmingham
Dec. 3, 1983	Auburn	23-20	Birmingham
Dec. 1, 1984	Alabama	17-15	Birmingham
Nov. 30, 1985	Alabama	25-23	Birmingham
Nov. 29, 1986	Auburn	21-17	Birmingham
Nov. 27, 1987	Auburn	10-0	Birmingham
Nov. 25, 1988	Auburn	15-10	Birmingham
Dec. 2, 1989	Auburn	30-20	Auburn
Dec. 1, 1990	Alabama	16-7	Birmingham
Nov. 30, 1991	Alabama	13-6	Birmingham
Nov. 26, 1992	Alabama	17-0	Birmingham
Nov. 20, 1993	Auburn	22-14	Auburn
Nov. 19, 1994	Alabama	21-14	Birmingham
Nov. 18, 1995	Auburn	31-27	Auburn
Nov. 23, 1996	Alabama	24-23	Birmingham
Nov. 22, 1997	Auburn	18-17	Auburn
Nov. 21, 1998	Alabama	31-17	Birmingham
Nov. 20, 1999	Alabama	28-17	Auburn
Nov. 18, 2000	Auburn	9-0	Tuscaloosa
Nov. 19, 2001	Alabama	31-7	Auburn
Nov. 23, 2002	Auburn	17-7	Tuscaloosa
Nov. 22, 2003	Auburn	28-23	Auburn
Nov. 22, 2004	Auburn	21-13	Tuscaloosa
Nov. 20, 2005	Auburn	28-18	Auburn

Nov. 18, 2006	Auburn	22-15	Tuscaloosa
Nov. 17, 2007	Auburn	17-10	Auburn
Nov. 18, 2008	Alabama	36-0	Tuscaloosa
Nov. 27, 2009	Alabama	26-21	Auburn
Nov. 26, 2010	Auburn	28-27	Tuscaloosa

In the 21st century, Auburn leads 8-3.

In the 19th century, Auburn won 3-1.

Alabama won the 20th century 36-23-1, with Coach Bryant's 19-6 record providing the margin.

For games played in Tuscaloosa, Auburn leads 7-1.

For games played in Auburn, Auburn leads 7-3.

For games played in Montgomery, the teams are 2-2.

For games played in Birmingham, Alabama leads 34-18-1.

Six of the 75 games have been decided by one point. Auburn won five.

23 of the 75 games, almost one-third, have been shutouts, 15 by Alabama.

Alabama has entered THE GAME undefeated 13 times in the modern series, since 1948 (61, 64, 66, 71, 72, 73, 74, 79, 89, 92, 94, 08, 09). Eleven of those times Alabama won THE GAME. Auburn won in 72 and 89.

Auburn has entered THE GAME undefeated seven times since renewal in 1948 (57, 58, 71, 93, 94, 04, 10). Five of those times Auburn has won THE GAME. Alabama won in 71 and 94.

Only in 1971 did both Alabama and Auburn enter THE GAME undefeated.

**Alabama center and linebacker (1960-62) Lee Roy Jordan,
No. 6 pick in 1963 NFL draft.**

Listing of Names

On the next few pages is a partial listing of the names appearing in this book. For each individual listed, the chapter where the primary reference to him appears is given. That is not necessarily the only reference to him in the book, but the one deemed most significant. For instance, consider the listings for quarterbacks Joe Namath and Patrick Nix. Namath was the Alabama starting QB for both the 1963 and 1964 games, but played much better in 1964. Therefore, 1964 is given as the chapter location for the primary reference to Namath. In similar fashion, Auburn QB Nix appeared in both the 1993 and 1995 games, but his 1993 performance was more dramatic and spectacular, so 1993 is the reference given for Nix. As another example, coaches Ralph Jordan and Paul Bryant appear numerous times in the book, but the chapter location given for each of them is his respective "Final Whistle" chapter.

Alexander, Shaun	1999	Davis, Stephen	1995
Alred, John	1981	Davis, Steve	1966
Aromashodu, Devin	2004	Davis, Terry	1973
		Davidson, Buddy	Halftime
Bailey, Greg	Final Whistle	Denny, George	Halftime
Baker, Robert	1995	Dooley, Vince	1966
Banks, Tom	Halftime	Dorsey, Charley	1995
Barfield, Doug	1979	Draper, Shawn	1999
Barker, Jay	1992	DuBose, Mike	1999
Barnes, Ben	Halftime	Duncan, Johnny	1966
Barnes, Wiley	1979	Duncan, L. N.	Halftime
Beard, Santonio	2002	Dunnavant, Keith	1966
Beasley, Fred	1995	Duval, Damon	2000
Beasley, Terry	1971	Dyas, Ed	1964
Beck, Dave	1972	Dye, Pat	1992
Bellew, Ronny	1982		
Bendross, Jesse	1982	Eagles, Tommy Joe	1992
Bernich, Ken	1972	Elmore, Grady	1964
Bethune, Bobby	Halftime	Evans, Heath	1999
Beverly, David	1971	Flynt, Wayne	1993
Billingsley, Randy	1973	Ford, Mike	1966
Bisceglia, Steve	1972	Fracchia, Mike	2006
Blackburn, Darrell	1995	Franchione, Dennis	2000
Borges, Al	2004	Franklin, Byron	1979
Bostic, James	1989	Frederickson, Tucker	1964
Bostick, Brian	2004	Freeman, Wayne	1964
Bowden, Terry	1993	French, Buddy	1963
Brackett, M.L.	Halftime	Fulghum, Robert	1989
Brooks, James	1979	Fuller, Andy	1995
Brown, Curtis	1995	Fuller, Rusty	1972
Brown, Ronnie	2004	Fullwood, Brent	1984
Bryan, Jimmy	Prologue		
Bryan, Tom	1966	Gafford, Monk	1963
Bryant, Paul	Final Whistle	Gandy, Wayne	1993
Bunch, Jim	1973	Gantt, Greg	1972
Burgdorf, Brian	1993	Giffin, Al	1967
Burkett, Jackie	Halftime	Gilmer, Creed	1964
Butler, Chris	2002	Gray, Andy	1981
Butler, Harry	Halftime	Griffith, Doc	1963
		Gross, Gerald	2006
Cahill, Tom	1966	Groves, Quentin	2006
Campbell, Jason	2004		
Campbell, Randy	1983	Hall, D.J.	2004
Carlson, Norm	Halftime	Hall, Lemanski	1993
Carter, Loran	1967	Hall, Mike	1967
Castille, Jeremiah	1982	Hall, Wayne	1993
Castile, Tim	2004	Hannah, David	1979
Chatwood, David	1966	Hannah, John	1973
Chizik, Gene	Halftime	Hardy, Ken	1979
Childs, Bob	1967	Harris, Jim Bob	1979
Christian, Tim	1967	Hayes, Bobby	1963
Clayton, Chuck	1981	Henley, Terry	1972
Cochran, John	Halftime	Holtzclaw, Johnny	Halftime
Cody, Bill	1963	Hood, Roderick	2002
Cole, Richard	Halftime	Homan, Dennis	1966
Cooley, Jon	1995	Housel, David	2002
Cox, Brandon	2006	Houston, Martin	1992
Crane, Paul	1964	Hudson, Ray	2004
Cribbs, Joe	1979	Hurston, Chuck	1963
Crowe, Jack	1985	Hurston, Dwight	1967
Croyle, Brodie	2002	Hyatt, Freddie	1967
Croyle, John	1973		
Cubelic, Cole	2000	Ingram, Mark	2009 & 2010
Currier, Mike	1967	Irons, Kenny	2006
Curry, Bill	1989		
		Jackson, Bo	1982
Daniels, Ronney	1999	Jackson, Wilbur	1971
Danley, Stacy	1989	James, Lionel	1981
Davis, Bill	1972	Jelks, Gene	1985
Davis, Paul	Halftime	Jett, Gardner	1972

Name	Year		Name	Year
Jilleba, Pete	1967		Neighbors, Billy	2006
Johnson, Brandon	2002		Nelson, Benny	1963
Johnson, Lyndon	1992		Newton, Bill	1972
Johnson, Robert	2002		Newton, Cam	2009 & 2010
Johnson, Rudi	2000		Nix, Patrick	1993
Jones, Jimmy	1967		Norris, Lanny	1972
Jones, Miles	1972			
Jones, Robbie	1979		Ogden, Raymond	1963
Jones, Terry	1999		Ogilvie, Major	1979
Jordan, Lee Roy	2006		Oliver, Bill (Brother)	1971
Jordan, Ralph	Final Whistle		Owens, James	Halftime
Junior, E. J.	1979			
			Palmer, David	1993
Kelley, Joe	1966		Parseghian, Ara	1972
Kelley, Les	1966		Partin, Jimmy	1964
Kennedy, Jackie	1992		Patrick, Linnie	1981
Kent, Mailon	1963		Payne, Ernie	1995
Kilgore, Jon	1963		Pennington, Spencer	2004
Kim, Peter	1982		Peoples, George	1981
King, Emanuel	1985		Perkins, Ray	1966
Kitchens, Brenda	1995		Petrino, Bobby	2002
Kitchens, Freddie	1995		Plagge, Richard	1967
			Proctor, Michael	1992
LaBue, Joe	1971		Portela, Jorge	1979
Langham, Antonio	1993		Propst, Eddie	1967
Langner, David	1972		Pruett, John	Halftime
Leard, Ben	1999		Pruett, Roger	1973
Lee, Kevin	1993		Pugh, Keith	1979
Lester, Brad	2006			
Lewis, Don	1964		Rawson, Larry	1963
Lewis, Walter	1982		Ray, David	1964
Linderman, Chris	1972		Raburn, Gene	1967
Locklear, Mike	1979		Reebals, Eric	1995
Lowry, Tommy	1971		Reitz, John David	1967
Lude, Mike	1992		Richardson, Greg	1985
Lunceford, Tommy	1967		Riddle, Dennis	1995
			Robbins, Mark	1979
McCants, Keith	1989		Robinett, Robby	1971
McClintock, Justin	1999		Robinson, Brian	1993
McElroy, Alan	1979		Rodriguez, Prechae	2006
McGeever, John	2006		Rose, George	1963
McGinty, Robert	1984		Rouzie, Jeff	1971
McGriff, Curtis	1979		Rutledge, Gary	1973
McIntyre, Secedrick	1973			
McLaughlin, Mike	2006		Saban, Nick	Halftime
McMilion, Reid	1993		Samuels, Chris	1999
McNair, Kirk	Overtime		Samples, Alvin	1967
McNeal, Don	1979		Sanders, Frank	1993
			Sanspree, Danny	1972
Malone, Toderick	1995		Schmaltz, Dick	1971
Maxwell, Ray	1973		Shealy, Steadman	1979
Melton, Larry	1995		Shelling, Chris	1993
Miller, B.M.	Halftime		Shula, Mike	1985
Miller, Robert	1966		Sides, Brownie	1967
Milons, Freddie	1999		Sidle, Jimmy	1963
Miska, Jason	1995		Simon, Ken	1979
Mitchell, John	1971		Simpson, Howard	1963
Mitchell, Roger	1972		Slack, Reggie	1989
Moore, Mal	1981		Sloan, Steve	1964
Moorehead, Kindal	1999		Solomon, Terry	1995
Morgan, Ed	1967		Spivey, Paul	1973
Morrow, Harold	1995		Smith, Freddie	1979
Mosley, John	1964		Smith, George	1972
Moss, Stan	1967		Smith, Kenny	2000
Muskett, David	1967		Smith, Tre	2002
Musso, Johnny	1971		Stabler, Kenny	1967
			Scott, Randy	1979
Namath, Joe	1964		Stallings, Gene	1992
Neel, Mike	1972		Stover, Nikita	2006

Name	Year
Strickland, Chuck	1971
Sullivan, John	1966
Sullivan, Pat	1971
Sutton, Donnie	1966
Taylor, Courtney	2004
Taylor, James	1973
Terretta, Gino	1992
Tidwell, Travis	1963
Tiffin, Van	1985
Tillman, Lawyer	1992
Thomas, Ben	Overtime
Thompson, Dickey	1967
Thornton, Jack	1963
Todd, Richard	1973
Tolleson, Tommy	1964
Trammell, Pat	2006
Trimble, Wayne	1966
Trotman, Charley	1979
Tuberville, Tommy	2007
Turner, Craig	1982
Unger, Harry	1972
Versprille, Eddie	1963
Wade, Tommy	1967
Wallace, Cooper	2002
Walker, Peahead	1964
Walls, Randy	1972
Warren, Frank	1979
Washington, Mike	1973
Watts, Tyler	2002
Weldon, Marcel	1995
White, Larry	Overtime
White, Stan	1993
Whitman, Steve	1979
Whitworth, J.B. (Ears)	2000
Williams, Carnell	2004
Williams, David	1972
Williams, Shaud	2004
Wilson, John Parker	2006
Win, Lyle	1989
Wheeler, Wayne	1972
Wright, Alexander	1989
Woodall, Woody	1963
Woodward, Dave	2006
Zow, Andrew	1999

Jason Campbell lettered four years at Auburn (2001-2004) and wound up second in the school's career records for passing yardage, completions, completion percentage and touchdowns. In the single season records he is second in passing percentage and third in yardage and touchdowns. He was drafted in the first round of the 2005 NFL draft by the Washington Redskins; In 2010 he was traded to the Oakland Raiders.

Photo Courtsey Todd Van Emst Auburn Athletic Department

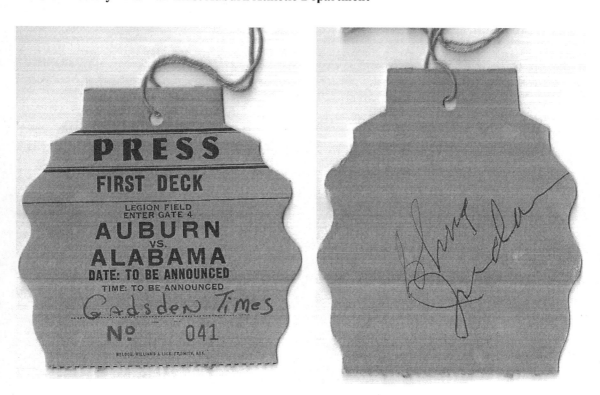

Shug Jordan autographed the author's press pass after his final game.

Bryant has four winners in fullback Steve Bowman (30), tackle Jimmy Fuller (73), quarterback Steve Sloan (14) and linebacker Paul Crane (54). These players were members of Alabama's 1965 that defeated Auburn 30-3; then defeated Nebraska 39-28 in the Orange Bowl and was named National Champions, winding up with a 9-1-1 overall record.

Former Auburn coach Terry Bowden on the sideline in Jordan-Hare Stadium. He coached the Tigers five full seasons and the first six game of a sixth season in 1998 for a 47-17-1 record. He made NCAA history by becoming the first football coach to start a Division 1-A career with 20 consecutive wins. He led Auburn to its first 11-0 season in his first season on the Plain in 1993; then won the first nine games of the 1994 season before winding up the year with a tie against Georgia and loss to Alabama. He won his first and last game against Alabama, winding up 2-3 against the Tide.

This is the gathering at an Auburn's spring press party (circa 1965), held at Bill Beckwith's cabin at a lake outside the city. From the left are: Jack Doane, Montgomery Advertiser; Carl Stephens, Montgomery TV; Bill Beckwith, Auburn SID (front); George Smith, Anniston Star (back); Coach Ralph Jordan; Bill Lumpkin, Birmingham Post-Herald; Hap Halbrooks, Florence Times (front); Jimmy Smothes, Gadsden Times; Sam Adams, Alabama Journal (front); and Elmore Hudgins, SEC public relations director.

Two veteran sports editors take time to visit in the press box at Bryant-Denny Stadium before starting to work covering another Alabama-Auburn football game. Left is John Pruett of the Huntsville Times; right is Jimmy Smothers of the Gadsden Times. Combined the two of them have 100 years experience in sports writing and have covered that many games between the Tide and Tigers.

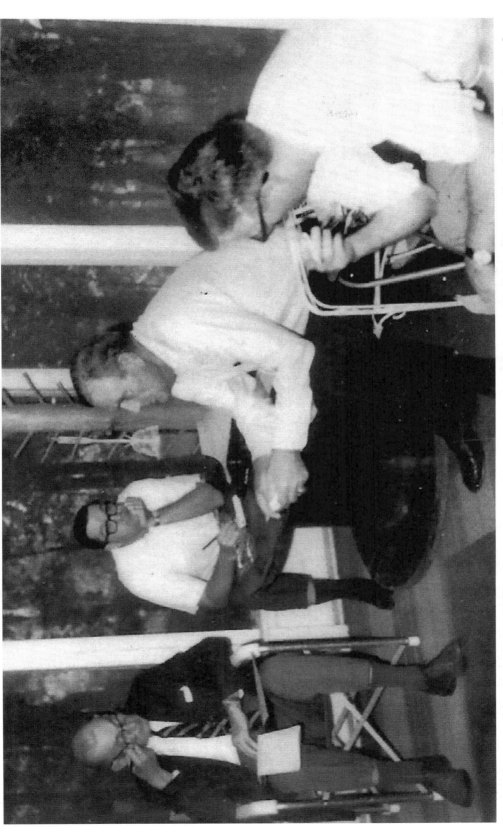

From the left are Bob Phillips, Birmingham Post-Herald; Jimmy Smothers, Gadsden Times; Coach Paul Bryant; and Benny Marshall. The three newsmen are talking football with the Alabama coach during a visit to his cabin on Lake Martin. All four men have since been inducted into the Alabama Sports Hall of Fame; all but Smothers were deceased when this book was published in 2011..

Made in the USA
Charleston, SC
20 November 2011